W9-BXM-372

THE SUPERNATURAL IN TRAGEDY

THE SUPERNATURAL IN TRAGEDY

BY

CHARLES EDWARD WHITMORE

ST. JOSEPH'S UNIVERSITY STX
PN1899.S8W5 1971
The supernatural in tragedy.

3 9353 00148 0084

PN
1899
S8
W5
1971

142302

PAUL P. APPEL, *Publisher*

MAMARONECK, N.Y.

1971

Originally Published 1915
Reprinted 1971

Published by Paul P. Appel
Library of Congress Catalog Card Number—74-162502
ISBN 911858-24-5

TO

GEORGE LYMAN KITTREDGE

PREFACE

THE present volume, save for a few excisions and corrections, is substantially the thesis presented by me at Harvard University in 1911 for the doctorate in Comparative Literature. It makes no pretence to exhaust the field which it undertakes to survey; indeed, I hope that its publication may serve to stimulate additional research, not only in the drama of countries not here dealt with, but in other departments of literary activity. I trust, however, that the principles here enunciated are sufficiently well grounded to be a useful basis for such investigation.

I desire to make a general acknowledgement of thanks to all the members of the Division of Modern Languages at Harvard whom I had occasion to consult in the course of the work, for helpful criticisms and suggestions; to Professor H. W. Smyth, for inspiration derived from his lectures on Greek literature; and to Professor E. K. Rand, for help in running down the quotation from Eusebius discussed in the section on the liturgical drama.

I have endeavored to make the bibliography a complete list of books and articles dealing specifically with the supernatural in tragedy; but some items, particularly in the modern section, may well have escaped me, and I should be grateful for additions or corrections.

CHARLES E. WHITMORE.

CONTENTS

                                                     PAGE

INTRODUCTION 3
    Definitions and Exclusions 3

PART I

ANTIQUITY

I. GREEK TRAGEDY 17
    1. Aischylos 17
    2. Sophokles 50
    3. Euripides 63
    4. The Contribution of Greek Tragedy 90

II. SENECA 97

PART II

THE MIDDLE AGES AND THE RENAISSANCE

III. THE MEDIEVAL SACRED DRAMA 113
    1. Origin and Growth of the Liturgical Drama 113
    2. The Miracle-Play in France 127
    3. The Miracle-Play in England 146

IV. THE RENAISSANCE IN ITALY 177
    1. The Sacred Drama in Italy 177
    2. Classical Italian Tragedy 186

V. THE ELIZABETHAN AGE IN ENGLAND 203
    1. Seneca in England 203
    2. The Growth of Native Tradition 221
    3. The Period of Achievement 235
    4. Devil-Plays and Witch-Plays 263
    5. The Period of Decline 273
    6. The Elizabethan Contribution 279

vii

PART III

SOME MODERN ASPECTS

VI. THE PERIOD OF SUBSIDENCE 291
1. Restoration Tragedy 291
2. The Eighteenth Century 298

VII. THE MODERN REVIVAL 305
1. The Revival in England 305
2. Henrik Ibsen 318
3. Gabriele D'Annunzio 332
4. Maurice Maeterlinck 335

CONCLUSION 345
Function of the Supernatural in Tragedy 345

BIBLIOGRAPHY 359

INDEX 365

THE SUPERNATURAL IN TRAGEDY

THE SUPERNATURAL IN TRAGEDY

INTRODUCTION

Definitions and Exclusions

It is a commonplace of literary history that what may be called, in the widest sense of the term, supernatural manifestations are very apt to occur in connection with tragedy. Such manifestations appeal to an interest deeply rooted in human nature, however much it may be ignored during certain periods, or in our own professed attitude. A certain respect for such matters, even a certain covert belief, lingers in the most skeptical; and the enduring character of the interest which we feel in the unseen is shown by the abundance of the literature which ministers to it, and by the real importance which it may sometimes assume. *Hamlet* without the ghost is as unthinkable as *Hamlet* without the Prince himself. In the case of tragedy, the body of material which attests this preoccupation with the powers beyond man is assuredly extensive; yet it has not, so far as I am aware, ever been studied as a whole, in order to ascertain how far such an interest is necessary or advisable for the expression of the tragic impulse in dramatic form. A survey of so wide a field can only be tentative; but an examination of the various epochs in which the connection of the supernatural with tragedy is most clearly marked can hardly fail to reveal some general tendencies, and to provide a basis for more detailed investigation of special aspects in the future. The whole subject is so much of a piece that such aspects can only be profitably studied in their relation to the entire development, which, by virtue of its origin in a universal human instinct, presents a fundamental unity. Our study, then, is primarily concerned with those periods in which examples of the supernatural in tragic drama are most numerous, in order to determine what the particular contribution of each case is, and thus secure data from which general conclusions may perhaps be drawn. It must be remembered that we are to deal with somewhat intangible matters; and accordingly we must clarify our ideas concerning the scope and office of the supernatural in literature at large, before we can profitably approach the more limited subject of its manifestation in the drama.

One need scarcely justify the assertion that the desire to arouse terror is the predominant reason for the introduction of the supernatural in literature where, as in tragedy, a serious effect is aimed at. I use " terror " as the most inclusive word available, denoting not only the mere shock of physical fear, but the subtler, more spiritual dread, which commerce with the unseen world may provoke; an emotion which may at its highest, as in certain religious experiences, pass into awe, with the element of terror almost or wholly obscured. The most general question, then, which confronts us at the outset of our inquiry, is this: what is the nature of the supernatural terror ? We may be helped to a concreter view of this question by the answer given it by the late Lafcadio Hearn, in an essay entitled *Nightmare-Touch*.[1] His answer is, I think, too explicit, but it certainly contains an element of truth, and may serve as a guide to a more adequate conception.

Hearn's explanation, though ostensibly covering only ghosts, would apply equally well to supernatural terror in general. It is simply this: the fear of ghosts is the fear of

[1] To be found in the volume entitled *Shadowings*.

being touched by ghosts. Furthermore, this fear results from dreams of being chased by ghosts, and is the product of a long evolutionary process, of accumulated and inherited impressions of dream-pain. Such transmitted dream-impressions are of course quite incapable of being proved; and it certainly is not true that dreams of ghostly pursuers are of universal occurrence. To dream of being chased is, indeed, a frequent form of nightmare; but that is something wholly distinct from the fear of a specifically supernatural pursuer. Hearn admits that such fear is vague and hard to define; and it is precisely in trying to particularize it that he falls into error. It is in the very uncertainty of the fear that its horror lies; in the sense of some indefinable presence, and in the utter inability to judge of the limits of the power which this presence can exercise, probably for baleful ends. The feeling is deeply rooted in the primitive consciousness that these forces of the other world are of doubtful friendliness to man; they surely have the capacity, almost certainly the desire, to harm. In the case of departed spirits this anger at the living may be due to some easily assignable cause, such as neglect of the due rites of burial, or desire for revenge on a murderer; but apart from such particular instances the attitude of mortals toward the other world is constantly one of distrust and uncertainty. Even to Herodotos, in one of the most devout periods of Greek history, the divine principle is wholly envious and troublesome.[1] The supernatural terror may accordingly be defined as the dread of some potentially malevolent *power*, of incalculable capacity to work evil. It is this sense of power which will later serve us as a criterion of whether the supernatural in a given work is really inherent and necessary, or detached and without significance.

[1] Τὸ θεῖον πᾶν φθονερόν τε καὶ ταραχῶδες, i. 32.

If now this vague sense of an unlimited hostile power is to take shape in a definite figure, that figure will be effective only in so far as its definiteness does not dissipate the envelope of uncertainty from which all its power of arousing terror derives.   If it is dissipated, we have a mere bugbear, which can at most threaten physical violence.   An element of the incalculable, then, is an indispensable accompaniment of any artistic use of the supernatural.   The art which deals with such themes must be not merely representative but evocative, calling forth all the dubious suggestions which may lurk in even the most commonplace objects and situations, and so creating an appropriate atmosphere. Here again we may be helped to a concreter view by analyzing an actual piece of literature which attains this end.   To facilitate impartial inspection and judgment I select something outside our ordinary sphere of knowledge and sympathy, in order that our search for the elements in question may be as clear of preconception as possible.   I choose then the little poem of *Balder's Dreams* from the Norse Elder Edda, and proceed to give a condensed prose version.

Soon were the Gods all in assembly, and the Goddesses all in conference: and of this the mighty powers deliberated; why had Balder bodeful dreams ?

Up rose Odin, and on Sleipnir he laid the saddle; he rode down thence to Niflhel, and met a whelp who came forth from Hell.

Bloody was he on the breast before, and at the father of magic song long he bayed.   Forth rode Odin (the earthway rang hollow) till he came to the high court of Hel [the Goddess].

Then rode Odin before the eastern gate, where he knew was the grave of a prophetess; he began to speak a compelling charm to the wise woman; against her will she rose, and spoke a word of death.

" What man is that, unknown to me, for whom I have increased the toil of my journey ?   I was snowed on with snow, smitten with rain, drenched with dew; dead was I long."

Odin questions her of Balder's fate; she answers reluctantly, ending each stanza with the line " Against my will I spoke, now will I be silent," to which Odin replies "Be not silent ! Thee will I question; till it is all known, yet will I learn." They break off defiantly, and the prophetess warns him of the coming Doom of the Gods.

The most striking feature of this astonishingly effective poem, is, I think, its indefiniteness; a quality to be sharply distinguished from vagueness. This distinction, which will recur in the course of our investigation, is an important one, not always duly observed by critics. Precision in the use of means does not imply clarity in the result, when that result is intended to be indefinite; one does not look for topographical detail in a painting of a mist-wrapped landscape. Vagueness is the result of unskilful handling of means, while indefiniteness can only be gained by a skilful use of them. A confused impression may perfectly well result from details concrete in themselves, but inappropriate to the effect sought. Underworld descriptions in particular are, as we shall see, very apt to err by too great multiplicity of detail resulting in mere confusion. In our Norse poem we have only Odin riding down over the ringing earthway into the chill silence of the nether world. There is no elaboration of the incidents of his journey, no striving for gruesome effects; a few simple words create an atmosphere of uncertain dread, of indeterminate awe.

This impression, when viewed more closely, is seen to be remarkably re-enforced by the use of words suggesting mysterious sound. The whelp bays long (everyone knows the uncanny suggestiveness of a dog's howl), and the way rings hollow under the tread of Odin's horse. In addition to these reproductions of physical sound there is in the very words of the original a fitness of sound to situation which culminates in the first stanza uttered by the prophetess. This quality is of course lost in translation; but even through the veil of prose one can hardly miss the remoteness, the deadly chill, which the words carry.   Furthermore, the brevity of the incidents allows none of the peculiar effect of each to evaporate; the prophecies are not detailed, and the poem ends in the gloom cast by a hint of coming destruction.   Finally, for a more technical point, one notes the use of the refrain to emphasize the emotion of the scene — the reluctance of the prophetess, the relentless questioning of Odin.

On the strength of this brief analysis we may provisionally lay down the principle that the effectiveness of an episode introducing the supernatural is likely to be in direct proportion to its brevity.   The condensation of the sense of power and awe into a brief compass allows none of its peculiar virtue to escape.   For a work like our poem, where such a brief episode suffices for the entire composition, this may be an adequate account of the matter; but the employment of such episodes in a work of large scope involves the necessity of coherently uniting the supernatural incidents with the main plot, and thus gives rise to a fresh set of artistic problems.

The attempt to introduce supernatural motives into the drama in particular at once encounters certain difficulties which are inherent in the dramatic form itself.   A piece of pure narrative, whether in verse or prose, can employ decorative touches at will, and weave them into the fabric of the composition; in the drama the necessities of presentation involve actual exhibition of the supernatural, whether in itself or in its effect on the characters.   Such actual presentment may be disillusionizing; or, if it escape that peril, it may still lack dramatic fitness.   The problem of evoking a continuous appropriate atmosphere, a necessary concomitant, as we have seen, of any artistic use of the supernatural, is here much complicated by the equal necessity of a due relation to the purely dramatic exigencies. This, then, is the essential problem of the use of the supernatural in drama: how is the indispensable atmosphere to be secured without a sacrifice of dramatic coherence? It is precisely the study of the various attempts to solve this problem which we shall undertake in the ensuing investigation.

A tragedy, as Aristotle says, cannot exist without plot; and it follows from our definition of the supernatural as a power that it can only be fully itself when it is a constituent force in the plot, with an actual influence on the characters. Under these conditions even an episodic manifestation of the supernatural must be the expression of a pervasive force, which it should be the dramatist's aim to keep duly in our minds. On the other hand, in inferior work such an episode may be introduced solely for its momentary effect, and lack any deeper connection with the course of the drama. Here, then, we have a fundamental distinction in the dramatic use of the supernatural, and I shall designate these two classes, for our convenience, by the terms *intrinsic* and *decorative*. Take away the decorative supernatural, and you have removed a superficial attribute; remove the intrinsic, and you have wrenched out one of the supports on which the whole play rests. To anticipate by choosing a couple of examples from the time of Shakespeare: the ghost in *Hamlet* is indispensable; without him the play could not possibly exist in its present form. On the contrary, the ghost of the Friar in Chapman's *Bussy d'Ambois* is, as a ghost, absolutely superfluous, and his excision, so far from causing any loss, would be a distinct improvement. We may now proceed to an exacter classification of the forms which the supernatural forces may assume.

These forms may be grouped into three classes. On the one hand are obviously superhuman forces, of which we may distinguish two sorts: the power of destiny which supposedly controls mortal affairs, whether left as an impersonal conception of overruling fate or made concrete in a more definite God or Gods; and lesser beings, still regarded as having more than human power, under which devils, angels and allegorical figures are evident sub-classes. On the human side we have again two divisions: mortals who are still alive, but who have traffic or affiliation with the powers beyond, more especially (for the needs of tragedy) with the darker powers of unalloyed malignancy; [1] and mortals who have passed by death into another world, but return from it, or in other words ghosts. The third class is in a measure intermediate, and of much less frequent occurrence: it consists in the assumption by some force of Nature, especially the wind or the sea, of that element of incalculable power which we found to be the essence of the supernatural.

With regard to tragedy in particular we may say that the representatives of these classes with which we shall chiefly have to deal are first, Fate; second, devils and angels, or in general figures embodying the good and evil impulses of humanity; third, witches (and in a subordinate degree magicians); and fourth, ghosts; with such examples of our third class as we may encounter and define. This may suffice as a general classification; since the several types make their appearance at various times, and under different conditions, we may defer their detailed consideration till the progress of our survey requires it.

[1] An important subdivision of this group, that of mortals who are carried into another world otherwise than by death, and who retain their mortal body throughout, is of very infrequent occurrence in drama, and may for our purpose be disregarded.

Any of the just-mentioned classes of supernatural powers may appear in a drama as either intrinsic or decorative; and actual representation is no criterion of the side on which a given instance should be placed. A ghost, for instance, may appear frequently, and be very active on the stage, without at all affecting the progress of the action; and on the other hand some power which never takes bodily shape, which may even be conceived of as remote, may have a most vital relation to that progress. Influence on the characters is the sole criterion of the intrinsic supernatural. We must remember, then, that the decorative supernatural may take shape in a represented figure, or may consist wholly of allusion. Such allusion need not deal directly with a supernatural theme, but may be of such a sort as to turn the mind in that general direction. References to death and its attendant phenomena are, as we shall see, a frequent means of attaining this result, especially where ghosts are in question. These decorative allusions are to be judged precisely as is architectural decoration. If they emphasize the main structural lines, and prepare for a significant manifestation of the supernatural, they are good; but if they correspond to no structural necessity, they are bad.

We may now briefly summarize the principles which the foregoing discussion has furnished us, and which are to guide us in our ensuing investigation. We have seen that there is inherent in mankind an interest in the things beyond mortal life and experience, which comes to apprehend, in this extra-human realm, a group of forces which may intervene with incalculable effect in human affairs. Furthermore, these powers are conceived to be by no means inherently friendly to man; hence their treatment in imaginative literature will be primarily with serious intent — in the case of the drama, in tragedy. Any literary handling of such motives demands the expression of this sense of incalculable power, accompanied by a continuous appropriate atmosphere, in which the sense of incalculability shall be preserved.   In the drama the actual presentation, whether of the forces themselves or of their effect on the characters, raises a special problem: that of making the supernatural force an indispensable part of the plot, and the appropriate atmosphere an element in the whole dramatic fabric.   It remains to delimit the periods in which our search is to be conducted, before proceeding to the collection and study of the various examples.

The field of tragedy which is open to us is obviously a vast one, and even a cursory survey of all its departments would be impossible here.   The deeper manifestations which we are in search of, however, do not appear in every epoch; and our progress, though in the main historical, need not be retarded to take note of every instance of trivial incompetence. I wish to lay most stress on the periods of chief importance, but in such historical perspective as shall enable us to discern their relation to the development as a whole.   These chief periods are the fifth century B.C., in Greece, and the Elizabethan age in England.   We shall begin by an inspection of those antecedent conditions of Greek tragedy which gave it an inevitable connection with the forces beyond man, and then study the varying fashion in which this connection is dealt with by the three Attic masters.   In antiquity we shall also discuss Seneca, comparatively unimportant in himself, but very significant as an influence.   Passing to the Middle Ages, we shall study the rise of a new dramatic tradition in the miracle-plays, and its varying fortunes in France, England, and Italy, as in the Renaissance it came into contact with the reviving classical tradition.   The progress of the latter we shall trace in Italy, and the contrast with England thus afforded will bring us to the Elizabethan era, where we shall follow the development in detail to the Closing of the Theatres. A survey of the Restoration period will show us the decay of the supernatural in a time of imitation and futility; and finally, in the nineteenth century, we shall indicate tendencies, apparent in several literatures, which seem to point to a renewal of the tragic supernatural in our own time. By thus dealing with the more fruitful periods our study will be more productive of results, while at the same time the historical continuity will be sufficiently maintained. Lastly, at such times as the nature of our accumulated material requires, we shall seek to formulate the generalizations which relate to our subject in its entirety.

It may be said here that for such an investigation as we are undertaking no rigid definition of tragedy is possible. A play which may very insufficiently satisfy any such definition may yet yield us an episode of decided interest, and the supreme achievements can only be fully appreciated in connection with such collateral evidence. We may fairly say that any serious use of the supernatural (by reason of its nature as already defined) has tragic implications, and conversely, that for our purposes any such serious use, even though episodic, is a sufficient token of tragic intention. The degree to which this intention is realized in artistic form will then determine the importance to be assigned to each case in our general scheme.

In the extensive body of material thus open to us I hope to reveal a fundamental unity in the relation of the supernatural to tragedy which shall both connect various manifestations of the tragic spirit widely separated in time and space, and show an intimate connection between the highest results of such manifestations and the supernatural itself.

We shall see this basic impulse, the interest of humanity in what lies beyond, working itself out in a fascinating variety of forms, refining on the crudity of early ideas, and at last reaching a stage where a purely atmospheric supernatural, free of any visible or tangible properties, may be charged with the utmost intensity of tragic terror.   To trace the stages by which these heights are attained will at once lead us to a better appreciation of their loftiness, and a warmer recognition of the services of the humbler artificers.

PART I

ANTIQUITY

CHAPTER I

GREEK TRAGEDY

SECTION I. — AISCHYLOS

GREEK poetry appears to us in its earliest manifestations already full of divine personages, keenly interested in mortals, and participating at will in the control of their affairs. The action of *Iliad* and *Odyssey* is wholly dependent on the Gods who direct it, and who frequently intervene to alter the course of events. The very character of the Greek religion, with its concrete embodiments of the divine nature, made such intervention a necessary corollary of the Gods' existence. The literary expression of this conception of them is by no means merely mechanical, even at the outset; the apparition of Athena in the hut of the swineherd Eumaios (v. 159) being perhaps the most admirable out of numerous examples of the sort in the Homeric poems. Passing to the lyric period, we have Sappho speaking in a dream with Aphrodite (fr. 87); and Pindar's odes afford unsurpassable examples of the splendor with which the commerce of Gods with men could be surrounded. It is wholly natural, then, that the drama of the Greeks should show an especial interest in the relations of man to the power beyond him.

In the case of the drama, indeed, the circumstances of its rise among the Greeks would have made such an interest inevitable, even if the general conditions just alluded to had been lacking. By virtue of its origin in a cultus of peculiar depth and emotional poignancy, Greek tragedy gained an association with religion such as has never since co-existed with a similar degree of artistic excellence. The worship of Dionysos, centering about the figure of a God scorned, suffering, but ultimately triumphant, and the representation, as we may suppose, in the earliest choral drama of the incidents of his beneficent progress and conquest of humanity, imposed upon the nascent art a connection with the supernatural world that was never entirely effaced. In that earliest tragedy the Chorus of Satyrs, and doubtless the presence of the God himself, familiarized the beholder from the outset with the spectacle of superhuman participants in the drama. We cannot trace in detail the other circumstances, such as association with the cult of heroes, that may have contributed to this state of affairs; [1] but the resulting intimate connection of tragedy with the Gods is perfectly evident. The development of this connection made them in time the inherent impelling forces by which the action of the tragedies of the fifth century was directed, and that not only in a conventionally religious but in a vitally artistic sense. Traditional this connection was; but each individual dramatist felt free to approach the problems which it involved in his own way, and to achieve therein some of the highest victories of his art.

Furthermore, the temper of the age in which tragedy began its independent existence was favorable to the employment of the supernatural. The peril of the Persian invasions, and the seemingly miraculous repulse of the huge Eastern armaments by the far smaller forces of Hellas, resulted in a marked quickening of religious emotion. The men of that time believed that they had actual evidence of

[1] See Farnell, *Cults of the Greek States*, v. 230 ff., for a good summary of the question, with valuable references. The most recent discussion is M. P. Nilsson, "Der Ursprung der Tragödie," in *Neues Jahrb. kl. Alt.* for 1911, pp. 609 ff.

the activity of the Gods in their behalf. Such incidents as the help afforded by Pan to the Athenians before Marathon, the apparition of the sons of Aiakos at Aigina, and the failure of the Persians to seize Delphi,[1] powerfully affected the belief of the people, and brought them a more vivid sense of the Gods as close at hand, and intimately concerned in the affairs of mortals. It follows that in such an age the appearance of the Gods on the tragic stage must have had a solemn reality, hard perhaps for us to understand, but which we must in some measure grasp if we are to form a true estimate of what such figures meant to the poet and his auditors.

In this age of renewed belief (" âge de croyance et d'energie," as Croiset calls it) the first master of tragedy arose. Reared at Eleusis, and undoubtedly responsive to the subtle influences of that potent religious centre; a warrior in the great struggle with Persia, sharing with his contemporaries a perception of the divine power manifested in the humbling of the arrogance of the mighty empire — he could not fail to evince an interest in the powers which shape the destiny of mankind. His own brooding, reflective nature made this interest a central fact in his personality, and led him to find the most characteristic expression of his art in the presentation in human terms of some variant of the inexorable equation $\kappa \acute{o} \rho o s + \ddot{v} \beta \rho \iota s = \breve{a} \tau \eta$. Fragmentarily in the *Seven Against Thebes*, and supremely in the *Oresteia*, he depicts the sombre evolution of the sinister forces to which man by his own act yields himself, and which with slow and irreparable deliberation work out the curse of a mighty house to the end.

Even the figures of the accepted mythology are shaped and shadowed by his compelling imagination. One has only

---

[1] See Herodotos, vi. 105, viii. 64, and viii. 37–39.

to compare his Zeus, the conception of whom in the Prome-
thean trilogy has aroused such conflicting views of the
poet's intention, who is so strangely invoked as " whosoe'er
he be," " most holy and most perfect," with the Zeus of the
second stasimon of Sophokles' *Antigone*, who is a beneficent
monarch, not very far removed from the human type.   In
this regard Aischylos is less Attic than Dorian; there is in
him the same sense of the tremendous breaking in of the
divine power that we find in the august gesture of interposition of the Apollo of the west pediment at Olympia, as
contrasted with the blending of divine and human in the
culminating scene of the Parthenon frieze, where Gods are
distinguished from mortals rather by superior grace and
dignity than by any manifestation of superhuman power.
Aischylos exalts his Gods, and sets them against the background of an enormous sweep of time.   Behind the new
rulers of Olympos we catch glimpses of that far past when
there was war in Heaven, and change of dynasties; when
" one who was great of old shall no longer be spoken of as if
he had been, and he who came after met a conqueror, and is
departed " (*Ag.* 168 ff.); when Apollo had not yet come to
Delphi, and the oracle was inspired by " Earth, primeval
prophetess."

But even more awful and more potent than the familiar
Gods are the dim forces who guide a mighty family to its
destruction; the μέλαιν' Ἐρινύς who directs the tragic fortunes of the house of Laïos, or the sister Furies who watch
the piling up of the tempest over the head of Agamemnon.
Slighter, but not less vivid, are such shapes as the Curse
that Eteokles sees beside him, or the phantom of Helen that
haunts the dreams of Menelaos.   These guiding forces of
the Aischylean drama are for the most part, as we should
expect, powers whose operation is baleful; yet behind them

all stands the eternal Justice, Themis or Dike, allotting to every mortal the fruit of his works, whether good or evil. In general, however, the sinister forces occupy the foreground, and immediately dominate the tragedies of Aischylos. Their dreadful manifestations of old, and their imminent coming, are told or sensed by shuddering choruses and wailing prophets; and at the supreme tragic climax they break in upon the action in visible form. Aischylos, virtually creating his own mythology, makes these naturally vaguer figures as realizable and impressive as the more definite divinities of common belief.

This supernatural world preoccupies the mind of Aischylos at the very outset, and manifests itself more pervadingly and triumphantly with the maturing of his art. The earliest of the extant plays, the *Suppliants*, has no overtly supernatural element, but the characteristic Aischylean ideas are already present. The king Pelasgos, for instance, as he deliberates whether he shall espouse the cause of the Danaids, is moved by the thought of the avenging spirit, the ἀλάστωρ, who is " all baneful, a grievous visitant, who frees not even the dead in Hades " (414–416). Later, when the favorable decision has been reached, the Chorus praises the Argives for having thereby shown due regard for the avenging watcher of Zeus. " No house that hath him on its roof rejoiceth; for he sitteth heavily " (646 ff). Here we have the idea of the avenging demon who haunts sinful houses clearly indicated; but for the bulk of the play he is overshadowed by the might of Zeus, who is invoked in the first words of the Chorus, whose power is recurrently proclaimed, and whose name rings out repeatedly in the final song of thanksgiving. The essential Aischylean attitude is as yet only adumbrated, and practically does not affect the plot.

The *Persians* registers a marked advance in the relation of supernatural to plot, though the adjustment of the two is not yet perfect. Aischylos is too full of patriotic enthusiasm to follow out in detail the malevolent workings of the φανεὶς ἀλάστωρ to whom the Messenger, at the beginning of his splendid narrative, ascribes the ruin of the Persian host. In general type, however, and in sundry matters of detail, the *Persians* is a curious anticipation of the *Oresteia*. There is in the mournful foreboding of the entrance-song of the Chorus — κακόμαντις ἄγαν ὀρσολοπεῖται/θυμὸς ἔσωθεν (10–11) — a suggestion of the mood which will be intensified to an atmosphere of awaited horror in the *Agamemnon*. This is parallel to the purely decorative allusions of the *Suppliants*; but Aischylos also attacks the problem of the relation of supernatural to action by employing two of the most widely available means — the prophetic dream, and the ghost. Atossa comes to seek counsel of the Chorus by reason of an ominous dream, in which she saw the failure of her son Xerxes to yoke to his chariot a woman personifying Hellas, while the shade of his father Dareios stood by in pity. When, on awakening, she sought the altar to make propitiatory sacrifice, a portent added to her terror — she beheld an eagle who offered no resistance when pursued by a hawk. The Chorus bids her persevere in her offering, making it now not only to the Gods, but also to the shade of Dareios, who has power to send blessings from the underworld, and whose appearance in the dream shows that he retains an interest in the fortunes of his family. Queen and Chorus then engage in a brief colloquy concerning Athens, following which appears the Messenger, with his tale of the battle of Salamis and the disastrous retreat of the Persian host. So Atossa's dream of disaster is confirmed; but none the less she decides to make her sacrifice to the nether

powers, in case some good may yet result.   When she
reappears, however, it is to offer libations to the dead alone.
While she pours them the Chorus sings a chant designed to
call up the shade of Dareios.   It recounts the virtues of the
dead king, and implores the powers of the underworld to
consent to his return to the light, most of the strophes
ending with a shrill cry of summons.   The ghost hears, and
rises over his tomb, asking the reason for this invocation.
It has been hard for him to return, for the powers of the
underworld are better at holding fast than at releasing.
However, he is here; but he bids those before him speak
briefly, for his time is short.   The Chorus, overcome with
awe, leaves to Atossa the task of informing him.   He sees
in the ruin of Xerxes the natural result of his impious attempt to bridge the Hellespont, and alludes vaguely to the
fulfilment of oracles, whose purport is not explicitly mentioned.   He then gives a brief summary of Persian history,
and of the achievements of his own reign, concluding with a
prophecy of Plataia, and a warning that Persia must abstain
from further efforts to subdue Hellas.   His last words are an
injunction to the Chorus to take their joy of life while it is
theirs: " for wealth profits not the dead."   So he vanishes,
and the direct connection of the supernatural with the plot
ends.

That the plot is a loosely woven one is evident.   The
supernatural does not enter deeply into the fabric of the
drama, and there is only an external climax.   We progress
from the premonition of disaster to the account of it, and
finally to the actual sight of the defeated Xerxes, who as it
were embodies the fate that has overtaken Persia; but
there is no corresponding deepening of the thought.   The
supernatural elements show a certain vagueness of conception.   Atossa's dream does not determine the nature of her

sacrifice; and the change of purpose by which she makes it
to the shade of Dareios alone is not adequately emphasized.
In the same way the ghost himself is not drawn with unfalt-
ering strokes.   A certain hieratic quality which he displays
is not misplaced, since he is not merely a human spirit, but
also in a way a symbol of the past glories of Persia.   But he
is more than a symbol; certain of his allusions to the lower
world have a solemn imaginative quality which gives him
distinct character as a ghost.   Yet it must be admitted that
he wavers.   We cannot make out the exact limits of his
knowledge of terrestrial affairs; but his memory of his own
exploits is very clear, and despite the shortness of his visit
to the upper world he has time to refer to them at considerable length.   Aischylos lets him impart more information
than the professed conditions of his return to the light would
lead us to expect; his expository function, that is, usurps an
undue amount of space.   This, however, does not seriously
impair his value as a stage figure, for his references to
Persian history were doubtless sufficiently novel to fix the
attention of the bulk of the audience on them, without
leaving them time to speculate on the propriety of such an
account under the conditions.   Moreover, the whole episode
had an effectiveness in representation which the mere
reading of the text cannot convey.   The movements of the
Chorus in their rich Eastern robes, and the strange shouts
which end the stanzas of their song, must have been picturesque, if nothing more, and well calculated for the more
impressible audience of the early fifth century.

If the various details of the play are not worked out with
perfect clearness, neither is the central thought, the divine
punishment of human presumption, made as evident as we
should desire.   It recurs at intervals, but it is not systemat-
ically developed and emphasized.   It is only late in the

play that we learn of the specific sin of Xerxes, the bridging of the Bosphorus, with its challenge to Poseidon that could only have emanated from a mind diseased. Xerxes himself recognizes the cause of his downfall — ὡς ὠμοφρόνως δαίμων ἐνέβη/Περσῶν γενεᾷ — but in a fashion that adds nothing to what has already been said. The chief interest of the *Persians* lies in the fact that it is the first known play in European literature to bring the supernatural into even external connection with the action, and that it does grapple seriously with the problems thus raised. It presents precisely the elements which Aischylos will later use for his sublimest achievement, and so has a historical interest for the study of his dramatic evolution. Yet that the importance of the play is not purely historical — that it has in certain details, notably in the handling of the ghost, marked aesthetic excellences — has, I trust, been sufficiently shown in the foregoing analysis.

In the *Prometheus Bound* we have a drama of a very different type, unique in that it is presented entirely by superhuman personages, with the exception of one mortal, Io, who has been for a time raised by the force of her destiny to the level of the Gods, and so figures as almost one of them. The most striking feature of this play is the gigantic scale on which it is conceived. The ordinary limits of space and time are amazingly expanded; the savage mountain landscape amid which the action is set, and the slow drift of time during its enacting, create an unparalleled effect of vastness, enhanced by Prometheus' tale of the wars of the Gods, the accounts of Io's wanderings, and the prophecy of the fate of Zeus. We look backward to the beginning of man's life on earth, and forward to the doom which is to overtake the usurper Zeus. Yet precisely in this unrelieved vastness lies the limitation of the piece.

There is no contrast of human and superhuman; even Io, who might readily have been made to afford such a contrast, has little of humanity about her.   That Aischylos might have drawn her in less exalted guise we learn from the fortunately preserved fragment of the *Kares* (fr. 99) in which Europa recounts her wooing by Zeus, with full recognition of its consequences to her as a mortal woman.   Likewise there is too little contrast between the conflicting wills of Prometheus and Zeus; our sense of the struggle between them is gained by reflection on the action, rather than by the spectacle of the action itself.   It is an intellectual reconstruction, not a direct impression.   The nature of the subject, which involves only a passive resistance on the part of Prometheus, is of course largely responsible for this; but from our present standpoint it remains a feature to be adversely criticized.   This double lack of contrast, then, makes the play an imperfect example of the successful use of the supernatural in tragedy; but of its imaginative grandeur there is of course no question whatever.   A detail to be noted is the brief passage (645 ff.) in which Io describes the haunting dreams which preceded her union with Zeus:

> ἀεὶ γὰρ ὄψεις ἔννυχοι πωλεύμεναι
> ἐς παρθενῶνας τοὺς ἐμοὺς παρηγόρουν
> λείοισι μύθοις.

Short as it is, it exhibits the peculiar Aischylean quality which is lacking in the corresponding passages of the *Persians*, and shows that Aischylos has advanced a stage in the progress to full expression of his individuality.

It is in the *Seven against Thebes* that we find him on the threshold of his most characteristic achievement.   In full mastery of narrative and lyric verse, and with a growing insight into the moral order of the Universe, he sets himself to his peculiar task, the depicting of the curse of a mighty house as it progresses to fulfilment. Since the extant play is the last of its trilogy, we cannot trace the working out of the motive in its entirety; but enough remains to enable us to estimate the advance which the poet has made. The drama centres wholly around Eteokles, in whom the action of the curse is to be made manifest. He appears as the prudent leader of the state, solicitous for its safety in the impending crisis, and yet overshadowed by the doom of his race. His consciousness of the fact finds expression in his invocation of the Gods at the end of the prologue, as he grimly includes in the list of divinities Ἀρά τ᾽ Ἐρινὺς πατρὸς ἡ μεγασθενής (70). The plan of the play, with its glowing descriptions of the terror and fervor of war in the panic-stricken appeals of the Chorus and the glorious picture of the seven hostile chieftains, defers the action of the curse until the very climax. When Eteokles, at the end of the Messenger's speech, realizes that his hated brother is indeed before the gates, madness descends on him like a thunderbolt. There is no time for subtle analysis; Aischylos trusts his audience to have caught the sense of impending doom, which was doubtless accentuated for them in the two preceding plays, and with one swift stroke shows us the culminating moment. Eteokles is utterly demented, obsessed by the conviction that the curse *must* be accomplished. He pictures it sitting beside him, " with dry tearless eyes," driving him, with the Gods' connivance, to his doom. The entreaties of the Chorus cannot touch him; " the woes that the Gods give cannot be shunned," are his final words, full of a sinister fatalism. The Chorus is left to rehearse the evil tale of the royal house of Thebes, from the day that Laïos transgressed the thrice-uttered oracle of Apollo, and roused a threefold wave of doom — the murder of Laïos himself, the incest of Oidipous, and the impending mutual slaughter of the two brothers. Almost at once the Messenger enters with the dread tale; the city is saved from invasion, but the two brothers are dead by each other's hand. Then begins the strange scene of the lament of Antigone and Ismene over the bodies, with its dubious conclusion, as Antigone defies the city's edict, and is followed by half the Chorus in her decision to bury Polyneikes. It would seem that Aischylos felt himself unable to dissolve his work into harmony at the close. The whole play gives an effect of incompleteness, of moral uncertainty, which is not solely due to the loss of the rest of the trilogy. A minor manifestation of this mood is discernible in the attention devoted to the tragic figure of Amphiaraos, the just man involved in the doom of the unrighteous. We cannot escape the conclusion that this sense of uncertainty is designed; for it could not have been resolved in a succeeding play, since the *Seven* is the third of the trilogy. The final word is to be found in the shuddering wail,

> ἰὼ Μοῖρα βαρυδότειρα μογερά,
> πότνιά τ' Οἰδίπου σκιά·
> μέλαιν' 'Ερινύς, ἦ μεγασθενής τις εἶ,

in which the shade of Oidipous is coupled with the Erinys as the bringer of doom. This, however, is the sole hint in the play of the woe which the wrath of the dead can directly inflict; the really potent force is the Erinys, who is of course the Curse personified, the Fury-Curse, as Eteokles himself calls her. The aim of the play is to depict the unswerving progress of sin to utter ruin, and to proclaim the inevitable punishment of presumption. When the end is reached, the rest is darkness. The principle that suffering brings wisdom is not yet enunciated; that task is left for the *Oresteia*.

From every point of view the *Oresteia* is its author's consummate achievement. It contains his deepest thoughts on life, his greatest edifices of lyric, and his most colossal and at the same time his most subtle character-drawing; but beyond all these it offers the most perfect example of interpenetration of supernatural and plot that I know of in any literature. All the various manifestations of the supernatural that we have seen in the earlier plays are here heightened and combined with astounding and unique effectiveness. As an example of successful evocation of atmosphere the trilogy stands unrivalled; yet this atmosphere is but the preliminary for a supreme fusion of the human world with the divine. The trilogy is a unit; but before judging it in its totality we must, so far as possible, isolate and analyze the various elements which combine to form the majestic whole.

The first part of the *Agamemnon* is chiefly occupied with creating an atmosphere of gloom and foreboding; an end attained with masterly skill. The brief prologue, with its hints of a sinister past and a dubious present, definitely establishes an appropriate mood; and this impression is steadily accentuated. The Chorus on its entrance speaks of the punishment which must follow crime; the Gods requite the wrongs of their servants by sending against the transgressors the late-avenging Erinys. In the case in hand, the expedition against Troy, there is perhaps fault on both sides; but " the issue tends toward what is fated." Stubborn passions are not to be assuaged by tardily repentant sacrifice; a saying in connection with which it is certainly legitimate to recollect that the souls of the dead are capable of displaying just such stubborn resentment. This prelude ends with the hope that the good news just received will repel the grief that devours the hearts of the Chorus; and we pass to the stasimon, which by its description of the sacrifice of Iphigeneia explains the previous hint that Agamemnon is not wholly free from guilt. By this deed of blood he first " entered the halter of necessity," and took sin upon him; and if the law of retribution holds, he has made himself subject to it. This suggestion of the vengeance which may come from the dead is taken up at the end of the speech in which Klytaimestra depicts the sack of Troy. She prays that the victors may commit no sacrilege in the city; but even if they do keep clean their hands, ἐγρηγορὸς τὸ πῆμα τῶν ὀλωλότων/γένοιτ᾽ ἄν. The multitude of those slain at Troy is a standing menace to those responsible for their death. The following stasimon re-echoes this thought. There is of course an appeal to the public in the motive as it is used here, since just before this time Athenian citizens had fallen in their country's service in many foreign lands; but there is also, I think, an allusion to the guilt of one who in any way causes bloodshed. Τῶν πολυκτόνων γὰρ οὐκ/ἄσκοποι θεοί, says the Chorus; and the thought at once calls up the images of the Erinyes, who obliterate the prosperity of him who is successful without desert — " and when one is among the dead there is no help." This is the first wholly explicit allusion to the Furies, who are in the issue to dominate the remainder of the trilogy; for the reference to them in the parodos is intentionally general. The entrance of the Herald, with his tale of the imminent arrival of Agamemnon, would seem to augur a more cheerful turn of events; but his mind is not really tranquil. He speaks of the sufferings of the army before Troy, and rejoices that all that is past; but there is a shadow over his satisfaction. " The dead are dead," he says in substance; " our toil is over, and they have no care to rise again; why perturb the living by recounting the number of the lost ? " The very

fact that he refers to the matter shows that he must argue
with himself that the dead are powerless; and despite his
effort at cheerfulness he ends with an account of shipwreck
and disaster.   A storm has swept Menelaos away from the
fleet, and his fate is in doubt.   The Chorus returns to its
preoccupation with the idea of sin and punishment, in the
figure of the lion's whelp, reared up as a pet only to revert
to its original nature, and become a murderous bane, " a
priest of ruin in the house."   The ominous word πολύκτονος
recurs (734), and in the next strophe Helen is called νυμφό-
κλαυτος 'Ερινύς (749).   The concluding words of this stasimon,
an anapaestic address to the approaching Agamemnon
which reminds us of some of the brief illustrative scenes in
Shakespeare, hint boldly at hidden evils in the State;   but
the warning just falls short of explicitness, and the king's
fate is sealed.   We might think that the Chorus, having
beheld the safe return of their lord, would now shake themselves free from their forebodings;   but the gloomy mood
recurs, finding expression in words unsurpassed for suggestion of impending woe.   The song, too long to quote in full,
must be read in its entirety;   but some of the most significant
phrases may be cited.   A settled fear flits about the prophetic heart of the Chorus, and an unbidden unpaid song
prophesies woe;   " my soul, self-taught, intones without a
lyre a dirge of the Erinys."   The attempt to cast off this
foreboding by reflecting that doom is often not absolute is
vain.   The thought of bloodshed intrudes: " when once the
black blood of a slain man has fallen on the earth, who can
recall it by incantations ? "   So the singers cease, in despair
of being able to " unwind aught profitable from the stirring
embers of their heart."

All these passages which we have been examining constitute as it were the statement of a great *Leitmotiv*, a

theme of the vengeance that follows bloodshed.   Parallel
to it are lesser touches, which contribute to the deepening of
the general gloom.   Most notable are those that refer to
dreams.   The old men of the Chorus compare themselves to
" dreams that wander about by day " (82), and dreams
figure largely in the marvellous passage which describes the
conduct of Menelaos after the flight of Helen (408 ff.).   It
begins by recounting how the seers of the house bewailed the
woes that had come upon it, and then how Menelaos in sleep
beheld deluding images of his lost wife, which brought him a
vain delight, slipping through his hands at the very instant
he thought to clasp them, and " following with wings the
paths of sleep."   Klytaimestra's description of the state of
captured Troy is a sort of waking dream; in the intensity of
her emotion she forgets the Chorus, and speaks half to herself, fascinated by the vividness of the picture she calls up.
She has had dreams in sleep, too, in Agamemnon's absence;
faint dreams, from which the buzzing of a gnat sufficed to
awake her, but in which she saw " woes outnumbering the
time that slept with her."   An analogous case is the Herald's
account of the divine figure which descended on the ship in
the midst of the tempest, and guided it on a safe course.
(662 ff.)   All these touches effect an imaginative expansion
of the drama, avoiding the monotony which might result
from too great insistence on the central theme.   The combined effect of the whole is to create an unsurpassed atmosphere of solemn and ominous expectancy; and Aischylos
now proceeds to bring his supernatural forces into closer
connection with the action.

    This he does by an actual uplifting of his drama into a
higher sphere, not, as in the *Prometheus*, by a mere expansion of the scene on a given level.   This exaltation begins
with the episode of Kassandra, in which he uses prophecy to

enlarge the limits of time, and likewise to reveal the presence of the visitants who are bringing doom upon the house. The Chorus are at first indifferent, if not scornful; reluctant also to admit this unlooked-for justification of their own forebodings. Kassandra's terrible words, however, gradually renew their mood of dread, which they vainly seek to fend off by questioning the validity of the mantic art. Kassandra's vision sweeps from the murdered children of Thyestes to the imminent crime of Klytaimestra against Agamemnon and herself; and she beholds the revel band of Furies, drunken with blood, who abide in the accursed palace. In a final access of inspiration she foretells her doom, and the vengeance which shall be exacted when Orestes returns, to put the coping-stone on the woes of the race. At the very end, as she prepares to enter the palace, she starts back in loathing at the stench of slaughter that issues forth; but she controls herself, and goes bravely to her death. The effect of this scene has been to show us that the impending murder of Agamemnon is but an episode in the bloody chronicle of the house of Atreus; but we are recalled from this wider view to the immediate crime. Above the chant of the Chorus, as it broods over the mutability of fortune, rings out the king's death-cry. It might seem as if Aischylos had touched the confines of tragic possibility; in reality he is only on the threshold of his highest achievement. Yet in order to secure a fitting contrast he begins by emphasizing the atrocity of the present crime. Klytaimestra comes forward, dripping with her husband's blood, and coolly avows her deed, dwelling with brutal explicitness on every ghastly detail. It is the extreme of mortal passion. Suddenly the mood changes; wailing lyric measures replace the spoken dialogue, and the march to the true climax is begun. Klytaimestra for a time keeps to the trimeter, as she expresses her confidence in the justice of her cause; then she too is carried away by the rising tide of lyric emotion.   The Chorus recall Helen, reproaching her as the first cause of the woes that have befallen Hellas; but Klytaimestra rebukes them, and they turn to the baleful power that haunts the house of Tantalos, while she ironically praises their change.   Once more we recall the chain of crime in which the murder of Agamemnon is but a single link.   The Chorus seek comfort in the thought of Zeus, all-causing, all-accomplishing, without whom nothing comes to fulfillment, and who must have some secret purpose in all these deeds of horror.   This brings a return to the present crime; and Klytaimestra, at the utmost height of her fearful exultation, avows herself to be that παλαιὸς δριμὺς ἀλάστωρ the very incarnation of the ancestral curse, who has taken bodily form that he may " sacrifice one full-grown in requital for children."   Agamemnon's sin against his daughter has found him out.   In this speech the drama reaches its true climax, a spiritual, not a material, one.   The Chorus reels before this revelation, and is mocked by Klytaimestra; yet it clings to the belief in atonement for crime, and gives it tremendous affirmation.   Reviling is met with reviling; it is hard to judge; but

> μίμνει δὲ μίμνοντος ἐν θρόνῳ Διὸς
> παθεῖν τὸν ἔρξαντα· θέσμιον γάρ.   (1563–4.)

We have utterly transcended the mortal world; the personages before us are no longer Klytaimestra and an Argive elder, but the protagonists in an eternal struggle, the drama of sin and retribution.   They have become, in Nietzsche's phrase,[1] " zeitlosen, ausserhalb aller Gesellschaftssphären lebenden," and that *Verzauberung* which he postulates as

---

[1] Die Geburt der Tragödie, c. 8, *Taschenausgabe*, p. 93.

the end of art is attained. The daring genius of Aischylos has set before us not merely a single tragic event, but the very forces from which all tragedy springs. The entrance of Aigisthos restores us to the world of men; but even here, in the clash of very human passions, the thought of the powers beyond recurs. " I shall not refuse to die," says Aigisthos, as he and the Chorus are on the point of coming to blows. In a flash they catch up the words. " Δεχομένοις λέγεις θανεῖν σε," they cry; a touch that Sophokles, with all his instinct for the theatrically effective, could never have conceived. It voices a consistent attitude, not a transient emotion.

Our analysis, then, reveals in the *Agamemnon* an atmosphere of foreboding evoked by the combination of a great leading motive, the idea of sin and retribution, with lesser motives which offer opportunity for imaginative expansion, and thus avoid the danger of monotony. To the mood created by this atmosphere is presented an actual crime in all its atrocity, and a revelation of the eternal forces which are behind this momentary outbreak. The two worlds are thus sharply contrasted, and each gains in power and vividness by the clear presence of the other.

The moving agencies in the *Agamemnon* are the dead who desire vengeance, and the Erinyes who punish transgression. The second of these is the predominant one, the first being used as a subsidiary, though occasionally it becomes more prominent, as in Klytaimestra's grief for the loss of her daughter, which she alleges in justification of her crime. In the *Choephoroi*, on the other hand, the first agency dominates the early part of the play, and is not at any time overlooked, though it changes its form at the end, when Klytaimestra, not Agamemnon, is the spirit who demands vengeance. The skill with which Aischylos makes his entire plot dependent on this motive is a measure of the advance in technique which he has made since the *Persians*. The elements are essentially the same, but they are employed with far greater mastery.

The fact which initiates the whole action of the drama as it takes shape before us is an ominous dream that Klytaimestra has had, only explicable as a sign that Agamemnon's shade is wroth against her. She has told us in the previous play (*Agam.* 275) that she would set little store by the fancy of a slumbering mind; but with an inconsistency not infrequent in skeptics she takes a very different course when confronted with an actual portent. In an outburst of terror and feigned repentence she sends Elektra with the Chorus to placate the angry shade by pouring libations over his tomb. It is this mission which gives the newly returned Orestes an opportunity to recognize his sister, and to leave the tokens by which he may be known in turn. This part of the drama, then, is strictly conditioned by the supernatural power that has sent Klytaimestra the ominous dream; and it is around the tomb of Agamemnon, a material token of that power, that the action centres.

We gain a fairly clear idea of this impelling dream from the entrance-song of the Chorus. It visited Klytaimestra in the dead of night, making her hair stand erect with terror, and causing her to summon trusty interpreters, who declared it to mean that those beneath the earth were sorely angered at those who had slain them. Klytaimestra devises her graceless offering to avert the threatened woes; but from such hands as hers it can accomplish nothing. " What atonement is there for blood once shed upon the ground ? " asks the Chorus. This thought, already present in the *Agamemnon*, becomes the central motive of the *Choephoroi*, and is promptly developed. " Through the

blood drunk up by the nourishing earth the stain of slaughter
that cries for vengeance is fixed, and floweth not away; and
enduring doom runs through the sinner, to fill him with
pollution past all cure " (66 ff.). Elektra now appears,
asking the Chorus for guidance in the unwelcome office she
is called upon to perform, and is bidden to pray for an
avenger, " one who will take life for life." Accepting this
advice, she invokes the chthonian powers and her father's
spirit, and goes off to perform the libation, bidding the
Chorus meanwhile utter a paean for the dead. Her errand
is soon performed, and she returns in great excitement over
the lock of hair which seems to betoken the desired return of
her brother. In judging the ensuing recognition we must
realize that it is, for the dramatist's purpose, a secondary
matter. For the needs of the play it has to be brought
about; but Aischylos has no desire to play with all the
possibilities of the situation in the manner of his more
sophisticated successors. He deliberately sacrifices the
exciting detail to the deeper spiritual logic, disposing of it
in a few swift strokes, and then turning to what really
interests him, the long choral scene in which Orestes and
Elektra invoke their father's spirit to aid their cause. To
censure this scene as too prolonged and motiveless is merely
to admit that one has wholly misconceived the aim of the
play, whose whole structure, as we have seen, rests on the
postulate that Agamemnon's soul desires vengeance, and
has power to accomplish it through the hand of his son.
The long lament is a double scourge, and its sound goes
home under earth, to rouse to action those who have power
to help (375 ff.). The scene is the finest example of the
skill with which Aischylos can rear a great lyric structure;
and with its accompaniment of action and music it must
have fully equalled the necromantic scene of the *Persians* in

external effectiveness, while far surpassing it in depth of
significance.   A minute analysis is not necessary here; but
a few passages may be pointed out which offer new variations on the central theme of vengeance for bloodshed.
This, for instance: " Yet it is a law that drops of blood that
fall to the ground demand further blood; for havoc calls the
Fury that brings from those who died of old another doom
upon doom " (400 ff.), reiterates the keynote of the whole.
The Chorus skilfully urges Orestes on by telling him how
his father's corpse was mutilated, and buried in dishonor;
such a contrast as we have already noted in the climax of the
Agamemnon.   At the close of the scene a note of hope begins
to sound; the final words of the Chorus, " προφρόνως ἐπὶ
νίκῃ," could have found no place in the preceding play.   The
deed is decided; and the issue must surely be for good.
There is now space for a detailed description of the all-
important dream, motivated by Orestes' natural inquiry as
to the reason for the sending of the tardy libations.   At
this point the expository portion of the drama ends, and we
are ready to proceed to the catastrophe.   For a time the
supernatural plays no direct part; but it is recalled to our
attention by two highly significant allusions.   One of these
is the final utterance of the Chorus just before the entrance
of the disguised Orestes: " The anvil of Justice is fixed in
place, and Fate the swordsmith is ready to forge; in the
fullness of time the famed deep-brooding Erinys brings to
the house a child to exact penalty for the pollution of ancient
bloodshed " (646 ff.).   The words κλυτὰ βυσσόφρων Ἐρινύς
are a transparent allusion to the name Κλυταιμήστρα, and to
that incarnation of the ancestral curse in which the mur-
deress found the justification of her crime.   She slew in
requital for a child; now in turn a child demands reckoning
for her deed.   The second reference, clinching the first, is

the frenzied cry of the slave who has found Aigisthos slain, and tries to summon help: " I say the dead are slaying one who lives! " (886). This single line sums up the essence of the two plays. Agamemnon fell in requital for the death of Iphigeneia; now from the underworld he impels Orestes, himself deemed to have perished, to the deed of vengeance. In the final colloquy between Orestes and Klytaimestra the hint of renewed woes becomes explicit, and the supernatural powers again prepare to shape the action. Klytaimestra, having exhausted all possible appeals to her son's tenderness, resorts to the threat, " See to it, guard against thy mother's vengeful hounds," for which Orestes has the ready answer, " How may I escape my father's, if I grant this ? " Klytaimestra realizes that all is over, and cries despairingly, " Alas for this serpent that I bore and reared! " Orestes grimly retorts, " A sure prophet is the fear that springs from dreams." These four lines, with inimitable brevity, concentrate the whole meaning of the drama. Klytaimestra's threat of vengeance finds prompt fulfillment. Orestes has hardly finished declaring to the people that he has exacted due penalty for his father's murder when his mind begins to waver. He determines to go as a suppliant to Apollo, who has impelled him to his act, and bidden him seek sanctuary at Delphi in time of need. Scarcely has he formed this resolution when he beholds the dread Erinyes, with serpents twined in their hair, and dripping blood from their eyes. The Chorus tells him that they are mere phantoms of his overwrought mind, but he knows better: " Clearly these are my mother's vengeful hounds." " You see them not," he says, " but I see them; I am driven forth, no longer can I remain." So he rushes away, leaving the Chorus in doubt whether to call him a savior or another bringer of doom.

" Where will it end, where will the might of woe be lulled to
a change, and come to rest ? "

The *Choephoroi* takes over all the atmosphere of gloom
that enshrouded the *Agamemnon*, and does not need to
enlarge on the means that evoked it there; but it adds new
shades of its own.   Chief of these, as we have seen, is the
potent wrath of the dead, which assumes an eerier character
through the closer relation with them brought about by the
invocation over Agamemnon's tomb.   As subsidiary
motives we have certain thrilling descriptions of terror.
One of these we have already noted, the effect of the dream
on Klytaimestra; others are the allusions which Orestes
makes to the woes threatened by the oracle in case he
neglects its commands — " woes that even a bow-shot cannot reach " (1033).   The atmosphere of the *Choephori* is no
mere replica of that of the *Agamemnon*, but has its own
individual traits.

With the final play of the trilogy the nature of the dramatic problem changes. It is no longer a question of creating
atmosphere, but of dispelling that which has already been
created, in order to attain that ultimate harmony which the
poet failed to achieve in the *Seven*.   The hint of Apollo's
protection which momentarily lightened the end of the
Choephoroi is made the dominant theme of the opening of
the *Eumenides* — a title which is in itself an indication of
the change of mood.   The first words of the Priestess, who
speaks the prologue, set forth the orderly succession of divinities at Delphi, and the might of the present master of the
shrine.   Her confidence in that might is not shaken by the
dreadful sight that she beholds within the sanctuary —
Orestes, with dripping sword, crouching on the ὀμφαλός, and
encircled by the loathsome band of Furies.   Loxias will
surely have power to banish them, even as he can cleanse

from pollution the houses of mortals. Forthwith the God himself appears, dismissing his suppliant, under the guidance of Hermes, and renewing his promises of aid. His first words, οὔτοι προδώσω, are a conscious reminiscence of those in which Orestes in the preceding play [1] declared his trust in the impelling oracle. For the first time we begin to feel confident that the powers of good will ultimately prevail.

But it is yet too early for these powers to have an undisputed field. Scarcely has Orestes departed on his journey to Athens when the ghost of Klytaimestra rises, to bid the sleeping Furies renew the pursuit of their victim. She tells them how she is mocked in the underworld because she has none to avenge her, and recounts the offerings which she has made them in time past. They stir in their sleep, uttering ghastly sounds; finally, awakened by the ever-increasing bitterness of her taunts, they resume the quest of the prey that has temporarily escaped them.

This actual presentation of the supernatural beings who were in the preceding plays only mentioned gives the question of stage management an importance which it has not previously had for us. Aischylos has determined to make the Furies his Chorus; he must, therefore, decide in what guise they are to be presented, and in what way they may be introduced with the maximum of impressiveness. An examination of the way in which he grapples with these difficulties cannot fail to be illuminating for our investigation.

At the outset he is confronted by the fact that the Furies have no definite aspect in the popular imagination.[2] No

---

[1] οὔτοι προδώσει Λοξίου μεγασθενής/χρησμός (*Ch.* 269). Cf. also Λοξία μεγασθενεῖ in *Eum.* 61.

[2] See Miss Harrison, *Prolegomena to the study of Greek Religion*, pp. 223 ff., for an excellent account of this evolution of the Fury.

one before him had tried to evolve for them a shape which should distinguish them from the other varieties of baleful spirits.   It follows then that before he can bring them onto the stage he must invent for them an appropriate embodiment, and that he can obtain a more striking effect by familiarizing the audience with this novel concept before actually disclosing it, rather than by presenting it suddenly in all its unfamiliarity.   We are thus led to expect an elaborate prelude to the introduction of the Chorus; and that is precisely what we find.   We have first the speech of the Priestess as she returns from the shrine horror-stricken at the dreadful sight she has beheld.   Around the crouching suppliant sleeps a wondrous band of women — yet not women, but Gorgons.   And yet they are not like Gorgons, but rather resembles Harpies, though they are wingless.   " Here precisely," says Miss Harrison (*op. cit.* p. 224), " came in the innovation of Aischylos; he takes the Harpy-type, loathsome and foul, and rids them of their wings."   Aischylos has thus acquainted the audience with the bodily semblance which he has bestowed on his creations; but he is not yet ready actually to reveal them.   It is true that Apollo says to Orestes, " And now *thou seest* these raging creatures overcome " (67); but this applies only to the actors, not to the audience.   Orestes from his place on the stage can see them; but the spectators cannot.   The line, however, conveys a vivid sense of their presence close at hand, an impression soon to be reënforced.

Some have held that at the end of the Priestess' speech the interior of the shrine was actually disclosed by the ἐκκύκλημα; but this is not likely.   The use of the machine at this period is not proved; and a platform large enough to accomodate the ὀμφαλός, Orestes, Apollo, Hermes and a Chorus of twelve would be difficult to manage under any circumstances.   It is much more natural, and at the same time more effective, to suppose the Furies still behind the scenes when the ghost of Klytaimestra rises. Her appeals to them, and their uncouth sounds as they gradually return to consciousness, show conclusively that they are close at hand. Finally, at her last words, " Follow, wither him in a second pursuit," they enter, thus producing an impressive climax. A significant hint that this was indeed the method employed is furnished by a phrase in the Life of Aischylos contained in the Medicean MS. of his plays. In the well-known description of the powerful effect on the spectators of the Chorus of Furies we read that it was brought about as they entered scatteringly — σποράδην εἰσαγαγόντα τὸν χορόν. This could not have been the case if the Chorus had been revealed by a machine, as they would all have appeared simultaneously; nor can it refer to the second parodos, before the Areiopagos, since only the first appearance could have produced so powerful an effect. If, however, they did not enter at all until after Klytaimestra had ended her appeal it would be perfectly natural for them to appear one by one, the awaking being supposed to take place just off the stage, and each Fury hurrying on as soon as roused.

We have thus a very skilful introduction of these novel and terrible figures — first the description by the Priestess, then the strange sounds that answer Klytaimestra, and finally the actual disclosure. The maximum of merely physical terror is thus attained; but Aischylos cannot be content with that. If the Furies remain merely physically terrible they will destroy that sense of their power which we have derived from the allusions in the preceding plays, and belie their deeper character as supernatural beings.

As a matter of fact the loathsome aspect of the Furies is a mere externality. They are keen-scented for blood, it is

true; but this is merely the outward indication of a power
that is really spiritual.   It is the scornful Apollo who bids
them repair to spots where the most revolting tortures are
practised, or to the blood-reeking dens of lions; they themselves know that their real dominion is over the souls of the
guilty.   The word " blight " recurs several times to express
the nature of the dread power that they exercise.   " Wither
him! " cries Klytaimestra in her last appeal to them; they
themselves declare that they will wither Orestes while he is
yet alive, and then drag him below (267); and the " binding
hymn " which they sing to bring him under their control is
" blighting to mortals," αὐονὰ βροτοῖς (333).   Their power
does not cease at the threshold of the grave.   " Though one
should flee beneath the earth, he is not freed," they declare
(175); and again, with a more imaginative restatement of a
line we noted in the *Suppliants*,[1] " even he who dies is not
over-free."   They bring the sinner to a goal " where joy is
nowhere a wonted thing " (423).   This skilful use of under-
statement produces a finer effect than any accumulation of
horrible details could compass.   The underworld in which
they dwell is no place of vulgar torture, but a realm governed
by moral ordinances.   A very significant passage (273 ff.)
presents its ruler Hades as " a great judge of mortals
beneath the earth, who observes all things with recording
mind."   Thus we see that the physically horrible touches
in the Furies are mere details on a background of spiritual
power.

Two choral odes in particular set forth the two aspects of
this power.   Its baleful manifestations against the trans-
gressor are the burden of the tremendous " binding hymn."
" Over the victim is this song, a frenzy, a maddening dis-

---

[1] *Supp.* 416 ὃς οὐδ᾽ ἐν Ἅιδου τὸν θανόντ᾽ ἐλευθεροῖ, a mere statement of
fact; here restated with impressive reserve: θανὼν δ᾽ οὐκ ἄγαν ἐλεύθερος.

traction, a hymn of the Erinyes that binds the soul, sung without the lyre, blighting to mortals." The phrase δέσμιος φρενῶν clearly marks the spiritual element in their power, which is exercised through the madness inspired in the guilty man. In his infatuation he does not realize the source of his woes, for his mind is wrapped in gloom; but the attack is irresistible. " The thoughts of men, though passing proud beneath the light of day, are melted and dwindle in dishonor beneath the earth at our black-robed advance and at the baleful dancing of our feet " (373-6). The mere presence of these dreadful beings suffices to bring doom upon the guilty.

But there is likewise a moral aspect. They do not assail him whose hands are pure of blood, but only the murderer who seeks to hide the stain of bloodshed (312 ff.). This moral aspect finds expression just before the actual trial begins. If this matricide is not punished, they will relinquish their pursuit of the guilty, and let loose every kind of murder. All invocation of them shall be in vain; it shall profit no one to cry " O Justice, O enthroned Erinyes," when his own kin turn against him. Suddenly they return to a theme first enunciated in the *Agamemnon*: " It is profitable to be wise after suffering." Arrogance is the child of impiety; but from a healthy mind comes desired prosperity. He who without compulsion is just shall not fail of it, nor be cut off utterly; but he who defies justice shall strike on the reef of reckoning, and be undone.

It is in this ode that the moral issue of the drama is solved, so far as it is solved by Aischylos. He conceives Orestes to be one who has learned by suffering, and made due atonement for his offence. Orestes comes before Athena fully convinced that he has been purified: " The bloodstain slumbers and withers from my hand, the pollution of a

mother's blood is washed away " (280 f.).   Aischylos
skilfully leaves this purification outside the action of the
drama, introducing it as a postulate, about which, so far
as the play itself is concerned, we are not at liberty to
argue.

This change of attitude is clearly indicated by the aban-
donment of the two great dominant motives of the preceding
plays.   The idea that blood demands vengeance is expressed
but once, and then in rather passing fashion: " a mother's
blood shed upon the ground is hard to restore " (261).   The
Furies are more interested in the blood which they will exact
in penalty from Orestes, as they practically go on to say.
Similarly the ghost of Klytaimestra, after she has roused
the Furies, has absolutely no further part in the action.
Orestes has no fear of her whatever, as he makes perfectly
clear when questioned on the point by the Furies.   If he
is condemned, he says, " my father will send help from his
tomb."   " Dost thou trust in the dead, thou who hast slain
thy mother ? " they ask indignantly; but he merely
replies, " Yes, for a double pollution fell on her " (598–600).
We can see why the motive of revenge for blood should be
dropped in this drama of reconciliation; but we may fairly
ask why, if the ghost of Agamemnon is sufficiently powerful
to shape the whole action of the *Choephoroi*, the ghost of his
wife should be utterly powerless in the *Eumenides*.   Both
he and she are ghosts eager for revenge; and there is no
reason, on general grounds, why one should be granted his
desire, and the other be cheated of hers.   We can only say
that for the needs of his play Aischylos has made the power-
lessness of Klytaimestra, like the purification of Orestes, a
postulate; and we may perhaps add that her impotence
symbolizes the defeat of the baleful powers.   It must be
admitted, however, that this second postulate is less justi-

fiable, more a product of the exigencies of the particular play. There it stands, however, to be accepted as a constituent of the plot. Of the merits of the ghost's appearance as a superb decorative episode there is of course no question whatever.

In essence, then, the moral problem has been solved before the court of the Areiopagos hears the case and casts its vote; and we need not linger over the scene of the trial, except to notice that in it Apollo loses to some extent the dignity which the divine personages in Aischylos elsewhere preserve, even in such trying circumstances as the angry colloquy between Prometheus and Hermes at the close of the *Prometheus*. The atmosphere of the Athenian law-courts, which is to have so prejudicial an effect on Euripides, already taints this scene, and gives Apollo somewhat the air of a blustering advocate. After the rendering of the verdict of acquittal Orestes has nothing more to do; and in his final speech he is merely the spokesman of the Argive people, promising their faithful allegiance to Athens. The political preoccupation which haunts Aischylos throughout this portion of the play is here perfectly manifest; but there is a return to the higher level of the trilogy in Orestes' declaration that after his death he will, as a hero, send help to Athens from his tomb. This may be regarded as the resolution of the theme of the power of the dead, a power previously exercised only in deeds of terror, but now to become an agent of beneficence. In the finale of the drama we have the great resolution, the gradual transformation of Erinyes into Eumenides, and their reconciliation with the new order. At first they are savagely resentful, and threaten to bring all manner of evils upon Attika; but they are at length won over, and leave the stage escorted by the grateful citizens to their new sanctuary in the city of Pallas.

It would be idle to assert that the *Eumenides* is not more local than the two preceding dramas, or that it has an equal claim on our regard.   It is designed for an Athenian audience, and appealed to them with a force which it cannot have for us.   Yet we may fairly say that in the respect which concerns us here, the treatment of the supernatural, it fully sustains the level reached by the *Agamemnon* and the *Choephoroi*.   Aischylos has brought his Furies visibly before us, subjecting them to all the possible disillusion of actual enstagement — and they have stood the test.

We may now, after this discussion of the individual plays, proceed to sum up their total contribution to our subject. We saw that the idea of the avenging spirit was present in the *Suppliants*, but merely as a decorative detail, with no direct effect on the plot.   In the *Persians* the connection of supernatural and plot is closer, though not minutely carried out.   There is, however, a curious anticipation of the plan of the *Oresteia* which deserves to be discussed in more detail than at our first mention of it.   The *Persians* begins with a vague dread of impending evil, made keener by Atossa's recital of her ominous dream, and particularized by the Messenger's story of Salamis.   The gloom is deepened by the prophecy of Dareios, which foretells a continuance of woe in the future, and finally we behold in Xerxes the visible symbol of the disaster that has overtaken Persia. We thus progress from anticipation through revelation to actual spectacle.   In the *Oresteia* precisely such a climax is effected, though with infinitely greater power, in the case of the Furies. They are at first mentioned in very general terms; then the allusions become more specific, and more closely related to the present action.   Kassandra's inspired vision sees them above the fated palace; but no one else in the *Agamemnon*, unless it be Klytaimestra, has so clear a sense of their pres-

ence. At the end of the *Choephoroi* Orestes in his frenzy
sees them close beside him, and we too feel that they are
almost within the scope of our own perception. Finally,
in the *Eumenides*, they are displayed to all; they form the
chorus, participate intimately in the action, and are the last
to leave the scene at the end of the play. They have thus
come from the very verge of consciousness into the focus
and centre of our perceptions, and reveal in unmistakable
fashion the power that they have exercised from the outset
of the trilogy. The resemblances between the two works
extend even into details. In the *Persians* the ghost of
Dareios disclosed to us something of the past and present
history of Persia; in the *Agamemnon* Kassandra reveals,
with far more thrilling effect, the appalling past and future of
the house of Atreus, while the earlier ghost is almost eclipsed
by the sinister phantom of Klytaimestra in the *Eumenides*.
The dream which only superficially alters the action in the
Persians becomes in the *Choephoroi* the principle which
conditions the entire play.

On his way to this supreme achievement Aischylos has
created in the *Prometheus* a drama in which Gods alone take
part, and which for all its grandeur lacks a fitting contrast;
he has also, in the trilogy to which the *Seven* belongs,
attempted his own peculiar problem, though not yet with
ability to solve it. Other essays he doubtless made in plays
now lost; but even in those which we have, the progress of
his mastery of the supernatural is singularly regular. In
the *Oresteia* he has absolute command of his means, and
makes them all subservient to the total effect. The Furies
are really the protagonists of the trilogy; and this fact
explains the lesser emphasis that he lays on details which
our modern taste would expect to find treated at greater
length. This is why he cuts short the recognition between

Orestes and Elektra, and at the end dismisses Orestes rather unceremoniously. For his dramatic purpose it is utterly immaterial what becomes of Orestes; his real interest lies in the reconciliation of the Furies with the new order of things. With a splendid disregard of merely theatrical exigencies and appeals he sternly subordinates the less essential human details to his main purpose. Yet he never slights the essential humanity of his characters, never falls into the lack of contrast which such neglect would involve. We never lose sight of the actual crimes which are the immediate causes of the woes of the present generation of the house of Atreus; but we never forget that these crimes are but incidents in a vast evolution, which leads to the absolving of the survivor whose virtue has been so sorely tested. It is for the doer to suffer, indeed; but through suffering comes wisdom. Aischylos shows us the reflection in the mortal world of the struggle between good and evil which pervades the Universe; he brings the supernatural into the sphere of our own experience, and shows us the human and the superhuman, each with its individuality, combining into one majestic whole.

SECTION 2. — SOPHOKLES

To pass from Aischylos to Sophokles is to come into a different world, a world of serene lucidity, in which the characters are no longer enveloped in portentous gloom, but revealed in clear lights, and in which even the most sinister trains of events tend to dissolve at last into quiet. The emphasis is primarily on the mortal participants; the Gods withdraw into their shining heaven, and the " divine event " to which the whole dramatic creation does after all move is indeed far off. Sophokles cannot, of course, forget the Gods: indeed, he sometimes causes difficulties by re-

membering them at the wrong moment. He is primarily
interested in the conflict of human passions, set before us in
definite characters and in sharply defined opposition. He
thus gains in pathos, and in purely theatrical effectiveness;
yet the Gods are there, behind the mortal passions which he
sometimes observes so intently as to forget the forces which
lie beyond them. As a result, he often falls somewhat
short of the deepest tragic terror and intensity, and at worst
into actual confusion and loss of connection in his treatment
of the supernatural. It is only at a relatively late period of
his development that he succeeds in establishing his own
synthesis between the powers beyond and the world of
mortals; yet his success, when finally achieved, has peculiar
merits of its own. In this earlier lack of interest in the supernatural, and in the perfection, on its own lines, of his ultimate solution of the problem, he is far more typically Attic
than is Aischylos. He does not set the two worlds in sharp
contrast, but blends them, just as the Parthenon frieze, at
its culminating point, brings the Gods into its very midst,
but without allowing them to overpower the mortal participants. Aischylos is interested in the supernatural
primarily because it reveals to him the springs of human
action; Sophokles regards it as one more thread to be woven
harmoniously into his design.

In his earlier plays, however, Sophokles is not over-careful
in his manner of bringing the supernatural into his fabric.
A comparison of his *Elektra* with the *Choephoroi* of his great
predecessor will afford an illuminating contrast, all the
sharper because of the identity of the material. We have
seen how the *Choephoroi*, receiving a large measure of gloom
and terror from the *Agamemnon*, steadily accentuates these
qualities, and adds new shades of its own. From sombre
opening to dubious conclusion the veil is never lifted, the

light scarcely suffered even to penetrate; and the fulfilment of the vengeance is only the prelude to new woe. The
Elektra, on the contrary, opens amid all the freshness of
dawn, and in full daylight the work of vengeance is brought
to a triumphant conclusion, over which no hint of fresh
calamity impends.   There are references enough to the
underworld, but they lack continuity, and seem designed
rather to secure contrast in a given passage than to express
any coherent view of the relations between the living and
the dead.   In any case, they create no uniform atmosphere,
whether one of such gloom as enshrouds the *Choephoroi*, or
one more appropriate to the spirit of the *Elektra* itself.
There is a continual shifting of conception and emphasis,
and a resulting uncertainty and " spottiness " of effect.   An
examination of certain passages will bear out this conclusion.
Elektra's first lament contains (110 ff.) an extensive invocation of infernal powers — Hades and Persephone, Hermes,
Erinyes, and ancestral Curse; but the Chorus promptly
reminds her (137 ff.) that no lamentations can recall her
father to the light.   Yet later, when she is directing her
sister Chrysothemis to make offerings at the tomb, she bids
her " fall down and pray that he himself may come with
favor from under earth, to help us against our foes " (453–
4).   This certainly suggests that she expects active assistance from the dead; and yet, when the supposed death of
Orestes has laid the burden of revenge on the survivors, and
Chrysothemis, seeking to learn whence they may derive
power to execute the vengeance with their own hands, asks,
" Am I then to make the dead to rise ? "   Elektra scornfully retorts, " I meant not that; I am not so void of wit "
(941.)   Again, after the recognition of Orestes by Elektra,
with all its play of tense emotion and sudden reversal, she
declares that even if her father should return to the light she

would not deem it a marvel, decidedly implying that under ordinary circumstances she would have no expectation of such an event. It seems impossible to avoid the conclusion that these passages are employed purely for decoration, that attitude being in each case adopted which seems likely to yield the maximum emotional effect. Sophokles is far more concerned with creating effective theatrical situations than with attaining a due relation of supernatural to plot. The supernatural elements, from the very nature of the plot, are there; but they are, as far as possible, disregarded. Klytaimestra's dream is of very little importance; she sees the ghost of Agamemnon, but he merely strikes his sceptre into the ground and makes it burst into leaf. There is no especial reason why it should have terrified her to any great extent, and it is promptly passed over. In a similar way, the impelling oracle is for the most part judiciously neglected. In true unity, therefore, and in deeper tragic impressiveness, the *Elektra* is decidedly inferior to the *Choephoroi*, though the vivid character-drawing, and the startling reversals of the plot, obscure the fact until a closer inspection is made. It seems clear, from other passages besides those just quoted, that Sophokles was trying to rival the *Choephoroi* on its own ground; but he certainly falls short of any such accomplishment. His references to the supernatural are not even consistent in themselves, and contribute very little to the tragic value of the play.

If the *Elektra*, as seems probable, belongs to the later part of its author's career, we may find additional proof of his lesser interest in the supernatural by turning back to the *Antigone*, one of the earliest of the extant plays. Here we have a more explicit attempt to synthesize the two worlds, but one which does not attain its object. The conflict between human and divine law, as personified in the head-

strong Kreon and the indomitable heroine, is the central
interest of the play.   To the minds of the spectators, for
whom the burial of the dead was a most sacred duty, which
it was the extreme of impiety to violate, Antigone indis-
putably has the right of the matter; and we may be sure
that Sophokles' conception of the problem did not differ in
kind from that of the average conservative Athenian.
Antigone accordingly must be regarded as under the protection of those chthonian divinities whose prerogatives she
is so anxious to maintain against Kreon's wanton aggression.
Here, then, is a clear relation between the action and the
powers of the underworld; but it is not closely united with
the dramatic fabric, nor adequately emphasized.   The
allusions to it are neither numerous nor striking, and assuredly sound no compelling note; our attention is almost
exclusively concentrated on the human aspects of the struggle.   The Chorus is quick to suspect supernatural intervention at the first news of the rite paid to the corpse of
Polyneikes; but this is an isolated hint.   In the choral odes,
where such thoughts might naturally be dwelt on and
developed, the only definite allusion is in the lines of the
second stasimon

κάτ' αὖ νιν φοινία θεῶν τῶν νερτέρων
ἀμᾷ κόνις, λόγου τ' ἄνοια, καὶ φρενῶν 'Ερινύς,   (601 f.)

and even here the pictures of the storm on the Thracian sea,
and of Zeus in his imperturbable majesty, which respectively
precede and follow, attract the attention more than the idea
of the ancestral curse.   That idea is indeed singularly
inconspicuous throughout the whole play, especially in
comparison with its prominence in the *Seven against Thebes*.
Ismene, in her account of the woes of the house which occurs
in the prologue (49 ff.) is content with a mere catalogue of

dreadful events; and the reference in the kommos which precedes Antigone's departure to her death-chamber (856) is
merely another touch in the prevailing pathos, with no profound moral connotation. Up to this point, then, the problem
has been worked out exclusively on the human plane, with
only incidental allusion to what lies beyond. This course,
if it had been adhered to, would have been perfectly legitimate; but now, at the climax, the supernatural suddenly
intrudes. The aged Teiresias, who, by reason of the prestige
which his long success as a prophet has given him, figures
with practically the authority of a divine personage,
thrusts himself into the action as a heavy beam might
break through a delicate marble relief. Thrilling this interposition undeniably is; but it is not justified by the logic of
the plot, and its effect is impaired by the violent altercation
with Kreon which lessens the dignity of the prophet's
abrupt entrance and withdrawal. This reversion to the
supernatural cuts the knot, indeed, but it comes in a measure ἔξωθεν τοῦ δράματος. Teiresias can scarcely be regarded
as the messenger of the outraged divinities of the world
below; and the might of destiny has not been so impressed
on us that we are prepared to accept its manifestation at
such short notice. Moreover, once the reversal has been
effected the Gods again withdraw, to make a not too
pointed last appearance in the closing words of the Chorus.

The *Antigone* thus affords an example of a play which
uses the supernatural only momentarily, to dispose of a
difficulty, and otherwise neglects it. Hence it is less praiseworthy in this regard than the *Elektra*, which consistently
relegates the supernatural to a subordinate position, and
does not call it into service to unravel the plot. In the
Antigone the might of the Gods has not been so emphasized
as to justify its sudden manifestation; and to say that the

Gods are not in question, because it is the mortal Teiresias who brings the message, is merely to quibble. It is, however, possible to perceive an attempt to increase our sense of the divine power in the way that the character of Kreon is presented. He may be conceived as a man professing disregard of any higher power, though conventionally " religious," but changing front abruptly when confronted by a manifestation of such a power, and as fain to obey as he was before to defy. He is clearly lacking in real respect for the Gods; he can pass from a solemn oath by Zeus to open blasphemy, and then excuse himself from that on the ground that his impious wishes are impossible of fulfilment. He is equally contemptuous of soothsaying; τάχ' εἰσόμεσθα μάντεων ὑπέρτερον, he says casually (631), in a way that is evidently more an unconscious expression of opinion than an intentional sneer. But the secret dread persists, and comes out in the burst of passion with which he receives the suggestion of the Chorus that some superhuman power has intervened in the bestowal of the last rites on Polyneikes. He is of course constantly liable to such outbreaks; but this particular one would certainly be better motivated if we regard it as the result of a concealed but lively dread. On this view we can also better appreciate his change of front after the departure of Teiresias, natural though that is under the circumstances. He makes every effort to placate the outraged power which he has always secretly feared, and we are supposedly impressed by the spectacle of condign punishment inflicted on the hard heart. But even if we accept this interpretation of Kreon's character, the *Antigone* cannot be regarded as a successful instance of the use of the supernatural to determine the course of a plot.

So far we have been considering cases of at least partial failure to unite the supernatural with a tragic action; we may now approach the pleasanter task of studying the successful solution of the problem by the matured art of Sophokles. The *Oidipous Tyrannos* may serve as our first example. Here the divine prohibition which Laios transgressed originates the entire tragic complication; but that transgression and its first consequences are well in the past at the opening of the play, so that the action starts securely on the human plane. The human aspects fittingly occupy the foreground, but leave scope for the thought of the powers beyond to appear at intervals. The clearness with which these human aspects are presented is such that any infusion of the higher element serves only to deepen their emotional effect, instead of clouding it. The prologue sets before us the two cardinal features of the situation — the heaven-sent plagues, and the eagerly awaited oracle that is to declare the cause of them. The parodos takes up these two themes, and develops them; they recur in the first stasimon, while the second adds to them the thought of the divine wisdom, which will surely be manifest when the present uncertainties are cleared up. One need not dwell on the contrast to the choral indifference of the *Antigone* which this reënforcement of the leading ideas presents. A contrast equally sharp may be found in the handling of Teiresias in the two plays. His entrance in the *Tyrannos* is much more adequately motivated than in the earlier play; Oidipous is eager to learn the will of the Gods toward Thebes, and Teiresias is by common consent their accredited spokesman there. It is natural, then, that he should be summoned; but he knows that the disclosure of the truth will be the undoing of the royal house. His situation, as he stands before us, reluctant to utter the fatal words, is far more tragic, and far more a problem in character, than his superficially striking but essentially irrelevant appearance in the

Antigone.   It is true that during most of the scene the human interest predominates; the prophet, for all his divine inspiration, is sufficiently of mortal mould to object vigorously to an accusation of imposture on his own account, as well as that of the outraged divinities.   Yet he preserves his dignity; and the dark hint which he drops at the end concerning the parentage of Oidipous maintains his impressiveness as a soothsayer.   The hint urges Oidipous on in his effort to discover the identity of his parents; and when the dread discovery is at last made we are fully prepared to recognize in it the manifestation of the Gods' unerring retribution.   The sense of their guidance tempers the horror of the climax; and at the very end of the play the fate of Oidipous hangs in suspense, while Kreon awaits a new oracle which shall decide his course.   Here, then, is a dominance of the Gods over the mortal characters which is kept in its due place with reference to the dramatist's aim, but which we are never suffered to forget.   At any moment we can look back over a perfectly coördinated sequence of thought and event, without, as in the *Elektra*, wondering how some of the details can be reconciled with one another, or being, as in the *Antigone*, bewildered by a sudden shift of emphasis.   The consummate clarity of the plot becomes the more evident, the more minutely it is studied.

In the *Oidipous Tyrannos* the interest which Sophokles feels in his problem is predominantly ethical; for the more purely aesthetic side of his solution we must turn to the *Oidipous at Kolonos*.   Here again the supernatural is intelligibly related to the plot.   Oidipous is presented as under the protection of the Gods, as one who has learned wisdom through suffering, and acquired strange virtues as a result of his trials.   This favor of the Gods toward their long-tried suppliant is at the basis of the whole play, determining not only the significance of the action, but the very place where it occurs. In this respect the play is a more luminous counterpart of the *Choephoroi*. We know by Antigone's first words that this is a sacred precinct, with its olive, laurel and vine, thick-winged with nightingales; the brief dialogue with the Stranger tells us to whom it is sacred, and arouses in the mind of Oidipous the recollection of the prediction of the later oracle (that which was still awaited at the close of the *Tyrannos*) that he should find rest at the seat of the Eumenides, and become a safeguard to the kindly land that should shelter him. His relation to the Gods is thus made wholly clear; and an added solemnity is given by the allusion, in the first strophe of the parodos, to the dread might of the August Goddesses, which confirms our belief that their power will indeed bring peace to Oidipous at the last. The entrance of Ismene brings an account of affairs at Thebes, with news of a fresh oracle confirming the benefit which some land is to derive from being the burial-place of Oidipous, and thus motivating the attempts of the Thebans to secure possession of his person which we are shortly to see enacted. The deftness of this union of divine sanction and dramatic exigency needs no praise. At the close of the scene the Chorus tell Oidipous of the rites of purification which he must perform; and so this part of the drama terminates, with its chief point, the relation of Oidipous to the Gods, firmly fixed in our minds. The long period of stirring action that follows — Kreon's bold attempt and its discomfiture, and the episode of Polyneikes — does not obscure this central idea; and when the summoning thunder breaks forth we have no trouble in picking up the thread and preparing for the imminent climax. The contrast of the storm in Nature and the terror of the Chorus with the majestic serenity of Oidipous as he realizes that the

end is at hand is a peculiarly Sophoklean one.   The feeble
old man, so long guided by others, is filled with superhuman
insight; erect and firm he passes out, now in his turn the
guide to that last resting-place which shall be a boon to
Athens as well as to himself.   He feels beside him the presence of Hermes the guide of souls, leading him to Persephone; and with words of blessing to those who have
befriended him he passes from sight.   The Chorus briefly
invokes the chthonian powers, and the whole is closed by
the Messenger's description of the last event of all — the
viewless passing of the toil-worn king to his long-sought
deliverance.   Dignity, compassion and triumph blend here
in reverent and exquisite reticence; in this scene, it may
fairly be said, the art of Sophokles culminates.

We thus see that the plays in which Sophokles deals with
the supernatural fall into two classes.   In the earlier he
utilizes it for temporary convenience, and lets it go the
moment it has served its turn; in the later he is perhaps not
much more interested in it, but he is careful to relate it to his
plot, and to make it enhance the effect of his human characters.   But the divine world remains throughout rather remote, and as a consequence of this remoteness only twice in
the extant plays do divinities actually appear on the stage.
It so happens that the two cases — Athena at the opening
of the *Aias*, and Herakles at the end of the *Philoktetes* —
belong respectively to the two periods of Sophoklean art
which we have just distinguished.   The appearance of
Athena cannot be called impressive.   " Appearance "
indeed is too decided a word; in fact she is but a voice to
Odysseus whom she accompanies, though she is visible to the
distraught Aias.   The Sophoklean clarity here becomes
rather blank; Athena is too much like the mortal she is
protecting, and Odysseus just here is not conspicuous for

any god-like attributes. We can feel the shortcomings of this Athena by comparing her with the Apollo of the *Eumenides*. He addresses his suppliant with perfect tenderness, yet preserves his divine dignity and serenity, while the shadowy figure of Hermes, who stands mysteriously in the background, adds just the depth which in the *Aias* is lacking. There is no real necessity for Athena's appearance, and it has no great aesthetic merit.

The apparition of Herakles is of a different sort, better in itself, and much more connected with the plot. The situation at the end of the play, just before he appears, is a conflict of decisions which only the intervention of a higher power can resolve. Troy cannot be taken without the aid of Philoktetes; but he will not consent to give his assistance, and there is no mortal force that can compel him to do so, now that Neopotolemos is on his side, and has sworn to restore him to his native land. But the Gods have willed that Troy shall fall; hence one of them must reveal to Philoktetes that his decision must be changed, and it is Herakles, who by reason of their long friendship stands in the closest relation to him, who performs the task. As he is but a demigod, he can combine the divine mandate with the persuasiveness of a human comrade, and so make his plea doubly effective. His words attain their effect, and Philoktetes, making his submission to Destiny, departs "whither mighty Fate bears him, and the will of friends, and the all-subduing divinity who has wrought this to fulfillment."

It is clear from such a survey as that which we have just completed that Sophokles is not irresistibly drawn to the supernatural by the constitution of his mind, but that he accepts it as a constituent of tragedy as it comes to him from the hands of Aischylos. He is at first content to treat it rather superficially, because it does not much interest him;

later, the defects arising from such a method become evident
to him, and he feels the necessity of making the supernatural enter into his dramatic fabric.   Hence arise the two
periods which we have discerned in his work.   Throughout,
however, his first concern is with his mortal characters, and
the powers beyond serve as little more than a background,
against which the mortals may be set in bolder relief, but
from which they are essentially detached.   We do not feel,
as we do with Aischylos, that the whole action depends on
the supernatural powers, who may intervene at any point.
Sophokles enunciates the principle πάθει μάθος, but he is less
interested in the process than in the result; he shows us
Oidipous at the end of his career, when he has attained wisdom by suffering, and leaves the Eumenides in the background; Aischylos, as we saw, is more interested in the
Furies who bestow the suffering, and lets Orestes at the close
depart almost unnoticed.   The Sophoklean method lends
itself in a much greater degree to purely theatrical requirements; but the art of Aischylos, by its very disregard of the
superficially effective, has a greater range and intensity than
the perfect but limited art of Sophokles.   Yet the beauty of
the latter's achievement is undeniable, and the *Oidipous at
Kolonos* forms a worthy pendant to the *Oresteia*.

In his earlier works, however, Sophokles cannot be ac-
quitted of the charge of a mechanical handling of the supernatural which prefigures the practice of Euripides, from
whom indeed Sophokles seems to have taken over the *deus ex
machina*, though to better purpose than his model.   It is very
probable that Gods appeared in certain of the lost plays,[1]
but it is not likely that such cases would materially affect
the conclusions already enunciated.   One loss, however, we
must profoundly regret — that of the *Polyxena*, in which the

---

[1] See E. Müller, *De Graecorum Deorum partibus tragicis*, p. 61.

ghost of Achilles appeared. Longinus, to whom we owe the record of the fact, speaks of the episode (*De Subl.* xv. 17) in terms of high praise, coupling it with the closing scene of the *Oidipous at Kolonos*. The opportunity to compare a Sophoklean ghost with those which Aischylos and Euripides present would be a welcome one, especially since Sophokles, so far as we have his plays, has little to say of the underworld, naturally preferring to look toward the radiant Olympians, who are more consonant with the spirit of his work. The opportunity, however, is not ours; and we can only close with a reminder that these lost works might, had they been preserved, have enlarged our estimate of the range of Sophokles' genius.

SECTION 3. — EURIPIDES

In the tragedies of Euripides we have something quite unlike what we have had to deal with in Aischylos and Sophokles. In their work the supernatural elements have had a relevancy to the several plots so marked as to render the study of their mutual relations comparatively simple. In Euripides, on the other hand, we have an author supposed, on good grounds, to have been by no means favorable to the established religion which had served his predecessors so well; yet in his work we find a greater number of divine apparitions than in Aischylos and Sophokles together. So paradoxical a state of affairs certainly demands discussion, and has on numerous occasions received it. The most recent treatment of the theme, that of Erich Müller,[1] gives a very good account of the constituent elements of the Euripidean Gods, and of the functions they perform; but its author seems to have slight regard for the fact that he is

[1] *De Graecorum deorum partibus tragicis*, Giessen, 1910. Chapter III, pp. 62–135, deals with Euripides.

dealing with drama, and hence has little to say concerning the relation of Gods to plot.   A review of the subject from our particular standpoint is therefore still worth making.

The supernatural characters in Euripides may be grouped under three heads, according to the point at which they appear in each play—a fact which at once indicates the distance we have traveled from Aischylos, or even Sophokles.   No one would dream of grouping the Gods of Aischylos according to the point at which they enter the action; the course of the play is throughout dependent on them.   In Euripides, however, this mechanical classification is justified by the facts of the case.   We have the God in whose mouth is placed a characteristic Euripidean prologue, and who may fairly be called the prologue-God; the God who appears at the end of the play, with more or less effect on the action, and usually a marked expository function, the familiar *deus ex machina*; and finally, in only a few cases, the God who intervenes before the action is wholly over.   Though the second and third classes sometimes overlap, they correspond in general to real distinctions in the Euripidean usage.

The first class derives a considerable variety from the fact that a single divine figure is never employed to deliver the prologue, unless some other divine manifestation occurs during the remainder of the play.   The only possible exception is the *Hekabe*; but there the prologue is delivered by the ghost of Polydoros, who cannot be regarded precisely as a divine personage.   This case may be dismissed for further consideration later.   The two instances in which we have Gods in the prologue and nowhere else are the *Troades* and the *Alkestis*, in each of which two appear.   In the former we have a dialogue between Poseidon and Athena.   Poseidon begins by describing the fall of Troy, and the destruction of

his favorite haunts there, which he is forced to abandon.
Then Athena expresses her anger at the desecration of her
shrine by the violence offered by Aias to Kassandra, and her
eagerness to make the return voyage of the Greeks as hard
as possible.   She secures the aid of Poseidon for this laud-
able undertaking, using as an argument his professed
tenderness for the city he has helped to found.   He ends
with some moralizing words on the folly of those who sack
cities without sparing temples or tombs.   Inasmuch as the
rest of the drama is concerned only with conditions in Troy
after its capture, and does not show us the hard home-
coming of the Greeks, this incident has no further effect on
the play, and serves only as a decorative prelude.

The *Alkestis* gives us a somewhat different type — a dialogue preceded by a monologue in regular form.   The first
speaker is Apollo; he recounts his services in the house of
Admetos, and his attempt to reward him by securing from
the Fates a promise that he shall escape death if another can
be found to die in his place.   Only his wife, Alkestis, will
consent to the sacrifice; and she is now at the point of death.
In fact, Apollo sees Death himself lurking near the palace in
wait for his victim, and a dialogue between the two divinities follows.   Death reproaches Apollo for robbing him of
Admetos, but Apollo answers that he should be content
with Alkestis, from whom he rather casually tries to dissuade him.   Death, however, is obdurate, even when Apollo
declares that Herakles is in the house and will rob him of
his prey; he proceeds to enter the palace, and make Alkestis
his own by the symbolic act of shearing a lock from her
head.   In the issue, however, very little more is heard of
any activity on Death's part; and the incident, if genuine,[1]

---

[1] The view that it is an actors' interpolation is maintained (not very
cogently) by F. D. Allen, in *Harvard Studies in Classical Philology*, ix. 37.

has only a decorative function.   These two cases of Gods in the prologue only may accordingly be dismissed, as showing no effect of the supernatural on the action.

The *deus ex machina* is the best-known type of the Euripidean usage of Gods, and the one which occurs most frequently in his work.   As simple an example as we can find is the Athena who appears at the end of the *Suppliants*. She appears without warning, just after Theseus has offered to yield to the Argives the bodies of the seven chieftains for which he has fought with Thebes.   She bids him not surrender them before he has exacted from the Chorus an oath that they will ever after be faithful to Athens;   a command which produces a prompt subsidence from the noble ethical level of his preceding speech.   She prescribes the ritual for the oath, and then predicts to the sons of the Seven their own expedition against Thebes, and its success.   Theseus expresses his willingness to obey, as do the Chorus, in the final words of the drama.

This speech of Athena contains two clearly marked parts — the prescription of the ritual for the oath, and the prediction of the second expedition against Thebes — both of them expository in character.   This expository element is practically constant in the Euripidean *deus*, usually, of course, in the form of prediction of future events, corresponding to the revelation of past events which we have in the prologue.   The interest in matters of ritual is less constant, but it crops out in other places, notably in the close of the *Iphigeneia in Tauris*.   It is explicable as an inheritance from the interest of Aischylos in such matters, augmented by Euripides' own antiquarian leaning.   The chief importance of the *deus* lies in the general expository function, which is precisely the way in which the power of the Gods appears to the least advantage.   " We grant," says Aristotle (*Poetics*,

c. 15), " that the Gods see everything "; accordingly the revelation of past or future by them results in no such sense of the exercise of superhuman power as that which we gain from the prophecies of a mortal seer. When, as in the case of the *Suppliants*, the divinity in question has no effect on the action, which terminates with his or her departure, we have a merely expository God, external to the action, and hence not satisfying our definition of the tragic supernatural. These two qualities of exposition and externality are the chief ones of the Euripidean *deus*, though with some variation in the several cases, as we shall now see.

We find the *deus* at its lowest point in the *Elektra* and the *Orestes*. At the end of the former, when Elektra and Orestes have executed their vengeance, and are in imminent peril of their lives, the Dioskouroi suddenly appear, and proceed to give directions for the future. Before giving them they hint at blame of Apollo for the oracle which has brought about the dreadful events just enacted; but he is their master, and they cannot speak too explicitly. They then proceed to dispose of the fates of the other characters. Pylades is to marry Elektra, and take her to his own country; Orestes, after seeking purification at Athens, is to settle in Arkadia. The Argives will bury Aigisthos; and Menelaos and Helen, just returned from Egypt, will perform the same office for Klytaimestra. Now follows a brief dialogue, in which the Chorus asks the Dioskouroi why they did not prevent the murder of their kinswoman; but the only answer is that Fate did not permit them to interfere. We then have the parting of Orestes and his sister, and a final injunction to him by the Dioskouroi. He is to flee the Furies, who are close at hand; while the two divinities will return to the Sicilian sea to save virtuous mariners.

It is evident that we have here a somewhat extended form, in which some of the results of the commands uttered by the Gods are portrayed in action; in this case the parting of Orestes and Elektra, with its attendant operatic lamentations.   This portrayal is, of course, scanty enough, in proportion to the number of things commanded, and is designed primarily to give opportunity for the duet of Elektra and Orestes.   The idea of the conflict of divine wills hinted at in the criticism of Apollo is not stated impressively, and falls rather flat.   The episode has little relevancy to the action, and still less power of its own.

An even worse case is the apparition of Apollo at the end of the *Orestes*.   As the situation stands, Orestes, Pylades and Elektra are still at Argos after the murder of Aigisthos and Klytaimestra, in imminent danger of being stoned to death by the outraged citizens.   In their extremity they conceive the brilliant idea of slaying Helen, just returned with Menelaos, and by this murder of the woman whom all Hellas detests winning such gratitude as will ensure their escape.   They carry out their plan, and in addition secure Helen's daughter Hermione as a hostage.   Menelaos learns of his wife's murder, and hastens in, to be confronted by Orestes with drawn sword at Hermione's throat, threatening to kill her if he is not allowed to depart in safety.   It is at this moment that Apollo appears, and proceeds to dispose of the characters in utter defiance of probability.   Helen, it seems, was not slain, but snatched away by divine power, and set among the Gods; Menelaos is bidden to seek another wife in her stead.   Orestes is to marry Hermione, whom he was just on the point of killing; Neoptolemos, who thought he was to have her, will never be her husband, since he is to meet death at Delphi.   Pylades, in accordance with a promise previously made him by Orestes, is to marry

Elektra. Finally, Menelaos is bidden to return to Sparta, and live on his wife's dowry. Both he and Orestes are perfectly satisfied with the new arrangement, and the confirmation of Apollo's oracles which it affords.

These two plays can be compared to nothing but the disordered visions of a nightmare; their events follow each other without any reference to an underlying principle. The *Elektra*, with its pseudo-realistic travesty of a great legend, is bad enough; but the *Orestes* almost passes the border of sanity. It makes little difference whether such plays as these are terminated by the intervention of a God or not; one more absurdity is no burden to a play which consists of little else.

A somewhat better example, though it contains elements resembling those of the *Orestes*, is the *Andromache*. Here the divinity in question is Thetis; and her intervention is sufficiently justified by her kinship to an important character in the play, Peleus. The piece deals with the fortunes of Andromache as the slave and concubine of Neoptolemos. He has recently married Hermione (in defiance of what we have just heard stated at the end of the *Orestes*), who is naturally not pleased at his previous relations with Andromache. Her enmity carries her to such an extreme that she decides on her rival's murder, and takes advantage of the absence of Neoptolemos at Delphi to put her scheme into effect, with the help of her father Menelaos, here represented as a thorough-going scoundrel. At the opening of the play Andromache takes refuge at the shrine of Thetis; but she is lured thence by the wiles of Menelaos, and brought into the power of her enemies. At this juncture, however, appears the aged Peleus, who speedily changes the complexion of affairs, and sends the baffled Menelaos about his business. Hermione, in abject dread that her scheme will become known to her husband, and bring punishment upon her, appeals to Orestes, who opportunely passes through the country, on the ground of their ancient love! He cheerfully consents to fly with her, and to slay Neoptolemos at Delphi. This plan is carried out; and the body of Neoptolemos is brought in to his grief-stricken father. After the due laments he appeals to Thetis, and she appears, to the amazement of the Chorus. As befits a Goddess, her ordering of the affairs of Peleus and Andromache is even more competent than that of the Gods we have previously encountered. She bids Peleus not grieve overmuch, but bury Neoptolemos at Delphi, and send Andromache to the Molossian land, where she will marry Helenos. Peleus, by reason of their former wedlock, is to be made immortal; he will dwell in the sea, and visit Achilles in Leuke. As soon as he has buried Neoptolemos she will come for him. He expresses his gratitude, and ends by moralizing on the advantages of marrying into a good family.

We have here a closer relation of the *deus* to the general action. Thetis is called to our attention at the outset by the fact that it is at her shrine that Andromache seeks refuge; and her actual appearance is justified by her former wedlock with Peleus, who plays so conspicuous a part in the rescue of the heroine. The direct invocation of her by Peleus is likewise something we have not had in the previous examples. Apart from this greater fitness of deity to circumstance, which still remains rather an external affair, we have essentially the same mechanical use as before, though with a less marked violation of probability.

Yet another type is to be found in the *Helen*. At the close of that play, it will be remembered, Theoklymenos, the king of Egypt, who has had Helen in his charge, has just learned that she and Menelaos have escaped through the connivance of his own sister Theonoe. He is naturally incensed at the deception; but the Dioskouroi intervene, to prevent his taking any severe measures. They make it clear to him that his sister has only followed the will of the Gods in facilitating Helen's escape and that he must acquiesce in it. Helen is to be deified, like Peleus in the *Andromache*. Theoklymenos is entirely submissive to these commands, and the play ends. We have thus an expository element much like that of the *Andromache*, but also a distinct affecting of the action. Theoklymenos is dissuaded from laying violent hands on his sister by the apparition of the Dioskouroi, who explain to him why his anger is without reasonable basis.

Essentially the same situation, with a finer aesthetic effect, is to be found at the end of the *Iphigeneia in Tauris*. Orestes and his companions have made good their escape with the stolen image, but a contrary wind has thrown them back into the power of the barbarian king Thoas. Just as he is on the point of starting in pursuit, Athena appears and bids him abandon his design; she then goes on to predict the arrival of Orestes at Athens, and the establishing of the cult of Artemis Brauronia. The impression produced by the interposition is admirable, the effect on the action marked, and the tone of the presentation sober and dignified. From the point of view of artistic handling this case is decidedly the best of those we have thus far examined.

We now come to two plays that combine the prologue-God and the *deus* — the *Ion* and the *Hippolytos*. In the first of these we have at the outset Hermes, who begins by telling us his ancestry, his function as messenger of Zeus, and the place of the action, Delphi, at which he has just arrived. He goes on to relate the love-affair of Apollo and Kreousa, and the birth and abandoning of their child Ion. Apollo, however, mindful of his offspring, bade Hermes convey him to Delphi, where he was reared at the temple, and became its steward.   Subsequently Kreousa married one Xouthos, a Euboean; they have had no children, and have come to Delphi to learn the cause from the oracle.   Apollo will there reveal Ion's relationship to them, and give him his real name, Ion, by which he is as yet not known.

It seems to be Euripides' purpose in this prologue to present the relations of Apollo and Kreousa in as unpleasant a light as possible; a purpose which he fully achieves.   There is no revelation of divine power in the events as Hermes describes them; even the conveying of Ion to Delphi is not a feat which demands the intervention of a God, for it might have been brought about (like the rescue of the abandoned Oidipous) by chance wayfarers, or something of the sort. The remainder of the play does not present the divine power in any better light.   At the end Athena comes, to speak for her brother, who is reluctant to appear, lest he be reproached for the manner in which he has managed affairs!   After the usual ordering of the future conduct of the other characters, she predicts the future glories of Ion's descendants.

Certainly such Gods as these are not at all calculated to inspire reverence in those who behold them; but neither do the mortals of the play command our respect.   If Euripides intended to set off despicable divinity against noble humanity, his sense of contrast cannot be called remarkable. The rather self-righteous Ion, the coarse, dull-witted Xouthos, Kreousa who in cold blood plans the murder of her husband's supposedly just-discovered son, with especial care that no suspicion may fall on herself, and the old servitor who falls in with her plan, and encourages her by villainous advice — these are assuredly not figures which display the virtues of humanity to any marked degree.

The truth seems to be that Euripides has attempted a "realistic" recasting of the legend which results only in destroying its beauty as a legend without making it credible as a matter of ordinary experience. One may grant that the less said of the Gods in it, the better; but neither are Kreousa and the rest to be regarded as very favorable specimens of their kind.

In the *Hippolytos*, on the contrary, we have a successful use of essentially the same elements as in the *Ion*. The prologue is spoken by Aphrodite. She extols her power, and tells us that she is wroth against Hippolytos because he has no heed of her. She goes on to declare that his life must be the forfeit of his arrogance, and explains how his undoing is to be brought about. All this exposition is strictly necessary, according to the usual Euripidean practice; there is no parade of erudition, and the Goddess makes it perfectly clear why she hates Hippolytos and intends to destroy him. We are thus convinced that the action of the play is to be guided throughout by the wrath of Aphrodite; and this conviction is enforced by numerous subsequent allusions. The scene between Hippolytos and his old slave which immediately follows the hero's entrance develops the motive. The slave bids his master pay at least outward homage to a divinity so powerful as Aphrodite; but the youth expresses his contempt of her and all her works in language which goes far to justify the fate which befalls him. The theme of Love's power recurs at intervals throughout the play; the Nurse uses it as an argument against Phaidra's resolution not to declare her passion (443 ff.), and the first choral song (525 ff.) takes it up. Phaidra, when she has determined to die, says that her death will delight Kypris (725–7), and after the announcement of the fatal accident which has befallen Hippolytos the

Chorus once more descants on the power of the Goddess, though in a manner which scarcely fits the gravity of the situation.   Now Artemis, the guardian Goddess of Hippolytos, reveals to Theseus the true state of affairs; an intervention fully justified by the facts of the case.   She explains to him the real nature of his wife's conduct, and then declares her hatred of Kypris for the deed that has been wrought.   She could not prevent it, for there is a νόμος of the Gods not to oppose one another.   The dying Hippolytos is now brought in, and she comforts him.   A marvellous fragrance reveals her presence, and the dying youth momentarily revives.   In requital for his death, she tells him, she will slay some favorite of Aphrodite's and give Hippolytos the honors of a hero.   Then she withdraws, since a God cannot be present at a death.   The reconciliation of father and son is effected, and Hippolytos quietly expires.   The last words of Theseus are a declaration that he will remember the many woes that Kypris has caused; the theme of the opening persists to the end.

Euripides here has frankly reverted to the method of handling the supernatural adopted by his predecessors; and the result seems to justify such a reversion.   The supernatural elements are intelligibly related to the plot, and delineated with appropriate touches, such as the fragrance which reveals to the dying Hippolytos the presence of Artemis.   The incidental allusions are sufficiently numerous to keep the power of Aphrodite before our minds, and the two divinities really display in action their capacities to affect the fates of mortals, instead of merely expounding their intentions or desires.   Yet we cannot feel that Euripides has penetrated very deeply into the spirit of the older tradition; his treatment here, despite its outward conformity to the practice of his predecessors, remains on the whole rather decorative than deeply rooted in the fabric of the drama.

The degree to which one regards such decorative handling as artistically satisfying naturally depends on one's view of Euripides' purpose in introducing divine figures at all. The late Dr. Verrall has made an exceedingly (perhaps excessively) ingenious attempt, in his *Euripides the Rationalist* and *Essays on Four Plays of Euripides*, to prove that Euripides wrote the majority, at least, of his plays with the intention of discrediting the traditional miraculous element in their plots; and that wherever that element is explicitly referred to or displayed it is designed to be unconvincing or even ridiculous. It follows from this that all the appearances of Gods are to be dismissed as purely mechanical, a mere concession to the prejudices of the uninitiated and to the conditions of the Attic theatre. Dr. Verrall himself states this conclusion in explicit terms: "The orthodoxy is pretended fiction, a mere theatrical trick, required in the first instance, and to some extent throughout, by the peculiar conditions of the tragic stage at Athens, but maintained in part out of a natural love for duplicity, ambiguity, irony and play of meaning, which was characteristic of the people and the time" (*Euripides*, pp. 231–32); and again, "In almost every case where superhuman or supernatural persons are introduced into tragedy by Euripides, we are compelled to suppose them unreal" (*Four Plays*, p. 167). Euripides, that is, used such figures purely as machinery, and without any serious intention.

This view, at first sight, does not lack plausibility; but it involves the supposition that Euripides degraded to a non-essential device what his predecessors had regarded as worthy of serious and dignified treatment. Admittedly such a concession to popular demands would impair the artistic effect of his plays; and it would seem that he might have found some way of conciliating the prejudices of the vulgar that would not have played havoc with his finales. Moreover, Dr. Verrall's theory compels him to treat the Athena of the *Iphigeneia* as the worst example of all: " To be more futile and unreal than the Athena of the *Iphigeneia* would be impossible " (*Four Plays*, p. 119).   As a matter of fact, we have just seen that she is precisely the example of the *deus* which best accords with our definition of the tragic supernatural.   A theory which leads to such curious inversions of the values in question seems to require some delicacy of handling.

It is not my purpose to discuss in detail the various bearings of this theory, but merely to point out that, though it is part of a general attempt to raise Euripides to a higher level of esteem than that which he usually occupies, it results, in this not unimportant matter of the supernatural, in a confession that he has fallen into a very incompetent method.   This conclusion we may eventually come to accept; but let us first see what light is thrown on the problem by our previous observations.

In the first place, we have noted the decided expository element in the Euripidean Gods, a trait in which they resemble the majority of the mortal characters.   There is no difference in kind between the information imparted by Gods and mortals, especially in the prologues; for the prediction of the future in the finales a God is of course more convenient, for reasons already stated.   But even where Euripides uses the more impressive methods of a mortal soothsayer to reveal the future, the expository matter remains essentially the same, as we see in the Kassandra of the *Troades*.   She enters (308) in a state of frenzy, and sings of her approaching nuptials with one of the conquerors. Hekabe tries to quiet her, and receives a long prophecy of the murder of Agamemnon and other impending events. The herald Talthybios intervenes, and is rewarded with a summary of the future wanderings of Odysseus! The imparting of assorted information is obviously the poet's chief aim. Only incidentally does Kassandra assume any deeper value, as at the end of her speech, where she declares that she will come a victress to Hades, after the death of herself and Agamemnon. To compare her with Teiresias, or the Aischylean seers, is impossible.

Such incidents as this, as well as the apparitions of Gods, have a marked spectacular appeal, which also fits in with the general tone of Euripidean tragedy, and which may account for their introduction in places where they are more or less inappropriate. But if they meant nothing more to their author than a temporarily convenient stage trick, would he have varied the manner of their appearance to the extent that he does ? Dr. Verrall exaggerates the conventionality of their use; in reality there is considerable variety of detail. The prologue-God does not appear as an isolated figure in the drama, except in the one case where he is replaced by a ghost; where the part of the Gods is confined to the prologue there are two of them, and even here variety is introduced by the more definite monologue of Apollo in the *Alkestis*, preceding the dialogue with Thanatos. Similarly, the *deus ex machina* appears unannounced — *Suppliants, Orestes, Helen, Iphigeneia* — or is perceived by the Chorus, or some character, before he speaks — *Elektra, Ion, Hippolytos*; while Thetis in the *Andromache* appears in response to an explicit invocation by Peleus. So evident a striving for variety is not what we should expect in the case of a purely mechanical expedient. And if its aim is solely to cast discredit on the received faith, would the orthodox

Sophokles have incorporated it in his *Philoktetes*, and that at the very end of his career, when its irreverent intent, supposing it to be real, must have been notorious ?

Moreover, what is to be said of the plays in which the Gods enter during the course of the action, instead of being relegated to the end ?   Artemis in the *Hippolytos* is really an example of such intervention, for the reconciliation of father and son is effected only in consequence of the facts which she discloses.   She thus clearly affects the action, and offers an interesting variant of the usual type of *deus*. But a more important case, and one on which Dr. Verrall has decided views, is the apparition of Iris and Lyssa in the *Herakles*, which we may proceed to examine.

The episode comes definitely in the middle of the play, at v. 822.   Herakles has just brought the tyrant Lykos into his toils, and slain him.   The Chorus sings a song of rejoicing, cut short by a sudden access of terror.   Above the house appears Iris, leading with her Lyssa, or Madness. Iris bids the old men of the Chorus not fear, since she does not come to bring woe on the whole city, but only on one man, Herakles.   Then she turns to Lyssa, and bids her fulfill her mission.   Lyssa declares her ancestry:

ἐξ εὐγενοῦς μὲν πατρὸς ἔκ τε μητέρος
πέφυκα, Νυκτὸς Οὐρανοῦ τ' ἀφ' αἵματος,

precisely in the style of the prologues, and then tries to evade the command of Iris, but without avail.   She enters the house, while Iris ascends to Heaven.   The Chorus utters a chant of terror; cries of pain are heard from within, and a messenger comes forth with the expected tale of woe.

At first sight this seems a clear case of the intervention of an actual divinity; but Dr. Verrall has an ingenious theory to explain the case away.   In the first place, he declares that this is a unique case in Euripides of the use of a God in the midst of an action, calmly ruling out the *Hippolytos* and the *Bacchai* as " debateable exceptions." But by analogy with the other divine figures Iris and Lyssa cannot be real; that is, they must be a represented vision, a nightmare, in fact. He cites the ghosts in *Richard III* as a parallel; but it is one which does not much help his case. Dr. Verrall, as he draws the comparison (*Four Plays*, p. 168), asserts that the actual appearance of a ghost in a professedly historical play would be a " dramatic solecism." This, however, is far from being a justifiable assumption[1]; nor could one argue from *Richard III* that the Elizabethans did not believe in the objective reality of ghosts. Dr. Verrall is considering the question from a very modern skeptical standpoint, which it is doubtful if any fifth-century Athenian, however " rationalistic " his trend of thought, had attained.

His assumption is that the Chorus, after their song of triumph, have suddenly been overcome by sleep; their leader then sees the vision, and, still asleep, utters the laments of 875 ff. Finally the entrance of the messenger rouses them, and they ask for precise information, since the impression they retain of the dream is so vague as to be practically negligible. The sudden falling asleep is, as Dr. Verrall says, unhinted by any reference in the text; he explains the lack by saying that it would be inappropriate, because of the involuntary nature of the slumber. Just why some brief allusion should have been impossible, is, to me at least, not clear; one would think that the sudden collapse of the Chorus would have somewhat surprised the spectators. But even granting this sudden slumber, the language of the ensuing lyrical passage, after Lyssa has

---

[1] What of *Julius Caesar* and its Elizabethan fellows ?

entered the house, is not very well adapted to convey the impression of a dream.   That a person under the influence of a nightmare should utter a sufficiently coherent lyrical passage of some thirty lines, responding appropriately to the cries from within, seems hardly plausible.   Imagine the effect in the opening of the *Eumenides*, if the slumbering Furies should sing an elaborate ode in answer to Klytaimestra's appeals!

If then we are to accept Dr. Verrall's interpretation of this episode, we must admit that Euripides has not handled it with any remarkable skill in psychological delineation. But we have seen that the interpretation strains the probabilities at several points, while the parallel adduced to support it really does not apply.   Richard certainly does not, while he is asleep, deliver elaborate speeches describing the ghosts that he sees; as we should expect, he utters not a word till he starts out of his dream.

In view of all this, the explanation that lies readiest at hand is that Euripides has here inserted an episode for decorative effect, without much care for its relevancy.   Dr. Verrall lays much stress on the fact that no mention of the apparition is made after the Messenger's entrance; but what has Euripides to gain by recalling it to our minds ? He cannot resist the temptation to insert it for the sake of momentary effect; but on any showing it is artistically defective, and the situation would not be improved by again calling it to our attention.   To seek a subtle significance in the incident is merely to exchange one set of defects for another.

What we have thus far deduced from our inspection may be briefly summarized as follows.   The supernatural in Euripides has indeed gone far in the direction of the purely mechanical, but has not yet actually reached that stage;

the care taken to secure variation of detail indicates that. It is true, however, that the Gods tend to appear at fixed places, in prologue or epilogue, with no very close connection with, or effect on, the action. In many cases they serve no real purpose; in others, as in the *Iphigeneia*, they have a real excuse for being, and show a reversion to the older practice. In one case, the *Hippolytos*, this reversion is so marked as to result in something which can fairly be judged by our previously established criteria. But in general the Euripidean Gods remain ornament, and not very good ornament; the next stage in their evolution, as we shall see, can only be a degradation to the state of machinery pure and simple.

We can estimate just how far Euripides has gone in this direction by comparing at this point the *Rhesos*, which has come down to us under his name, though the accuracy of the attribution was questioned even by ancient scholars. As the writer of the Greek argument justly remarks, the play has rather a Sophoklean character. It is a dramatic version of a single Homeric episode, the slaying of Rhesos, the Thracian ally of the Trojans, by Odysseus and Diomedes. Two Goddesses figure in it—Athena, and the Muse Terpsichore, mother of Rhesos. Athena appears when the two daring Greeks have invaded the camp, but are on the point of withdrawing again. She reveals to them the arrival of Rhesos, and bids them slay him, to avoid the losses which he will inflict on the Greeks, if suffered to live. They follow instructions; Paris comes up, and Athena pretending to be his guardian Goddess Aphrodite, mocks him in a scene of cruel irony. The murder is discovered, and the murderers are detected as they slip away; but the ready wit of Odysseus extricates them from the perilous situation. The charioteer of Rhesos enters, and accuses Hektor and the

Trojans of having treacherously slain his master; the resulting quarrel is checked by the appearance of the Muse, bearing her son's body in her arms. She laments, and then narrates how he was born, and how she will now make him a hero, ransoming his soul from " the Bride below," Persephone. She ends with a prediction of the death of Achilles, and tells how she and her sisters will come to sing his funeral song.

The blending of Sophoklean and Euripidean usage in this play is highly interesting. The episode of Athena follows the former; the Muse is more like the *deus ex machina*, but the expository element in her speeches, though marked, has not the stereotyped Euripidean manner, but is freely and imaginatively conceived. The author seems to have been one who had sufficient individuality to combine suggestions from other dramatists into something of his own. Indeed, the scene in which Paris converses with the pretended Aphrodite shows an irony not elsewhere paralleled in Greek tragedy in such a colloquy between a God and a mortal. Its nearest counterpart, the interview between Pentheus and Dionysos in the *Bacchai*, to which we shall shortly come, differs in being a colloquy between a mortal and an avowedly hostile power; while Paris imagines himself to be talking with one who has been his protector.

Thus far, with the exception of the *Iphigeneia in Tauris* and the *Hippolytos*, we have found little to praise in the Euripidean method of handling the supernatural; but we now come to a play which seems to defy our previous strictures, and stands forth as one of the marvels of Greek tragedy — the *Bacchai*. Here we have a play in which a God figures throughout as one of the chief personages, and reveals his power to the confusion of the impious and incredulous. At first he passes himself off as merely the

God's priest and initiate, and it is as such that he is known to the Chorus; but his true character becomes increasingly clear, and at the end he appears, like the usual Euripidean God, to dispose of the fates of the characters who have, too late, realized the terror of his might. He likewise appears at the very outset, to inform us of his identity and his previous adventures, in the customary Euripidean style. He has spread his worship through Asia, and now comes to Hellas, and to the city of his birth, Thebes. There his true lineage is unknown; but he has already shown his power by rousing the Theban women to Bacchic madness, and will shortly make himself known to all. To favor the execution of his plans, however, he has for the nonce assumed human form. He departs to Kithairon, where the Maenads are revelling, and the Chorus enters, to sing of the joys which attend the initiate. Then appear the aged Kadmos and Teiresias, to discourse piously of this new worship that has come among the Thebans, and to announce their determination to take part in it. Then comes in Pentheus, king of Thebes, in a violent rage against what has just seemed to the old men worthy of reverence. He is so wrapt up in his passion that it is some time before he realizes their presence; but when he does he mocks them for their absurd appearance, and declares his hatred of the orgies. Teiresias enters on a long defence of the new God, and Kadmos endeavors to dissuade his grandson from his folly, but without avail. Pentheus orders his attendants to take the mean revenge of destroying the seat from which Teiresias is wont to observe omens, and then to seize the leader of the Bacchai and bring him before him. The errand is soon accomplished, and Dionysos is brought in by a guard. Their leader relates how peacefully he yielded himself to them, ordering them to bind him and lead him to the king.

The Bacchai who were imprisoned, however, were mysteriously loosed from their fetters, and are now ranging the hills with their companions. " Full of many marvels does this man come to our Thebes; but it is for thee to provide for the rest."   Pentheus bids them unbind the captive, since he is safely in the toils, and scoffs at his womanish aspects; then he questions him as to his origin.   The stranger skilfully parries the attacks of Pentheus, and makes light of the threat of imprisonment.   " The God himself will release me *when I will*," he says, with a sinister double meaning which is even clearer in his next words. Pentheus, however, is wholly unaware of his true situation, and sends the stranger to a dungeon near the horses' stalls.   The Chorus reproaches Thebes for its ingratitude, and invokes the help of the God.

We now have the first clear manifestation of the power of Dionysos.   As the choral song ends his voice is heard from within, calling to his worshippers, who respond in great excitement; he calls again, proclaiming himself the son of Semele and Zeus.   An earthquake shakes the palace, and the flame that has hovered over Semele's tomb leaps up fiercely.   Appalled by these tokens of the God's presence the Chorus throw themselves on the ground, but Dionysos comes forth, bidding them not fear.   He tells them how he mocked Pentheus when the king came into the dungeon to bind him, making him see a phantom, and wearying him with a vain struggle.   The baffled Pentheus in turn appears, astounded to find before him the man whom he thought safely imprisoned.   He is manifestly distraught and Dionysos now begins to subdue him to his own will.   A messenger enters, with a tale of the Bacchic revel which he has beheld and the way in which the revellers put to flight the soldiers who attempted to seize them.   He bids Pentheus reverence the deity who has wrought such marvels, but only succeeds in stirring the king to new wrath, and a command that his hosts be summoned. Dionysos now intervenes, and by playing on the curiosity which the messenger's report has aroused in Pentheus prepares to lead him to his doom. He persuades Pentheus to disguise himself as one of the worshippers, and promises to conduct him to a place whence he may watch the revels in safety. He yields wholly to the God's persuasion, and enters the palace to assume his disguise, while Dionysos declares his purpose to the Chorus, telling them how madness shall come upon Pentheus, and how he shall be made a laughing-stock in his impotence, and later slain; then he goes to assist him in donning the fatal garb. The two come forth, Pentheus obviously a prey to madness; he sees two suns and two cities, while his companion appears to him in the likeness of a bull — a sinister apparition, in view of the God's frequent assumption of that form. Indeed, he tells Pentheus that he now sees him as he should; that is, he might know the God for what he is, if madness had not obscured his wit. Pentheus bids Dionysos give the final touches to his woman's garb, declaring, with bitter truth, that he is wholly in his hands. He exults in the thought of the deeds he will perform, and Dionysos with cruel irony turns his boasts against him. At last they depart, and the Chorus invokes the hounds of madness to seize on the guilty king, after which a messenger brings the expected account of his death at the hands of the Maenads, in which his own mother Agaue played the chief part. She is now returning to the city, with her son's head in her hands, deeming that she has slain a lion. In a moment she comes in, to engage in an excited dialogue with the Chorus, and eventually to be recalled by Kadmos to a knowledge of what she has really done.   At this point a portion of the play is lost; and after the break we find Dionysos, in the rôle of *deus ex machina*, revealing to Kadmos the woes of his race, and his own future destiny.   Agaue admits that they have sinned in not recognizing the God, but declares that he has punished them too severely; but he answers that it is the will of Zeus that has been fulfilled, and the play closes with the laments of Agaue and Kadmos.

Viewed from this angle the *Bacchai* seems to present a singularly effective treatment of its theme, in which irony becomes the means through which contrast is secured.   Pentheus is quite unaware of the true nature of the person who is temporarily in his power, while Dionysos is throughout the master of the situation, utilizing the madness of Pentheus as the instrument of his doom.   The rationalistic interpretation would seem to have no application here; yet it has been applied, and with no little skill, by Mr. Gilbert Norwood.[1]   According to his view, the play is an attack on the Dionysiac religion; the person who appears in its earlier part is not the God himself, but merely a follower, who is possessed of remarkable powers, but suffers from acute religious mania.   The episode in which " Dionysos " escapes from his prison is a mere sham; the palace is not shaken into ruins, but " Dionysos " by hypnotic power makes the Chorus, his easy dupes, believe that it has been. The other miracles are explicable as mere distorted products of the overwrought imaginations of those who report them.

It is obvious that this interpretation deprives the *Bacchai* of all interest from our point of view.   If " Dionysos " is a self-deluded impostor, we can have little concern for any

[1] In *The Riddle of the Bacchae*, Manchester, 1908.   Dr. Verrall has discussed and modified Mr. Norwood's views in *The Bacchants of Euripides*, Cambridge, 1910.   For a review of the question see R. Nihard, "Le Problème des Bacchantes," in *Musée Belge*, xvi, (1912) pp. 91 ff., and 297 ff.

merely abnormal powers that he may exercise. But Mr. Norwood's theory rather lacks evidence at critical points. For its *crux*, the explanation of the supposed " palace-miracle " through the hypnotism of an entire chorus, he has of course no evidence; but he suggests that Euripides may have " heard amazing reports of the magical powers possessed by Oriental wizards, and believed that the miracles and influence of Dionysos were due to the same cause " (*op. cit.* pp. 126–7). In that case such ideas must have been sufficiently familiar to the Athenian public of the day to make an unannounced use of them in drama perfectly feasible. Mr. Norwood admits that evidence for this is lacking; but adduces a good parallel from Lucian! A theory which can find no stronger backing is hardly to be called sound. Lucian has as much bearing on the state of thought in the fifth century B.C., as the editorial page of the New York *Sun* has on the mental habits of the Elizabethans.

The fact is that the rationalistic view, though intended to rehabilitate Euripides as a great dramatic poet, loses in one direction what it gains in another. Granting its truth, we may indeed admire the skill with which Euripides makes his real purpose unintelligible to the uninitiate; but all the treatment of the supernatural falls to the ground as trivial and unmeaning, and it is so conspicuous an element in some of the plays that such a bungling treatment of it in every case would constitute a real blemish. Dr. Verrall delights to enlarge on the great repute which Euripides enjoyed in antiquity as evidence that we too *must* regard him as a supreme dramatist. As a matter of fact, his repute was largely due to his skill in packing moral observations into quotable iambics, and had often little enough to do with any opinion of his ability as a dramatist. The recent rediscovery of Menander has shown with painful clearness the inexpediency of trusting too far the ancient estimates of plays.   The drop from the ecstatic rhapsodies of older critics to the disillusionized contempt of our own enlightened scholars is almost comic.   We are fully justified in asserting that the testimony of antiquity, even if it were as decisive as Dr. Verrall claims, is not necessarily binding on us.   In any case, we are nowhere told that the ancient fame of Euripides rested on his treatment of the supernatural, whether in a simply artistic or an ingeniously rationalizing way.

In the case of the *Bacchai* the application of the rationalistic theory is made more difficult by the strong element of folklore and ancient ritual practice which Mr. A. G. Bather [1] has revealed in the play.   Even if one does not accept all his conclusions, enough remains to make it almost certain that here, at least, Euripides is trying to achieve mythical verisimilitude.   It is not surprising that some of the elements in the complex conception should escape him; our previous examination has scarcely revealed him as a very competent depicter of divinity.   But a good part of the idea, with its strange duality, he has retained.   Dionysos is a double figure; the giver of many blessings, but likewise a dark and sinister power.   It is this sinister aspect that constitutes the tragic element in the *Bacchai*; and to overlook it, or seek to explain it away because not accordant with our own religious ideals, is futile.   " Our king is a hunter," cry the Chorus; and this cry is the text of the drama, increasingly applicable as Pentheus draws nearer his doom.   Throughout the *Bacchai* runs the primitive conception of the power outside human control which can bestow blessings, but can also bring doom on the unsubmis-

[1] See his paper " The Problem of the Bacchae," in *Journal Hellenic Studies*, xiv. 244.

sive; and it is by virtue of his reflection of this older attitude that Euripides has brought into his play some sense of
the true Dionysiac spirit, and made it his contribution to
the successful employment of the supernatural in tragedy.

In conclusion, something should be said of the ghost of
Polydoros in the *Hekabe*. He differs from the Aischylean
ghosts in his appearance as speaker of the prologue, with
resulting exposition. His first lines:

> ἥκω νεκρῶν κευθμῶνα καὶ σκότου πύλας
> λιπών, ἵν' "Αιδης χωρὶς ᾤκισται θεῶν,

are not without impressiveness; but he at once drifts off
into the customary account of his ancestry and previous
career. At the end he speaks of Achilles' demand for the
sacrifice of Polyxena, and of his own desire for burial, declaring that when it is granted he will appear to his mother,
whose enslaving he laments; but this, as the issue proves,
refers only to the discovery of his body, which is later
washed ashore. This expository function at once dis-
tinguishes him from the ghosts in Aischylos; even Dareios,
as we noted, does not appear solely for the purpose of
imparting information. It is precisely in virtue of this trait,
however, that Polydoros, through Seneca, becomes the
ancestor of many ghosts in Renaissance tragedy.

The preceding discussion has extended to greater length
than is warranted by the intrinsic merit of the plays considered; but the variety of theories to which the Euripidean
drama has given rise has made it necessary to examine all the
available material, in order to facilitate the reaching of
tenable conclusions. What we seem to have in Euripides
is a writer unable to find a satisfactory form for the expression of his ideas, especially in connection with the supernatural. He can no longer simply accept the legends,
but lacks the courage to cut loose from them altogether.

Circumstances compel him to employ the traditional figures; and he seeks, with varying success, to transform them, often with the result of producing mere travesties. From the point of view of our investigation he is most successful when, as in the *Hippolytos* and the *Bacchai*, he most closely adheres to the established canons in the treatment of the supernatural. Historically considered, he is no doubt the source, through Seneca, of the purely mechanical handling of the supernatural, which he himself closely approached, and into which an imitator could not fail to fall, as soon as the last link with vital tradition was snapped.

SECTION 4. — THE CONTRIBUTION OF GREEK TRAGEDY

Our examination of the three great Attic dramatists clearly shows that they represent three distinct attitudes toward a material common to them all. We saw that Greek tragedy, in virtue both of the general bent of the Greek mind and of the particular circumstances of its origin, had a connection with the supernatural which entered into its very heart, and became one of its indispensable constituents. The presence of this constituent naturally involved a definite attitude toward it on the part of each dramatist who essayed to write tragedies. Aischylos, standing nearer to the religious origin, and himself profoundly religious, accepted the supernatural elements without demur, and informed them with a new, intense vitality. Under the impress of his creative imagination a whole world of mythical figures comes into being, and even the more familiar Gods assume a fresh significance. It is in his Furies that Aischylos achieves the most extraordinary expression of his creative impulse; out of a few scattered elements he shapes supernatural beings of an amazing impressiveness, and brings them into his dramatic fabric with consummate skill. His introduction of the ghost is also a most significant innovation — the first appearance of what is the best represented and the most enduring supernatural type of all. The Aischylean theatre, under the double influence of the character of the time and the wonderful genius of its creator, attains a height of tragic power never since surpassed; and its peculiar merit is largely due, as our analysis has shown, to the surpassingly skilful use of the supernatural which it displays.

With Sophokles we come into a different sphere of thought, in which the supernatural has receded into the background, and no longer immediately dominates the drama. Sophokles has no profound interest in the supernatural, but accepts it as a traditional feature of what is now the developed tragic form. His indifference leads him at first to introduce it merely where it will suit his convenience, without relation to the deeper logic of a play; but gradually he progresses to an original and very skilful use of supernatural elements, subordinating them, indeed, but making them really contribute to the whole design. It is a somewhat impersonal method, and one which lacks the range and intensity of the Aischylean; but at its best it achieves effects of individual and very perfect beauty.

In Euripides we have yet a third stage, one of clearly marked decline. Euripides no longer respects the old conventions, and is ill at ease in their presence; but they are too well established, and also too convenient, to be given up altogether. The Gods, reduced to the mechanical status of deliverers of prologues and epilogues, afford one more vent for the perpetual stream of exposition which Euripides' characters pour forth. He has a mania for the imparting of information on all possible occasions, and the " all-seeing "

Gods may be presumed to have stores of that commodity, on which he levies unsparingly. It is the uniformity of this expository element, in his Gods as in his mortals, which constitutes one of the gravest objections to the rationalistic theory. " The mistress would speak, and the slave no less, and the master and the maiden and the old woman too," says the jibing Aristophanes; and the Gods are quite as afflicted with this incessant loquacity as are the mortal characters. We saw how Kassandra's prophecy in the *Troades* was used to bring in a summary of the *Odyssey*; how the ghost of Polydoros must tell us about his ancestry and his hapless career; and how the Gods of prologue and epilogue are chiefly noteworthy for the abundance of the facts which they are ready to detail. Euripides is usually satisfied to let his Gods do nothing but talk, unconscious, it would seem, of the unsatisfactory nature of that method of presenting them. Yet on occasion he feels the need of a more vital handling, and goes back to the older canons, creating a *Hippolytos*, or a *Bacchai*, and writing, from our point of view, his most excellent pieces. It is of course undeniable that he often reveals the Gods in an unpleasant light, and has no real reverence for them; but how far this is the result of definite purpose, and how far of mere incompetence, it is sometimes hard to decide. In any case, as the adherents of the rationalistic theory admit, his Gods are for the most part artistically worthless; and the predominantly mechanical handling of the supernatural in him, in whatever way to be accounted for, is beyond doubt.

Three classes of supernatural beings may be distinguished in Greek tragedy — the Gods of the ordinary mythology, the new powers, such as the Furies, which Aischylos practically creates, and the ghosts. Of these, the Furies are unquestionably the most impressive, the most dramatic, and the most original. For the Olympians we must turn rather to Sophokles, though in his work we find them, as was noted, rather in allusion than in actual presence. The ghosts, again, are most strikingly represented in Aischylos. The ghost of Dareios has a twofold function — that of presenting in a visible figure an image of the past glories of Persia, and that of supplying information which shall give us a proper knowledge of those glories. The expository function is thus a distinct product of the deeper purpose, and is far removed from a mere purveying of facts. The average Athenian of the day cannot have had much detailed knowledge of the Persian empire, and needed a recital of the kind which Dareios gives, in order to appreciate the changes which the defeat of Xerxes involved. The audience must have realized this need, just as the audiences of Shakespeare's day, to take an obvious example, must have felt a real interest in the account of the Salic law in *Henry V*. We saw that the expository portion occupies a somewhat undue amount of space; but this can be largely excused by the novelty of the subject, and the relative inexperience of Aischylos in the management of the supernatural. This sort of information is far removed from that supplied by the ghost of Polydoros, much of which is not necessary for the purposes of the drama in which it appears. Moreover, Aischylos gives much more attention to the ghostliness of Dareios, using all the opportunities afforded by the choral incantations and the contrast with the mortal characters to enhance his impressiveness. The ghost of Polydoros, on the contrary, appears alone, and no such contrast is possible in his case — a fundamental defect in the conception of the isolated prologue-ghost which we shall see further exemplified in Seneca and his followers. Finally, the ghost of Klytai-mestra has no expository function at all, and though she is not necessary to the progress of the play, she is splendidly decorative,[1] personifying in a single baleful figure that sleepless wrath of the dead which has been so important an element in the preceding plays of the trilogy.   Her appearance is strictly in accord with the spiritual logic of the *Eumenides*, and impresses us with the idea which she personifies to a degree not otherwise attainable.

Greek tragedy, as it took shape in the hands of Aischylos, possessed in the chorus an unrivalled aid to the artistic treatment of the supernatural.   The chorus is a sensitive instrument, which records the presence of supernatural powers before the more active characters are aware of it; it is also a representative body, which displays the feelings which we ought to have in contemplating the action, and so arouses in us the same emotions of dread which shake itself. It is thus a doubly powerful means of stirring us; it both reveals and excites.   Moreover, the chorus is sufficiently detached from the action to be free to comment on it; it can lead us to a wider view of the significance of the events, or can emphasize thoughts which the other characters are unwilling or unable to express, thus effecting an imaginative expansion of the drama which adds immeasurably to its depth and impressiveness.   The chorus can thus reveal to us the presence and influence of the forces on which the action ultimately depends, and lavish all its purely lyrical power in enhancing the awesomeness of these forces.   One cannot imagine the *Oresteia* with the chorus excised; and when in the *Eumenides* the Furies who dominate the action themselves become the chorus, the highest stage of which the Greek form is capable is reached.   We saw that Sophokles took some time to realize the advantages which the

---

[1] It must be remembered that I am using *decorative* as a strictly technical term, implying no aesthetic judgment of the object to which it is applied.

chorus gave him; and when he does, his lyrical inferiority to Aischylos keeps him from any chance of rivalling his predecessor. He does, however, adjust the chorus to his own aims with remarkable skill. Finally, it is significant that in Euripides, for whom the supernatural has largely lost its meaning, the chorus too dwindles to a mere lyrical adornment, often wholly unrelated to the action. It is perhaps too bold to call this an instance of cause and effect; but the fact remains that the chorus is the generative principle of Greek tragedy, and the means by which Aischylos achieves his incomparable success; and that when tragedy succumbs to the invading forces of rhetoric the chorus loses its identity, and lingers only as a purposeless survival.

The examination of Greek tragedy which we have just completed fully bears out our principle that the supernatural in drama must be represented as a power, whose effects are manifested in the action. It is in Aischylos that we find this condition most perfectly fulfilled; Sophokles attains a similar result in his finest work; but Euripides seems for the most part quite unconscious of the need of making the supernatural a real constituent of the dramatic fabric. He is usually satisfied with mere superfluous exposition; yet the older successful method sometimes haunts him, and he rids himself of his defects sufficiently to approximate to the achievements of his predecessors. Such reversions are, however, exceptional in his work, the general tendency of which is wholly in the direction of mechanical and meaningless handling. In less than a century Greek tragedy passes through a whole cycle of growth, achievement, and decay.

A second conclusion which may be drawn from our survey thus far is the need of proper contrast in the presentation of the supernatural. The more clearly the mortal characters are conceived, the more clearly do we discern the gulf which divides them from the supernatural. But the distinction must not be made too sharp; we must also recognize the bonds of relation between the two worlds. Aischylos draws his mortals, especially in the *Oresteia*, with perfect conformity to his whole design; and when, as at the close of the *Eumenides*, he lets them pass out of the centre of interest, it is because a higher interest has intervened. Sophokles uses his remoter Gods to increase the saliency of his mortals; but Euripides abandons the deeper elements of the legends to follow a realistic method which results in no equivalent gain for what is lost. The true value of each Greek tragedy is thus seen to be largely dependent on the success with which it weaves the given supernatural features into itself; so that the finest of them, the *Oresteia* and the *Oidipous at Kolonos*, derive their peculiar merit largely from the skill with which their authors shape the two worlds into a coherent whole, wherein each element contributes to the impressiveness of the other.

CHAPTER II

SENECA

THE early tragedy of Rome is preserved in such scanty fragments that nothing of significance for our purpose can be ascertained in regard to its treatment of individual themes. It must have followed Greek models with considerable closeness, and taken over from them some at least of the supernatural motives which we have already discussed. It is worthy of remark that Roman deities to some extent replaced the Greek, as we learn from Plautus:

> Ut alios in tragoediis
> Vidi Neptunum, Virtutem, Victoriam,
> Martem, Bellonam commemorare, quae bona
> Vobis fecissent. — *Amphitruo*, 41 ff.

For us the only Roman tragedy preserved in such shape as to admit of discussion is that of Seneca. His pompous rhetorical plays have little intrinsic merit; but because of their great influence in the Renaissance, when Seneca was regarded as one of the chief tragic masters, if not indeed superior to his Greek predecessors, it becomes important to see just what modifications of Greek usage he introduced. The question of his historical identity does not concern us; for those who imitated him in the Renaissance he was the tutor and victim of Nero, and we may be content to accept that opinion, as we are in any event concerned with the plays, not with the man.

In Seneca the supernatural has lost all connection with religion, and become a mere decorative survival, completing the revolution foreshadowed in Euripides. The Gods are

now machinery and nothing more.   It is from Euripides
that Seneca derives his supernatural figures; but in accord-
ance with his own taste.   Of the types available he rejects the
deus ex machina entirely, and uses the prologue-God in but
a single instance; whereas he gives to the ghost a prominent
place.   The single divinity who appears in his work is Juno
in the opening of the *Hercules Furens*.   She laments that,
though queen of Heaven, she is flouted by Jupiter in favor of
his mortal loves; she will therefore visit Hercules, the offspring of such an *amour*, with madness, and calls up the
Furies and other spirits of the deep to bring it about.   Otherwise she has no effect on the drama, which she merely introduces, like Poseidon and Athena in the *Troades*.

A distinguishing feature of her speech, and a hallmark of
the Senecan style in general, is the amount of erudition
which it contains.   It is clogged with learned allusions,
prominent among which are references to the lower world.
Juno speaks of Hercules' expedition thither, and mentions
Erebus and Styx.   Such references crop up throughout the
plays, in season and out of season.   A frequent form which
they assume is that of a list of the four great sinners —
Ixion, Sisyphus, Tityus and Tantalus — sometimes named,
sometimes described by periphrasis.   This stylistic trait
occurs not only in the mouths of ghosts, where it has greater
appropriateness, since they have just come from the regions
they describe, but on all possible occasions.[1]   The rivers of
the underworld are mentioned with even greater frequency:
Acheron, for instance, ten times, Lethe ten, Phlegethon six,
and Styx no less than fifty-nine.   These features were not
found in Greek literature by Seneca in any such profusion.

---

[1] See, e. g., *Herc.* 750 ff., *Phaed.* 1229 ff., *Med.* 740 ff., and also the index
in the Teubner text of the tragedies (Peiper and Richter, Leipzig, 1902)
under the proper names noted, and also sub vv. *Dis, Furiae, Inferi, Manes,
Tartarus.*

The grouping of the four sinners goes back to Pindar (O. i. 61); but he alludes to them only in passing, as he does to the punishment of sinners in the world below, of whom he says simply that they suffer " pain that may not be looked upon " (O. ii. 74). In Greek tragedy, as we have seen, such allusions are very rare: in the *Eumenides*, where, if anywhere, we should expect them to occur, they are wholly lacking. The same is true of the names of the infernal rivers. Acheron is referred to several times, and Aischylos speaks rather casually of a " Stygian gloom " (*Pers.* 669); but otherwise Greek tragedy yields little in the way of such ornamental allusions.

So far as I am aware, there is but one passage in classical Greek literature which can be adduced as indicating a use of such allusions in tragedy; I mean the lines in the *Frogs* of Aristophanes (469 ff.) in which Aiakos threatens Dionysos and his servant, on their arrival in Hades, with dreadful tortures. The serio-comic threats end in a series of puns; and the only question is whether Aristophanes is parodying a tragic passage, or merely concocting his tirade from phrases gathered at large. An inspection of the vocabulary shows that some of the words really belong to the diction of tragedy, while others are those of ordinary speech. The scholiast says that Aristophanes is parodying the *Theseus* of Euripides; but the lines which he cites from that play have no special resemblance to the supposed parody, and wholly lack the enumeration of torments which is the point at issue. Seemingly what Aristophanes has done is to draw up a list of tortures, and then clothe it in semi-tragic language, without giving a parody of any actual passage.

We find, then, no evidence that the Senecan style of underworld description had a counterpart in Greek tragedy. It is of course not impossible that such a counterpart should have existed in some of the scenes which we know occurred in tragedies now lost. Of the content of such lost works, however, we know nothing; ὄσα ἐν ῎Αιδου is Aristotle's pleasingly vague way of referring (*Poetics*, c. 18) to such motives, which he stigmatizes as merely spectacular. So far as ascertainable facts go we seem justified in denying that Greek tragedy, except possibly in unimportant instances, ever used allusions to the underworld as a consistent and extensive decorative device.

In Roman tragedy, on the contrary, this sort of description was a feature long before Seneca, as we see for instance, from the quotations which Cicero gives in the first book of his *Tusculans*. He speaks of the effect produced by the impressive lines:

> Adsum atque advenio Acherunte vix via alta atque ardua
> Per speluncas saxis structas asperis, pendentibus,
> Maxumis, ubi rigida constat crassa caligo inferum, (c. 16.)

which, however, are obviously more imaginative and less erudite than Seneca. We seem justified in seeing in such conceptions a distinctly Roman attitude, which likewise finds expression in a love of bloodshed and corruption for their own sakes. The words in which the Thyestes of Ennius wishes that his brother's corpse may hang and rot on some cliff:

> Ipse summis saxis fixus asperis, evisceratus,
> Latere pendens, saxa spargens tabo, sanie et sanguine atro,
> (c. 44.)

are wholly alien to the spirit of Greek art. In casting about for possible sources of this attitude we inevitably think of the Etruscans, whose art shows such delight in scenes of weltering bloodshed, and in the depicting of horrible demons of the underworld, subjects which contrast so strongly with their Greek prototypes.[1] Such motives, whether or not derived from the Etruscans, were well known to the Romans; in the *Captivi* of Plautus (998) a character speaks of having often seen pictures of " what is done beside Acheron." There can be no doubt of the presence in Italy of a marked taste for scenes of blood and horror, quite unlike anything Greek; and Seneca merely accentuates an already existent native tradition. We shall have occasion to recur to this question in connection with Seneca's conception of the ghost.

Having thus disposed of the external stylistic features of Seneca, we are prepared to turn to his chief contribution to our subject, the Senecan ghost. Three ghosts actually appear on the stage in his plays, and three others are described in detail; so that we do not lack material for discussion. Of the first group, two appear in the prologues of the plays in question; and the simplest type is that of the ghost of Thyestes in the *Agamemnon*. He begins by describing the region whence he comes, in imitation of the Euripidean Polydoros:

> Opaca linquens Ditis inferni loca
> Adsum, profundo Tartari emissus specu,

with references later to the " tristes lacus " and the four great criminals, but in periphrasis, not by name. He goes on to speak of his own crimes, and to predict the impending murder of Agamemnon, after which he withdraws, in order to permit the sun, which is unwilling to shine on such a criminal, to rise. His rôle is thus seen to be exclusively descriptive and expository.

In the prologue of the *Thyestes* we have a more elaborate form. Here the ghost is that of Tantalus, and he is accom-

---

[1] See J. Martha, *L'Art Etrusque*, pp. 179–180 and 392 ff., for demons and underworld in Etruscan art.

panied by a Fury who brings him to the light, after the
fashion of Iris and Lyssa in the *Herakles*. He asks why he
is thus recalled, and goes on to mention the four criminals,
himself included.   While his house exists, he declares,
Minos shall never have leisure in the world below.   The
Fury proceeds to give a catalogue of the future crimes of
Tantalus' descendants, which so appals him that he starts
back for Hades, preferring the tortures there; but the Fury
intercepts him, and bids him bring woe on the house of
Pelops.   He is reluctant, but at last obeys.   The Fury
declares that the house feels him near and shudders at the
contact.   The whole earth is blighted by his presence;
Alpheus is dried up, the snows melt on Cithaeron, and even
the sun is on the point of halting!   Such frantic hyperbole
is of course utterly futile as regards giving any sense of
supernatural power in the ghost.   He is confined to the
prologue, not the slightest reference being made to his baleful power in the subsequent course of the drama.

In the *Octavia* — a play probably not by the same hand
as the others, and certainly not by the historical Seneca —
we have a ghost in the midst of the action.   It is that of
Agrippina, the murdered mother of Nero, who brings a
marriage-torch for the unhallowed nuptials of her son and
Poppaea.   She seeks revenge for her own death; but the
motive is not accentuated.   Her threat of vengeance brings
the usual catalogue of sinners, after which she predicts
Nero's death, and wishes that she had never borne him.
The ghost returns in a dream narrated by Poppaea:

> Inter tubarum saepe terribilem sonum
> Sparsam cruore coniugis genetrix mei
> Vultu minaci saeva quatiebat facem.   (721–3.)

Here is the element of mysterious sound, though in a rather
forced manner.   Beyond this the ghost has no share in the

action; and we have again mere decorative episodes, not closely related to the plot.

These three cases, then, comprise a purely expository ghost, a ghost supposed to be capable of exercising baleful power, but described in such absurdly exaggerated terms as to lose all impressiveness, and a ghost appearing in the midst of the action, but without any other effect on it than a subsequent appearance in a dream. Agrippina is the only one of the three who approaches the type of the revenge-ghost; but she is not a good example of one, since the result which her wrath is supposed to bring about is not shown us in the play. In none of these cases is a satisfying artistic result attained; and the same is true of the ghosts who are merely described. We may begin with the ghost of Achilles in the *Troades*. His apparition (168 ff.) is preceded by a tremendous convulsion of nature; the earth groans, rocks fall from Mount Ida, the sea is troubled; at last the ground is cloven by a chasm reaching to Erebus, through which the ghost ascends, to demand the sacrifice of Polyxena. He then descends; the chasm closes, and nature resumes her wonted calm. The absurdity of the episode is absolute.

More elaborate is the introduction of the ghost of Laius in the *Oedipus*; he does not come spontaneously, but is raised by necromantic arts. We begin with a long description of the place in which the ceremonies of evocation are conducted; it is an ancient wood encircling a marsh. Next the rites themselves are described; their success is indicated by the barking of Hecate's hounds. Horror seizes the wood; the earth yawns, and the lower world is revealed — giving an opportunity for a heaping up of abstractions and much erudition concerning famous sinners. Finally Laius appears, " per artus sanguine effuso horridus, Paedore foedo squalidam obtectus comam," and predicts the dire woes that are to befall the royal house of Thebes.   The description ends, with curious abruptness, at the close of the quotation of his words; so that the elaboration of the introduction is not maintained, a hint that the author is seeking only a momentary effect.

The third described ghost likewise occurs in the *Troades*, a little later (438) than that of Achilles.   Andromache relates a dream in which the ghost of Hector appeared to her, not as he was in life,

> Sed fessus ac deiectus et fletu gravis,
> Similisque maesto, squalida obtectus coma.

The tone of the incident is unexpectedly quiet.   Hector warns his wife to save their son Astyanax, whose life is in danger, and then vanishes.   There is no attempt, as in the other two instances, to force the note of horror; but all three show a distinct conventionality.   Laius and Achilles both return to the light through a chasm miraculously cloven in the earth; Laius and Hector alike appear with unkempt hair (squalidam obtectus comam).

In this conception of the ghost as showing the marks of the ill-usage which his body received in death, we have again something which, so far as literary treatment goes, is distinctly Roman, though as a primitive conception it has left traces in Greek, as when Oidipous declares (*OT* 1371) that he has put out his eyes in order to avoid seeing his father and mother in Hades.   It is the same primitive and material conception that lies at the basis of the custom of " arm-pitting," the mutilation of the murderer's victim to make the ghost correspondingly powerless.[1]   In this connection it is highly significant that when Aischylos refers to the practice in the *Choephoroi* (439 ff.) it is merely to excite

---

[1] Cf. G. L. Kittredge, "Arm-pitting among the Greeks," *Am. Jour. Phil.*, vi. 151.

Orestes by the thought of the outrage done to his father's
body; the deed is kept from any contact with the idea of the
ghost and his power, which Aischylos desires to accentuate
and spiritualize.   The Romans, however, had no scruples
in taking the more material view, which was more consonant
with their habit of mind.   The ancestor of the Senecan
ghost is Vergil's Hector, who appears to Aeneas

> Squalentem barbam et concretos sanguine crinis
> Volneraque illa gerens, quae circum plurima muros
> Accepit patrios. (*Aeneid*, ii. 277.)

The Homeric Patroklos, on the other hand, appears to
Achilles under similar circumstances " in his habit as he
lived: "

> ἦλθε δ' ἐπὶ ψυχὺ Πατροκλῆος δειλοῖο,
> πάντ' αὐτῷ μέγεθός τε καὶ ὄμματα κάλ' ἔϊκυῖα,
> καὶ φωνήν, καὶ τοῖα περὶ χροὶ εἵματα ἔστο. (Il. Ψ 65.)

The Roman attitude was favored by the attendant indifference to bodily corruption which we have already noted.
The coarser Roman imagination seized on the repugnant
details which the finer Greek taste passed over.   Sophokles,
in the *Antigone*, alludes in passing to the stench which
comes from the unburied corpse; but it is treated as a mere
detail, to be mentioned because it is there, but not to be
dwelt on.   The watcher simply says that he and his fellows
sat to windward of the corpse, that the stench from it might
not reach them (412).   The Romans, on the contrary, had
a distinct interest in such matters, best seen, perhaps, in the
Pharsalia of Lucan, whose imagination was doubtless somewhat colored by the fact that he was Seneca's nephew.   The
description in Book VI of the witch Erichtho and her use of
corpses for purposes of magic has an ingenuity in horror
which is not Senecan, though very Roman in its materiality;
but there is accompanying erudite allusion that is wholly in
the Senecan manner.

A significant token of the Roman attitude toward corpses is to be found in that cemetery on the Esquiline on which Maecenas built his famous gardens. Before his day a part of the ground was used as a sort of Potter's Field, where the bodies of slaves and criminals were thrown into pits, along with every kind of refuse. When in recent times the region was uncovered in the course of excavations for a new street, some of the pits contained, in Lanciani's vivid phrase,[1] " a uniform mass of black, viscid, pestilent, unctuous matter, whilst in others the bones could in a measure be singled out and identified." Clearer evidence of the indifference of the Romans toward bodily corruption could scarcely be desired.

The link which unites this attitude with the ghost is the conception of the spectre as skeleton, again a distinctly Roman one. The use of this conception in art, and the whole interest in the macabre which it implies, is wholly alien from the true Greek spirit.[2] Literature, it is true, keeps rather closer to the Greek model; but the Roman substratum shows through, as in the ghost of Hector, noted above, and the ghost of Cynthia in Propertius (IV. vii), with her crackling finger-joints and the traces of the funeral fire. Among the common people the idea must have been far more vigorous, surviving until, in the Middle Ages, it crops up again, though with altered emphasis, in the Danse Macabré.[3]

The Senecan ghost is thus in a measure the result of a native tradition; but that tradition is lacking in the subtler imaginative qualities, and Seneca can bring to its aid only

---

[1] *Ruins and Excavations of Ancient Rome*, p. 410.

[2] See Daremberg et Saglio, *Dict. des Antiquités grecques et romaines*, s. v. *larva*, with the accompanying cuts and references. Interesting, though rather discursive, is L. Collinson Morley, *Greek and Roman Ghost Stories*, London, 1912.

[3] Cf. P. Vigo, *Le Danze Macabre in Italia*, Bergamo, 1901, pp. 9–15.

an elaborate apparatus of learned allusions which neither gives it the lacking qualities nor makes it more appealing to our tastes. It is only fair to add that these erudite references are in reality the dramatist's only way of securing the contrast necessary for the presentation of his ghosts as really supernatural. Since the power of the ghost is not exhibited in action, and alluded to, if at all, only in terms of such absurd hyperbole as to destroy all plausibility, it is obvious that the ghost can best assure us of his true character by describing the lower world whence he comes. We are thus informed that he is a ghost, while at the same time the dramatist secures yet another outlet for his store of erudition. Moreover, the prologue-ghost cannot be set in contrast with mortals, since he is either alone, or accompanied by another supernatural figure, such as the Fury in the *Thyestes*. Such contrast as we find in Seneca is thus attained in a very mechanical way, and can impart no sense of supernatural power. Practically, then, the Senecan ghost is a mere decorative figure, who has to assure us of his identity by an elaborate description of the underworld, (a contrast blunted, by the way, by the frequency of such allusions in the plays at large), and with a supposed power which we do not see in action, and which, on account of the absurd manner in which it is described, cannot impress us.

It would seem then that Seneca's failure to treat the supernatural worthily is partly due to his own lack of poetic imagination, and partly to a general inability in the Romans to conceive the supernatural except under a material and often repulsive aspect. An interesting example of the gulf between Greek and Roman in this regard, and one worth noting because of its general relevancy to our subject, is the treatment of the love-charm in Theokritos and Vergil, in which the latter is consciously following the former. We are all familiar with the power displayed by Theokritos in his second idyl, with its invocation of Hekate, " at whom the dogs tremble as she comes along the mounds of the dead," and the thrilling cry of the sorceress as she feels the charm working: " Thestylis, the dogs are barking for us up and down the city; the Goddess is at the cross-roads; let the gong sound straightway! " Greater sensitiveness to sound and its uncanny implications, and finer use of mere suggestion of the presence of the supernatural, could scarcely be asked. What now do we find in Vergil, who in his eighth Eclogue treats the same motive ? He begins with much detail about the incantations; and his sorceress pauses in her work to describe at large the nature of her drugs:

> Has herbas atque haec Ponto mihi lecta venena
> Ipse dedit Moeris; nascuntur plurima Ponto.
> His ego saepe lupum fieri et se condere silvis
> Moerim, saepe animas imis excire sepulchris,
> Atque satas alio vidi traducere messis.

This is mere antiquarianism, wholly out of place in the context. At the climax, when the dog barks, it is merely to welcome the returning lover. The poem is skilfully versified; but the thrill of mystery which should accompany such a theme, and which does accompany it in the Greek, has gone out of it utterly. The Greek sorceress speaks to herself, or to her servant; Vergil's speaks to the reader.

Returning now to Seneca, we may define his contribution to the tragic supernatural as a purely mechanical handling, in which the tendency foreshadowed in Euripides reaches its logical conclusion. He lacks real imagination, and can achieve no vital contrast in his supernatural figures; but he endeavors to make up the lack by an abuse of erudite references to the underworld, often without appropriateness to the situation. He makes the ghost, his favorite supernatural being, a mere decorative figure, without influence on the action, but sufficiently unlike any Greek type to be, at first sight, striking. Precisely these traits, by reason of their externality, make his supernatural susceptible of imitation; but its lack of inherent vitality makes such imitation sterile unless it is developed by a native aptitude in the imitators which will result in something essentially different from the model. Seneca found imitators enough in the Renaissance; but their efforts produced nothing of value except where they introduced elements so different from anything in their master as practically to result in a new creation.

PART II

THE MIDDLE AGES AND THE RENAISSANCE

CHAPTER III

THE MEDIEVAL SACRED DRAMA

SECTION I. — ORIGIN AND GROWTH OF THE LITURGICAL DRAMA

Bibliographical Note. — The ample store of erudition and the wealth of bibliographical matter contained in the two volumes of Mr. E. K. Chambers' *Medieval Stage* have made it unnecessary for me to give explicit references in the ensuing chapter, except for certain specific points.   The best general accounts of the period are, for France, Petit de Julleville's *Les Mystères;* for England, the introduction to Professor Gayley's *Representative English Comedies*, and that to *The Non-Cycle Mystery Plays*, edited by O. Waterhouse for the EETS (Extra Series civ. 1909); and for Italy, D'Ancona's *Origini del Teatro Italiano.*   For the liturgical drama the most convenient collections of texts are still those of Du Méril and Coussemaker.   The editions of the great French and English cycles are indicated in Chambers. Works especially concerned with the topics of the present investigation are of course noted in the appended bibliography.

IN approaching the wide field of the drama of the Middle Ages we shall find it necessary to adopt a somewhat different method of procedure from that which we have hitherto followed.   Ancient tragedy presents itself as a distinct art-form, which we can study without the need of much preliminary definition; but the Middle Ages offer us no such clear-cut type.   The words " Greek tragedy " call up in our minds a definite concept; no such clear concept responds to the term " miracle-play."   The miracle-plays have been little studied from the standpoint of dramatic art; and if we are to estimate the value of the supernatural as an element in plot, it becomes necessary to ascertain just what measure of conscious plot a given play possesses. Moreover, the movements of this period in the field of drama are broad and overlapping, rather than sharply defined. That there is among them a distinct movement in the direction of tragedy, I am convinced; but it is not always easy to make out, and may in some cases be best thrown into relief by a comparison with other tendencies not tragic in character. I shall, however, keep this part of the inquiry as subordinate as may be to the main issue.

We have seen that in Roman literature, tragedy, at least after the Republican period, and so far as complete examples are preserved, was never a really vital thing. A mere traditional form, based on foreign models, and wholly eclipsed in popular favor by gladiatorial show and pantomime, it remained the diversion of the learned, and lost all semblance of life with the fall of the Empire. The few reminiscences of the classical definitions of tragedy and comedy which survived in the medieval lexicographers and compilers grew steadily vaguer, until men lost all sense of the fact that these terms referred to forms of drama, and came to apply them to any form of composition, in prose or verse, according to the more or less serious intent of its author.[1]   Greek tragedy had of course long ceased to exercise any influence; and from the tenth century to the thirteenth even Seneca was lost to sight.   Yet throughout this period a new form of drama, the miracle-play, was almost unconsciously following a tragic tendency which resulted in a very real, if unformulated, tradition; and the lack of any dramatic models from antiquity compelled that tradition to work out its own independent forms.   When the stricter idea of tragedy returned in the Renaissance, ostensibly under the guidance of classical precept and example, it could not fail to be in some measure affected by this previous development of several centuries; and it is precisely

[1] Cf. W. Cloetta, *Komödie und Tragödie im Mittelalter*, Halle, 1890.

in this matter of the supernatural that I believe the influence of the medieval tradition is most clearly to be traced. In this view, modern tragedy is the result of the formative influence of classical models on previously accumulated native tradition; and it is our task to see what the nature of that tradition was in certain of the European countries, and to what extent the classical influence contrived to work upon it.

It is of course not asserted that classical tradition in general played no part in the long medieval development. We can find various instances of the use of classical tags, lines of Vergil, for example, inserted in a miracle-play; [1] indeed, Vergil himself is called in, as the prophet of the Gentiles, to give his testimony to the divinity of Christ. Later, with serene indifference to anachronism, the great authorities of antiquity, such as Aristotle and Cicero, are cited by Biblical heroes. All this, however, is merely matter of detail. Of the influence of classical drama *as drama* in the early stages of the miracle-play there is absolutely no trace. When, however, in the course of time examples of that drama were restored to men's notice, they found in this already diffused tradition an ally which had by increasingly numerous allusions made antiquity familiar, and thus facilitated the return to the ancient forms. But if the miracle-play owed, on the formal side, nothing to antiquity, it proved itself incapable of working out a consistent form of its own. Greek tragedy had had its chorus as an agency compelling unity; but medieval drama had no such unifying force. It results from this that the great service of the return to antiquity was, as has been said, the regaining of a formative influence.

---

[1] Cf. the adaptation of Aeneid viii. 112–114, in the Fleury *Magi* (Coussemaker, p. 159), and the quotation of the famous lines from the Fourth Eclogue in the Towneley *Prima Pastorum*, v. 387.

Antiquity being thus at the outset excluded, we may safely regard the traditions and the ritual of the Church as the sole source of medieval sacred drama.   The traditions of course included not only the canonical Scriptures, but also the apocryphal books, and the vast body of legend dealing with Saints and martyrs, all equally available for dramatic treatment.   One characteristic was common to all the phases of this huge mass of possible material: the presence and intervention of the supernatural.   The Bible gave on the one hand the story of God's constant manifestation of himself and his power in behalf of his chosen people, and on the other the sublime tragedy of his own sacrifice of himself to redeem mankind; while saintly legend supplied countless instances of the conflict of celestial and infernal powers in the incessant struggle for the souls of men.

The impulse to shape this material into dramatic form came from the liturgy, where indeed it had been latent almost from the first.   Naturally the age of the Fathers, with its savage attacks on the theatres and games of the Pagans, could not give expression to any such impulse; and yet a curious anticipation may be found in the writings of the very men who were the fiercest assailants of pagan amusements.   Tertullian, for instance, in the *De Spectaculis* (cc. 29 and 30), draws the contrast between the vanity of worldly shows and the grandeur of the spectacles revealed to the true believer, especially the pageant of the Last Judgment, when all the passions of mankind, noblest and basest, shall be displayed in very truth, not in the shams of the stage.   Eusebius [1] refers even more explicitly to the

---

[1] Quoted by John of Damascus in his *Parallels* (Migne, *PG*, xcvi. 312). The identity of this Eusebius is not certain, but he is probably not the bishop of Caesarea.   See Migne, *i. c.*, 229–300.   In this connection cf. Lactantius,

dramatic connotations of the liturgy, in a passage worth examining at some length.   It is a portion of a sermon dealing with the desecration of Sunday.   " Those who fear the Lord," says the preacher, " wait for Sunday that they may send up their prayers to God, and enjoy the body and blood of the Lord.   But the slothful wait for Sunday that, keeping aloof from work, they may solace themselves with evil.   And that I do not lie, the facts themselves bear witness. . . .   The herald summons to church, and all hold back, as if by reason of sloth.   There comes the sound of a lyre or flute, and all run as if winged."   Then comes the contrast between worldly joys and the splendors of the ritual.   " We behold the spectacles of the Church; we see the Lord Christ lying on the altar, the seraphim singing the thrice-holy hymn, the voices of the Gospel, the presence of the Holy Ghost, the prophets bearing witness — all spiritual, all conducive to salvation, all forerunners of the Kingdom.   But what does he see who runs to the theatres ? Devilish songs; women dancing."   There is further description of these profane sights, and a renewed assertion of the sanctity of Sunday.

Such passages as these seem to show a distinct sense on the part of their authors that the ritual of the Church contained elements which might serve to satisfy those human desires which, if left unchecked, led men to the perilous delights of the world and the devil.   A different class of sermons, more in the manner of Tertullian, satisfied these cravings by vivid rhetorical accounts of events in sacred history in a form

Divin. Inst. vi. 21: Itaque si voluptas est, audire cantus et carmina, Dei laudes canere et audire jucundum sit.

The Eusebius passage, so far as I am aware, has not previously been cited in its entirety.   It is translated by D'Ancona (*Origini*, i. 13), from the incomplete paraphrase in Douhet, *Dict. des Mystères*, p. 65, which does not at all give its context or its real significance.

already more than half dramatic, which might very easily pass over to a presentation as pure dialogue, and later, in certain cases, did actually so pass.   But in its own day all this rhetorical embellishment could not lead to any real drama. The only attempt at such a thing, apart from the curious essays of the Arians, was in such hybrid productions as the Χριστὸς Πάσχων, mere classical centos, with no vitality in themselves, and no influence on posterity.   It was left to a later age to bring to expression the latent drama of the liturgy.

We find the first movement toward this expression in the growing elaboration of the ritual from the ninth century on. Not only the great symbolic drama of the Mass, but episodes in the service which admitted of similar symbolic treatment, took on an increasingly dramatic character from the desire to make them as vivid to the people as possible.[1] By the eleventh century this impulse had reached a point where we may fairly speak of the existence of liturgical drama.

We are of course not deeply concerned with the liturgical play till it has developed to the point of taking shape in independent dramatic units; but a survey of the previous evolution is desirable, to show us just what stage in the whole process that point represents.   We find the starting-point in the *Quem Quaeritis* trope of the Easter service, a dialogue between the Maries and the Angel at the Sepulchre; a supernatural participant, then, at the very outset.   This simple episode was enlarged by lyrical expansions and by the addition of closely related incidents, such as the visit of the Apostles to the Sepulchre, or the apparition of Christ to Mary Magdalen.   Meanwhile the *Quem Quaeritis* had generated a parallel trope in the Christmas service, showing

[1] See Chambers ii. 3–6 for examples.

the shepherds who come to adore the new-born Child. This
incident underwent a like process of accretion.   A third
important centre of growth was the *Prophetae*[1], based not on
any part of the liturgy itself, but on a sermon ascribed to
Augustine, in which the prophets are called on to bear witness to Christ.   This is one of those sermons which show an
adumbration of dramatic form so marked as to render
peculiarly easy the change to delivery by several chanting
voices, a change shown in an eleventh-century manuscript
from Limoges (Coussemaker no. ii, p. 11).   Moreover, in
addition to the strictly Biblical prophets we have representatives of the Gentiles — Nebuchadnezzar to cite the
miracle of the fiery furnace, and Vergil and the Erythraean
Sibyl.   The *Prophetae* obviously differs from the other two
centres in being a succession of detachable incidents, not a
single incident around which others might cluster.   Accordingly we find that the appearance of Nebuchadnezzar
gives rise to a little scene of the three brethren cast into the
fiery furnace; and (more significantly) Balaam is added to
the list contained in the original sermon, and a similar scene
presents his affair with the ass and the angel.   By the end of
the eleventh century, then, we have two cycles, centering
around the Nativity and the Resurrection respectively, and
a loosely connected sequence, the *Prophetae*, from which
various incidents were breaking away and assuming separate form.

Now that the dramatic presentation of such motives
had been established, the next step was to round certain
episodes into definite dramatic units, which can really be
called "plays."   We encounter an example early in the
twelfth century, in the little piece called the *Sponsus*, which

[1] See Chambers ii. 52. For a different view see Hardin Craig, "The
Origin of the Old Testament Plays," in *Mod. Philol.*, x. 473 ff.

presents the parable of the Wise and the Foolish Virgins.
Largely lyrical in character as it is, it produces a genuinely
dramatic and unified impression.   It begins with a Latin
chorus descriptive of the Bridegroom, which is followed by a
lyrical dialogue between the two groups of Virgins, in which
French mingles with the Latin.   The Prudentes warn the
Fatuae not to fail in their watch; the latter confess that they
are unprepared for the Bridegroom's coming, and beg a share
of the oil, lest they be driven from the doors.   The Prudentes refuse, and bid them buy of the merchants; they
lament, but follow the advice.   The merchants likewise
repulse them, and bid them seek help of the Prudentes.
Realizing their helplessness, they implore the Bridegroom:

> Audi, sponse, voces plangentium;
> Aperire fac nobis ostium
> Cum sociis; praebe remedium.

Abruptly he appears; not with mercy, but with judgment.
He renounces them in Latin, and adds a curse in French; at
once, as the rubric directs, " Accipiant eas demones, et
praecipitentur in infernum."   This brief use of the devils,
who are destined to play so large a spectacular and eventually comic part as the miracle-play develops, is commendable for its restraint; and indeed the whole play is
effective largely by reason of its brevity.   Moreover, there
is a distinct, though perhaps unconscious, presentation of the
supernatural personages of the drama as detached forces,
really intervening in the action.   Certainly there is unmistakeable terror in the appearance of the Bridegroom; and
the piece is a little like a forerunner of Maeterlinck.

Illustrative of the strictly liturgical play is the set of ten
from the abbey of St. Benoît at Fleury-sur-Loire, a set consisting of two sorts of plays.   First, there is a group of six
Biblical plays, covering the Gospel narrative from the Ado-

ration of the Magi to the Apparition at Emmaus, with a detached play dealing with the Conversion of St. Paul. These pieces stick closely to their text, and the supernatural plays little part, except for brief warning apparitions of angels; to the Magi, e. g., or to Joseph and Mary before the Flight into Egypt. These episodes are short, and without distinctive artistic value. The St. Paul play is on a somewhat different footing. In the episode on the road to Damascus the Lord figures as a " vox ex alto," which might seem an attempt to secure an effect of dignity and mystery. Before long, however, we have the rubric, " Tunc veniat Dominus ad Ananiam, et dicat," which certainly suggests that the divine person participated in visible form, and cannot be regarded as proving a consciously artistic handling of the point.

The second group of the Fleury plays consists of four which deal with miracles of St. Nicholas. We shall meet with other instances of the favor which stories of this Saint enjoyed, and these particular cases may be rather briefly dismissed. Here again we can hardly speak of a distinct supernatural element; the miracles are brief, and little emphasized. Both groups of plays are written in clumsy Latin, and show little attempt at dramatic illusion; their chief importance is in showing the liturgical play advanced to a point where separate handling of incidents is possible.

We reach a somewhat more developed stage, and at the same time the first known dramatist of the period, in the work of the English monk Hilarius, at one time pupil of Abelard. He has left us three plays, which happen to illustrate the three main sources of the sacred drama. For the Old Testament, we have a *Historia de Daniel;* for the New, a *Suscitatio Lazari;* and from the body of Saints' legends a *Ludus super Iconia sancti Nicolai.* The first two, being of the regular liturgical type, need not concern us further.   The play that deals with St. Nicholas, on the contrary, is of a decidedly lively character, and is handled with real gusto.   It presents the familiar tale of the Barbarian who confides his property to the care of a statue of the Saint, in order to test his reputation as a guardian against thieves.   The experiment does not at first succeed very well, as robbers promptly appear and carry off the treasure. The Barbarian discovers his loss, and curses the Saint roundly, threatening to flog the statue if restitution is not made.   The Saint himself accordingly appears to the robbers, and by his menaces frightens them into bringing back all their booty.   The grateful Barbarian rejoices, and apologizes to the Saint, who now appears to him, and bids him thank only God.   The Barbarian, duly impressed, is converted to Christianity.

This lively little play, artistically much superior to the Fleury group, illustrates very well the early form of the Saint's play — the frank intermingling of natural and supernatural on the same plane, in merely physical relations, and the ultimate conversion, when the play contains any character not a Christian at the outset.   Such a form is of course not tragic at all, and its development can only lead to a comedy of manners.   It is not till later that a growing taste for martyrdoms brings a touch of tragedy into such pieces, in a manner which we shall examine in its place.

It may be said here that in the drama which still remains close to its liturgical origins the supernatural is practically never treated with conscious artistic intent, so as to bring out any distinctive quality in its representation.   We have already had examples of this; an additional one is the *Resurrection* from Tours (Coussemaker p. 37), which shows the *Quem Quaeritis* with several additions, not fused into a

coherent whole.   One of the rubrics is interesting as showing the crudity with which the supernatural power is
depicted in this period.   As the soldiers are guarding the
Sepulchre, " Veniat angelus et injiciat eis fulgura; milites
cadant in terra velut mortui."   The *Sponsus* is the only
play which seems to betray a consciousness of the need of
distinguishing the supernatural forces from the surrounding
dramatic fabric;   in general the episodes involving the
supernatural are brief, and without any marked characteristics.[1]   As we should expect, angels with messages or
warnings are the most frequent embodiments of the supernatural.

With the play of *Adam* we encounter a novel and decidedly interesting type.   It is the first known play in the
vernacular, and is no longer presented in the church, but in
the square before it, with a degree of scenic elaboration
strikingly shown in the detailed Latin rubrics.   In its present form it might be described as a sacred drama in two
acts and an epilogue.   We have the Creation of Adam and
Eve, the Temptation, and the Expulsion, for the first act;
the second, of much briefer compass, shows us the murder
of Abel;   and finally we have a *Prophetae*, not preserved in
its entirety.   The scenic elaboration just referred to sufficiently indicates that we have reached a period of conscious
art;   an indication confirmed by one or two points in the
structure of the piece.   Adam and Eve, contrary to the
Biblical account, are made to die before the murder of Abel,
thus setting that episode in bolder relief;   and the hint, in
the Expulsion scene, of the final coming of a Savior justifies

---

[1] A partial exception may be made in favor of the episode of the shepherds in the *Carmina Burana* Christmas play, where the devil whispers
skeptical suggestions into their ears, and an angel offers counter-suggestions,
till they are finally convinced by the *Gloria in excelsis*.   See Schmeller's
edition, p. 90.

the addition of the *Prophetae*, with its predictions of that
Savior's advent. But the chief interest of the play lies in
the handling of the characters, which we shall now examine
in some detail.

The play begins with a dialogue between the Creator
(called *Figura* in the rubrics) and Adam, in which the latter
is given instructions for his life in Paradise, and Eve for his
companion; both promise obedience to the injunction not to
taste the forbidden fruit. The ensuing action is given in a
long rubric. The Creator retires to the church, and Adam
and Eve walk about, "honeste delectantes in Paradiso."
Meanwhile the devils run to and fro in the square, with
appropriate gestures, occasionally coming near to Paradise,
and pointing out the forbidden fruit to Eve, as if urging her
to taste it. Then the chief devil comes to Adam (who
betrays absolutely no surprise at his appearance), and proceeds to tempt him, without success. The devil returns to
his fellows, and after a brief delay, and another *excursus per
plateam*, he returns jubilantly to Adam, promising even
greater joys as the reward of compliance, but only to be
repulsed again. Then, "sad and with downcast face," he
returns even to the gates of Hell, and holds a conference
with the other devils; yet another *discursus*, and the tempter
approaches Eve. She, as little surprised as her husband,
does not receive the devil favorably, but consents to hear
him. There is genuine psychology in the ensuing episode.
The tempter begins with a covert depreciation of Adam,
and proceeds by judicious flattery and a request for secrecy.
Naturally Eve is touched. After the devil's departure
Adam returns, and is angry with Eve for having allowed
him to address her. He rejects the tempter's counsel; then
a serpent, "*artificiose compositus*," coils up the trunk of the
forbidden tree, and whispers in Eve's ear. She listens, and

then, taking the apple, offers it to Adam. He is still reluctant, but at last yields, and at once recognizes his sin. He laments at some length; then comes the Creator, " as if in search of him." Confession and imprecation naturally follow; but the latter is tempered by the promise of a Savior to come. An angel now appears, clad in white, and with a flaming sword; he is stationed at the gate of Paradise, and Adam and Eve take up their earthly life. Again the devil intervenes, planting thorns and tares in the ground they have plowed and sown. The discovery of this act leads to a lament, and a lively quarrel between the two. The ensuing rubric, which ends this part of the play, deserves, long as it is, to be given in full, because of the light that it throws on the rôle of the devils. " Then shall come the devil, and three or four devils with him, bearing in their hands chains and iron bands, which they shall place on the necks of Adam and Eve. And some shall drive them, others drag them, to Hell; while other devils shall be near Hell to await them, and shall make great revelry among themselves at their perdition; and certain single devils shall come to them, and make signs, and raise them up, and cast them into Hell; and therein they shall make a great smoke arise, and they shall raise a clamor, rejoicing in Hell, and they shall clash their cauldrons and kettles, so as to be heard outside. And after some delay the devils shall come forth, and run about through the square; but some shall remain in Hell." With this the more important part of the drama terminates; the murder of Abel offers no striking features till the end, where the devils reappear. They " lead off Cain to Hell, with many blows; but Abel they shall lead more gently." Even in the *Prophetae* they are not ignored; after each prophet has given his testimony, he is escorted to Hell by a devil.

It is obvious that the devils are here established participants in the drama, whom it is perfectly natural to encounter in Eden, or find doing escort duty for a prophet. They constantly share in the action, and with equal zeal rush out to terrify the spectators.   Their chief has his own personality in the temptation scene; but in general their part is purely spectacular, confined to appropriate gesture and noise, but not yet definitely comic in intent.   They represent the crafty rather than the awful aspect of fiendishness, and accordingly have no tragic implications; they are simply effective stage figures, neither tragic nor comic, but very impressive for the spectators.   They represent as it were a state of balance, from which progress may be made in the direction of either comedy or tragedy.

The twelfth century, then, is the first in which we can speak of a genuine dramatic development.   We have the liturgical drama gradually working out of its fixed place in the liturgy in the plays of Hilarius, which could be given at matins or vespers, as might be most convenient, and migrating from the church to the square before it in the *Adam*. That play also shows us the change from Latin to the vernacular; a change indeed which has no direct bearing on the dramatic evolution, except in so far as it shows a desire on the part of the playwrights to reach their public more fully and intimately, and correspondingly facilitated freer treatment by enabling them to employ their native tongue. Even in the Latin plays the growing interest in stage effect is shown by the curious *Planctus Mariae* from Cividale (Coussemaker no. xx, p. 292), where the text is accompanied by rubrics that give elaborate directions for the delivery of every phrase.   Lastly, we find the play based on Scriptural material and the play dealing with Saints' legends existing side by side, and offering two distinct channels for the subsequent development, with the element of tragedy best represented by the former.   With regard to the treatment of the supernatural, the drama has not yet reached a point where such motives are treated as distinct from the surrounding material, except in a few isolated cases.

SECTION 2. — THE MIRACLE-PLAY IN FRANCE

The evolution of the strictly liturgical play, complete by the middle of the thirteenth century, demanded, for the further progress of the form, secularization.   The passing of the drama from the exclusive control of the clergy was favored by the removal of plays to the open air, a step necessitated by the growth of scenic elaboration.   With the accomplishment of this change the course of the development in the different countries begins to diverge, and we can now order our treatment geographically, first tracing the sequence of events in France, and then turning to England.

We may begin by noting certain general results of the new conditions.   One natural consequence was the enlarging of the two rudimentary cycles which we have already observed. The Christmas cycle found a prelude in the Fall, which was the primary cause of the Nativity, and in the *Prophetae*, which announced the Redeemer's coming.   To the Easter cycle were added a more detailed representation of the Resurrection, and (a theme most important for the developed cycles) the Harrowing of Hell.   Two groups were thus formed which might be combined to cover both the Old Testament and the New.   Their ultimate fusion in the all-embracing cosmic cycle is of course best shown in England, and its consideration may be postponed until we turn to that country.

So long as the miracle-play remained within the church the limitations of the building itself were a check on inordinate expansion.   It is even possible that a development of the choral aspect, as we see it for example in the *Sponsus*, might have led to something analogous to Greek tragedy. With the transfer to the open air, however, all formal limits disappeared; and the union of a huge outdoor stage with a very complaisant [1] and enduring audience led in France to results sufficiently indicated by the number of verses in the plays of the culmination — 50,000, for instance, in the *Mystère du Viel Testament*, and 35,000 in Greban's *Passion*.   In French religious sculpture the very necessities of the architectural spaces had compelled the treatment of the great cathedral façades as unified wholes; but in the drama no such salutary forces were operative. It was in France, indeed, that this tendency to unlimited expansion, combined with a certain dearth of imagination, worked most balefully; whereas in England a modification of both these circumstances led to marked success.

As we resume our study of the temporal sequence of the development in France we find in the thirteenth century two plays which strikingly illustrate the two tendencies which we noted in the twelfth.   These plays are Bodel's *Jeu de S. Nicolas* and Rutebeuf's *Miracle de Théophile*.   The first shows the transformation of the Saint's play into a comedy of manners.   The miracle which lies at the root of the piece is that of the Barbarian and the robbers, already familiar to us from the Fleury plays and Hilarius; but it is almost lost to sight in the material which Bodel has added.   The play deals with a Pagan kingdom which is threatened by an army of Crusaders.   At the outset

---

[1] A complaisance illustrated by the remark in the prologue to Greban's *Passion* that the matter shall be set forth " sans prolixité."

the king consults an idol, in order to discover the issue of the war; the image both laughs and weeps, a dubious portent which is variously interpreted by the courtiers. The crier is sent out to proclaim the result, and summon the people to battle; he has occasion to pass near a tavern, where the seductive announcements of the proprietor cause him to linger, thus introducing a long and vivid drinking-scene.   Finally the proclamation is made, and the two armies gather for the fray.   Before the conflict an angel warns the Crusaders that they are doomed to perish, but promises that they shall receive crowns of glory.   The prediction is fulfilled, and the angel utters a lament over the fallen.   All this while we have heard nothing of the Saint who gives his name to the piece; but he is now introduced, and by a rather ingenious device.   The victorious Pagans find on the field a single Christian survivor, kneeling before a statue of Saint Nicholas.   He is led before the king and mocked, but privately encouraged by the angel.   He vaunts the power of his patron, especially his efficacy as a guardian of property, to such a degree that the king, somewhat impressed, decides on an experiment.   The Christian is imprisoned, and the statue set to guard the royal treasures.   The crier is sent out to announce the test, and another tavern-scene is brought in.   We see three villains who have drunk beyond their means, to whom the proclamation suggests an easy way of obtaining money to pay their reckoning.   They have no trouble in appropriating the unguarded treasure; the robbery is discovered, and the Christian condemned to death.   He invokes the Saint, and the angel appears and comforts him.   The conclusion is of course the same as in the earlier plays; the Saint, appearing to the robbers, compels them to restore their booty, with the result that the whole realm is converted.

In this play we have obviously travelled far from the liturgical form.   The miracle has become a mere pretext; the chief interests are the lively tavern scenes, and the episode of the Crusaders, which must have appealed strongly to the age in which that great movement was actually going on.   There is an evident attempt to " give the public what it wants," but also a dawning sense of construction.   We have seen how the miracle is not dumped bodily into the piece, but introduced by a rather neat transition.   There is a certain measure of suspense in the fortunes of the captive, and a pathos in the battle scene.   The happy ending inherent in the form of play that ends with a conversion keeps the piece well removed from anything but the momentarily serious; but Bodel must be given credit for his sense of structure, and for his imaginative reconception of his material.

Of a very different and genuinely tragic type is Rutebeuf's *Théophile*.   The story of the man who sells his soul to the Devil, but is saved by a tardy appeal to Heaven, was of course immensely popular in the Middle Ages; but this seems the first attempt to give it dramatic presentation. Rutebeuf's conception, though on rather simple lines, is by no means unimpressive.   The play is a succession of brief scenes, rather than an organized whole; the author's aim is to illustrate by salient episodes a story well known to his audience.   Théophile, as we know, was archdeacon of a town in Cilicia, who was dismissed by his bishop for misconduct in office.   The play opens immediately after his fall, with a vigorous monologue in which he curses his foes, and thirsts for vengeance on them.   He decides to attain his end by resorting to a magician, Salatin, who is reputed to have commerce with the Devil.   The magician tells him that renunciation of God is the price of the revenge he desires; he consents to the terms, and makes an appointment for the next day, when the Devil is to be called up for him. On returning to his house he is tortured by remorse, and thinks with horror of the pains of Hell; but his desire for vengeance is too strong. He keeps the appointment; the Devil, already informed by Salatin of his demand, rises, and mocks at his terror. He is then given the terms of his covenant with the fiend, whom he is to serve with all his might when restored to power. Fulfilment is prompt; he is given his former office, and for seven years governs tyrannously. At the end of that period remorse again seizes him, and he prays (at great length) to the Virgin. She hears his prayer, and after some chiding goes to the Devil, wrests the charter from him, and restores it to Théophile. He in turn delivers it to the bishop, by whom it is read to the assembled people, and thus his salvation is accomplished.

For us the tragedy of the play evaporates with the intervention of the Virgin; but the men of its own time did not share our objection to the suddenness and absolute efficacy of the conversion. In any case, the earlier portion is tragic to a marked degree, and imaginatively realized. Théophile is perfectly aware of what his decision involves; he knows the torments to which he is condemning himself, but his thirst for vengeance overcomes his fear. The story indeed differs from the other offshoots of the parent story of Cyprian precisely in this accentuation of the intellectual element; revenge, not love, is the motive that impels its hero to traffic with the powers of Hell. There is a marked and sinister irony in the scene where the Devil mocks the terror of his new adherent which strikes a deeper note than the light mockery of the temptation scene of the *Adam*. In virtue of these traits the *Théophile* is the spiritual ancestor of Marlowe's *Faustus*.

The play we have just considered belongs to a class known technically as " miracles of Our Lady," a form whose vogue in the following century is shown by the forty examples preserved in the Cangé manuscript. As the name indicates, each play, however different from the rest in subject-matter, presents at some point the Virgin intervening in behalf of her adherents. The form is obviously a very conventional one, and the supernatural element is treated with little power or variety. The chief importance of the series for the evolution of the drama is the first appearance therein of themes drawn from secular history. We have the baptism of Clovis, on the basis of Gregory of Tours, and a very curious play on Julian the Apostate, in which that most inveterate pagan Libanius is converted, and becomes an enthusiastic devotee of the Virgin! Another noteworthy motive, not a historical one, is that of Robert le Diable, in which the man who is the Devil's son first appears in drama. There is of course a large amount of *diablerie* in these plays, but nothing which really demands extensive treatment here.

The orderly progress of the dramatic evolution renders it unnecessary to pause here for a summary, and we may proceed to the fifteenth century, which marks the culmination of the miracle-play in France, so far as size and number of compositions are concerned. Dramatically, however, there is a distinct retrogression; the hints of skilful characterization in the *Adam*, and the attempt at a closely woven plot in Bodel, come to no issue in their successors. Theology absorbs drama, and the underlying structure is obscured by extensive and often trivial digressions. Typical plays, which will sufficiently serve our purpose, are the already mentioned *Viel Testament* and *Passion*. They embody that side of Church tradition which, as we have seen, was richest in

tragic possibilities; but these possibilities are very inade-
quately realized.   The sacred text is in general closely
followed, and the result is a uniform body of verse, almost
wholly devoid of imaginative grasp.   Such attempts at
unity as there are result primarily from doctrinal, not
artistic, considerations.   I purpose to discuss these plays in
a general way, setting forth their main features, but reserv-
ing some specific points of comparison until we take up the
English cycles, which after all concern us more intimately.

It would scarcely be fair to demand any high degree of
unity from the *Viel Testament*, which is the result of an
attempt to create a cycle covering the entire Old Testament
by the fusion of a number of previously existing plays.
This attempt was abandoned when the meeting of Solomon
and the Queen of Sheba had been reached, and there are
added six detached mysteries, dealing with Job, Tobias,
Daniel, Judith, and Esther, and a final one on the apocryphal incident of Octavian and the Sibyl, which forms a link
between the two parts of Holy Writ.   The stories treated
are in general those which were conceived to be prototypes
of the life of Christ; certainly such incidents are those
treated at greatest length.   Furthermore, the earlier part
derives a certain unity from the so-called Procès de Paradis,
in which Justice and Mercy plead before God touching the
destiny of mankind.   It is a device which, if moderately
employed, would not lack dignity, nor even grandeur;[1] but
it becomes a mere wearisome substitute for a chorus.   When
it is first used, just before the Expulsion from Eden, it has a
certain appropriateness; but when it merely serves as a
mouthpiece for expounding the theological significance of
the doings of the Patriarchs, its impressiveness inevitably

---

[1] One thinks of the soul-weighing scenes in the *Iliad*, and of the dramatic
use of the motive by Aischylos in the lost Ψυχοστασία.

evaporates.   After the story of Moses the Procès as such ceases; and God himself takes on its rôle of expositor, very much to the detriment of his divinity.   God made a mere showman's expounder is one stage worse than " God the Father turned a School-divine."   This may suffice as a general account of the work, which, it can easily be seen, is not notable for either unity or proportion.

The lack of imagination just alluded to of course tells fatally against the force of the episodes dealing with the supernatural.   Such episodes, from the very nature of the material, occur in considerable number; but they do not result in any quickening of the imagination of writer or of hearer.   Either they are so brief as to lack any distinctive features, or so expanded as to lose all dramatic effect.   A detailed demonstration of this assertion would be unnecessarily tedious, and would require more space than we can here devote to it; a few examples will serve as sufficient illustration.

The chief besetting sins of the cycle are diffuseness and inability to appreciate really dramatic moments.   The prolixity of the speeches is normally so great that the movement of the plot is hopelessly retarded; and when a crisis is reached, it is generally interrupted by the Procès, in a manner that destroys all dramatic effect.   For instance, after the sin of Adam and Eve has been discovered by God there is a long scene in Heaven, in which Justice and Mercy debate, for nearly 400 lines, the fate which the sinners have deserved, and the Expulsion is not accomplished till this discussion has ended.   Similarly, when Abraham is on the point of slaying Isaac, Mercy pleads for the latter's life; her plea results in the sending of an angel, but the delay, coupled with monologues by both Abraham and Isaac, wholly destroys the proper feeling of suspense.   The desire to empha-

size points of doctrine is always prominent in these scenes of
the Procès, being indeed openly (and amusingly) avowed in
this speech of Mercy, during the adventures of Jacob:

> Puisqu' Abraham vous a prefiguré,
> Tuer son fils voulant, du tout ploré,
> Nous n'avons eu prefiguracion.   (16714–16)

One could scarcely ask for clearer evidence of the desire to
emphasize doctrine at the expense of drama.   The result
is an elaborate commentary on the story of Joseph and its
significance as prefiguring the life of Christ, even to such a
point as his sale by his brothers, which is equated with the
Betrayal.

The use of God as chorus is even more baldly expository,
and leads to a curious identification of him with his angel,
the shift from one to the other being sometimes made without warning, as in the giving of the law to Moses.   This
feature seems peculiar to the *Viel Testament*, but appears to
have no especial significance.[1]

Only occasionally does an episode appear which has
genuine force.   The first of the sort is the portrayal of
Cain, whose conduct is depicted with real impressiveness.
Before he can bring himself to the murder of his brother
there is a conflict in his soul; and after the deed he becomes
a voluntary outcast, conscious of his damnation, and at last
invoking it as a release from his earthly sufferings.   The
scene of the murder itself is brief and vivid; the voice of
Abel's blood, unseen, cries to Justice for vengeance —
and the Procès comes in to dilute the effect.   The punishment inflicted on Cain — to tremble incessantly — is a
truly imaginative touch.   Yet he remains undaunted, and
in his life as an outcast he experiences a fierce joy " d'avoir

[1] Cf. Heinze, *Die Engel auf die mittelalt. Mysterienbuhne Frankreichs*,
p. 32.

avec moi des semblables," even in Hell.   Perhaps the
finest expression of his mood comes after the death of Eve,
in the lines

> D'autre chose je n'ay envye
> Que de mourir; tout mon soulas
> Fut que mon ame fut ravie
> Desja en Enfer le plus bas;
> Car, veu la grandeur de mon cas,
> Aussi bien m'y fault-il descendre:
> *Il m'ennuye de tant attendre.* — (3692–98)

In a subsequent monologue he summons the devils to come
and seize him: and after he has been unwittingly shot by
Lamech he dies with a similar call on his lips.   Surely this
is a picture of a man accursed which yields to few in vividness and force, and reminds us rather of the better work
of an earlier period than of the quality of the surrounding
matter.

There are but two incidents in which the supernatural is
introduced which have any artistic value.   The first of these
occurs in the deliverance of the Israelites from Egypt, when
God curses Pharaoh (in an elaborate ballade), and at once
the sign of the pillar of fire is revealed to the departing
multitude.   Here for a moment there is some perception of
the supernatural as a power.   The second episode, somewhat similar, is that of the destroying angel who punishes
the sin of David.   After his work of destruction has been
completed he hovers between heaven and earth, where
David sees him:

> Je voy l'ange de Dieu en l'er;
> Vers Jerusalem a la face:
> Il semble qu'encor nous menace;
> Le voyez-vous pas comme moi ?   (32704–07)

Only here, in the whole cycle, do we feel that the power is
manifested in striking fashion; and the quality of even these

episodes is obviously of no very high grade.   The six detached mysteries need not detain us;   they present nothing new, and that of *Job*, where we might expect to find something of interest for our purpose, is perhaps the dullest part of the entire cycle.

It is evident from this survey that the part of the supernatural in the *Viel Testament* is essentially mechanical. Its brief manifestations are lost in the general flood of verbiage, from which no vivid imaginative handling intervenes to save them.   The Procès de Paradis, which might have served as a unifying element, and which a more sparing use might have made really impressive, becomes a mere stage device, monotonously handled, and fatally retarding the action at critical points.   One strongly realized character, Cain, and two or three rather striking episodes, are practically all that this large body of verse yields for our purpose. Of the supernatural directing the action in any vital way there is, except for the episodes noted, scarcely a trace.

In Greban's *Passion*, on the other hand, we have a work which does attempt to present its material, in this case the Gospel narrative, in unified dramatic form.[1]   Greban conceives his subject as a gigantic struggle between the powers of Heaven and Hell for the souls of mankind; but again, as in the *Viel Testament*, deficient imagination and pervading prolixity warp and obscure the underlying conception.   It is very difficult, in the space here available, to give a fair idea of Greban's drama.   The action is presented in a medley of diversified scenes, and the underlying plan which can be extracted from them is very hard to distinguish when the work is read in its entirety.   All that can be attempted here is a general sketch of the manner in which the

---

[1] For the previous history of this subject in France, consult E. Roy, *Le Mystère de la Passion en France du xiv au xvi Siècle*, Dijon and Paris, 1904.

supernatural is made a vital factor in the shaping of the plot.

It must be granted that the *Passion* shows a much greater interpenetration of the action by the supernatural than does the *Viel Testament*.   From the very nature of the terms in which it is conceived it sets continually before us the powers beyond man, especially the powers of evil.   The Procès reappears, but only at the beginning and end is it extensively employed; for the bulk of the play it is the devils and the souls in Limbo who are the chief supernatural participants, the former as movers of the action, and the latter as the symbol of redeemed humanity.   The part of the devils is in general grotesque, but not, on the whole, comic in intent; while the humor, when it does appear, is often grim, and by no means a matter of mere horseplay.   The devils are throughout the antagonists of Christ, whose true nature they become aware of only gradually; at first they suppose him to be merely a man, of exceptional virtue, indeed, but one who will eventually succumb to their temptations.   Their perception of his true character, and of their inevitable and impending defeat, introduces a measure of genuine climax, culminating in the moment when the Redeemer breaks down the gates of Hell, and leads forth the souls who have so long awaited his coming.

It is clear that Greban consciously uses the souls in Limbo as the unifying principle of the major part of his work.   Some of the scenes are laid there; and allusions also serve to keep its inmates before our minds.   The plan of the drama is thus to portray the struggle of the powers of evil against Christ; but it cannot be said that Greban makes this plan conspicuous.   He does not emphasize the incidents which illustrate it, nor can it, in actual representation, have produced any strong impression on the spectators.   He has an irritating trick of inserting needless scenes to enlarge a given episode, and his verbosity is nothing short of astounding. In the Procès, for instance, which occurs early in the play he outdoes his predecessors by introducing, beside Justice and Mercy, the figures of Peace, Truth, and Wisdom.   The first and second two argue severally at great length, and after the decision that mankind shall be redeemed has been reached, Wisdom enters and has to be told all that has preceded, in order that she may contrive means for that redemption.   Greban can never forget that he is a bachelor of theology, and his fondness for doctrinal quibbling is pushed to inordinate lengths, as in the episode of Christ and the Doctors, which occupies some 1600 verses.   However, he does contrive, in a group of scenes in which the devils figure largely, to devote some attention to his central theme, as the following brief examination of the most important of these scenes will show.

The first scene in Hell is one in which Lucifer calls up his legions; Satan says to him,

> Lucifer, roi des ennemis,
> Vous hurlez comme un loup famis,
> Quand vous voulez chanter ou rire,

to which he replies with a curse, and a lament for his changed estate, which shows real power.   The devils assemble, and sing a chorus, so hideously discordant that Lucifer implores them to cease.   He then informs them that there is a plan on foot to rob them of the prey that they have made of mankind.   Satan, when asked his opinion, expresses a like suspicion, and cites passages of Scripture which seem to him to confirm it.   Lucifer adds that he has noted that the prophets are continually calling on God for help, which he thinks they would not do if they had not some ground for thinking it would be granted.   In any case, he decides,

Satan had best be sent to earth, to see if he can find any man of such surpassing virtue as to make it possible that mankind should be saved; if he does find such a man, he is to tempt him with all his skill.   Satan approves of this decision, and goes forth; his suspicions are aroused by the mysterious circumstances surrounding the Nativity, and after the Flight into Egypt he returns to Hell.   Against his will he is forced to confess the virtues of the Virgin and her Child, and is tortured for the unwelcome tidings, after which he is allowed to suggest a remedy.   He declares that he has already inspired Herod to order the Massacre of the Innocents, and is much praised by his master, who sends him with two other devils to fetch Herod's soul.   This is eventually accomplished; Herod expires in torment, appalled by the sight of " more than a hundred thousand devils," all eager to carry him off.   In his agony he stabs himself to death, and is removed by the exultant fiends, to be warmly received in Hell, and rewarded for his services by a bath of molten lead.

With the progress of the action we begin to encounter scenes which portray a growing consciousness on the part of the devils of the gravity of the conflict in which they are engaged.   When Satan returns to Hell after his failure to tempt Christ in the wilderness, he admits that he does not know what to make of his antagonist, but suspects him to be something more than mortal.   The devil who is cast out of the Canaanite woman (12229) reports to Lucifer after the miracle, and is tortured for his testimony to Christ's power. An even more significant scene follows the raising of Lazarus; the devils discover the loss of the body, and see in it a striking proof of their opponent's might, so that Lucifer gives orders for the strict guarding of the gates, lest any further loss be suffered.   It may be noted here that the

actual raising of Lazarus is not impressive, nor is a subsequent speech descriptive of Hell, and almost wholly concerned
with the topography of that region.   We shall later have
occasion to contrast this passage with an English parallel.

The next scene in Hell follows a monologue in which
Satan laments his ill success, and introduces another torture
scene, here evidently by way of comic relief.   Then there is
a serious discussion of how Christ's death can be brought
about.   Lucifer bids Satan and Berich stir up the enmity
of the Pharisees; but Satan suggests the avaricious Judas
as an easy prey and a fit instrument.   Lucifer approves, and
the two set out.

The treatment of Judas in the ensuing portion of the play
is the one point at which Greban seriously grapples with a
real problem of characterization.   Judas' first speech
(11017) is a monologue, in which he sets forth his utter de-
pravity, though expressing a hope that his sins may perhaps
be remitted if he becomes Christ's follower.   Our view of
his character depends on how far we regard this desire for
salvation as sincere; and the dramatist has not given us the
means of forming a secure judgment on the point.   It is
clear that Judas, even before he is approached by Satan,
is uncertain of his fate, and discontented with his poverty;
and before the Last Supper he is obviously hypocritical in
his professions of devotion, and jealous of the favor shown
to John.   As the disciples sit at table Satan enters and bids
Judas fulfill his contract; he hesitates, and Christ, knowing
his thought, bids him do what he intends without delay.
He does not quite realize that his purpose is known, but
decides to go on the devil's errand; the other apostles,
surprised at his sudden departure, think that Christ must
have sent him on some mission.   This touch of tragic
irony sets us definitely on the road to the catastrophe.

The third part of the work, which is wholly concerned with the Passion proper, shows Greban's constructive skill at its best, and for a time presents Judas as the protagonist. His remorse at his deed finds expression at 21120, though in language the reverse of simple.   Foiled in his attempt at atonement by the return of the thirty pieces, he realizes that he is lost, and invokes the devils.   Lucifer hears, and sends Despair to fetch him.   The opening of the scene between the two is one of the few really excellent things in Greban.   Despair begins:

> Meschant, que veulx-tu que je face ?
> A quel port veulz-tu aborder ?
> J. — Je ne scay; je n'ay oeil en face
> Qui oze les cieulx regarder.
> D. — Se de mon nom veulz demander,
> Briefment en aras demonstrance,
> J. — D'où viens tu ?
>   D. — De parfont d'enfer.
> J. — Quel est ton nom ?
>   D. — Desesperance.   (21790–97)

The effect of this fine opening is, however, lost in an interminable quibbling dialogue.   Judas hangs himself; but his soul cannot escape through the mouth that has kissed Christ, and the devils have to cut open his stomach in order to secure their prey.

The imminent catastrophe now begins to have its effect in the world below.   Michael comes to Limbo to announce that the time of deliverance is at hand, and the souls raise a song of thanksgiving.   Lucifer hears their rejoicing, and realizes what it portends.   For him Christ is still only a man of surpassing virtue, but a foe of whom he must needs stand in dread.   Meanwhile Satan, on earth, rejoices that he has at last brought about the downfall of his enemy. " J'ay tout gaigné, j'ay tout gaingé," he exults, " J'ay fait un hault fait, un chef d'oeuvre."   He returns in triumph to

Hell, only to find that he has wrought the very reverse of what Lucifer desires, and to be sent with all speed to Pilate's wife, that by a dream he may cause her to persuade her husband to secure Christ's acquittal.   The errand is soon accomplished; but it is too late.   Pilate, despite his efforts, cannot turn the stubborn enmity of the priests, and Satan is constrained to return with a report of his failure.   Hell is put in a state of defence, and Satan once more returns to earth, in the hope of some last turn of luck, which he finds among the soldiers who are casting lots for Christ's raiment. In changed semblance he accosts one of them, and furnishes him with dice, the devilish traits of which are satirically described.   After Christ has expired on the Cross Satan, dubious as to what has become of his soul, decides to return to Hell.   The doubt is soon solved by the Harrowing of Hell, the true climax of the work.   Satan brings warning of the Redeemer's approach; then a voice is heard chanting the psalm *Attolite portas*, to which the souls in Limbo respond.   The Cross breaks down the gates, and the victor enters.   He tells the devils that their power is overthrown, and leads out the redeemed, who glorify him.   The devils lament at great length, after which Satan is sent for the souls of the two robbers.   The resulting scene is disappointingly brief; Michael, in a quatrain, says that he will carry off the just soul, and Satan does the same by the other. There is no conflict, no allusion to the fact that this is the last chance for the devils to display their power.   In view of the space which Greban often allots to absolutely unessential episodes, one regrets that he could not have given more attention to this, which is really a part of his main plot.

The fourth part of the work falls decidedly below the level of the third.   It consists almost wholly of detached and

uninteresting scenes, and at the end reverts to the theological subtleties of the beginning.   Satan makes a last effort
by spreading false reports among the Jews, but is overcome
by the spectacle of the Ascension, and returns to Hell with
the news of his utter failure, to be rewarded with the fiercest
torments.   The Ascension is followed by the most curious
portion of the entire work, the actual presentation of the
reception of Christ into Paradise.   Naturally such a scene
is wholly repugnant to our feeling; and it can scarcely be
said to justify itself even for its own day.   Even a worthy
poetical setting would scarcely help it; and that of course it
does not receive.   It ends with a promise by the Father
that the Holy Spirit shall be sent to the Apostles.   The
depicting of Pentecost leads to a "moralité finable," in
which the Procès is solved; the four abstractions embrace,
the Father proclaims the accomplishment of the Redemption,
and the play is at an end.

It must be repeated that such a summary as the preceding gives an inaccurate idea of the proportion of organized
plot to the entire fabric.   I have no desire to underestimate
Greban's technical skill; but I am also unwilling to have
such a presentation of parts of his work regarded as typical
of the whole.   For the *Viel Testament* such a process of
excerpting does well enough, since in that case there is
practically no underlying plan whatever; but with the
Passion we must remember that the really articulated
portions are isolated in the midst of loosely connected
groups of scenes, and hence lose in effectiveness the more
the entire play is considered.

The development in France, then, as illustrated by the
Viel Testament and the *Passion*, shows us on the one hand a
drama which contains no intrinsic supernatural, and very
little that is really decorative, and on the other a drama in

which an underlying union of supernatural and plot is obscured by irrelevant episodes and tedious theological digressions. Practically nowhere in the *Viel Testament* is there any attempt to distinguish the supernatural from the surrounding matter; the angels, frequently though they appear, might equally well be mortal heralds, so far as any wonder which they arouse in the other characters is concerned. When the higher supernatural forces intervene, it is generally in such a way as to arrest the action at a critical point, and to diminish or destroy the dramatic effect. Greban to a certain extent avoids both of these defects; his supernatural beings, especially the devils, are really distinguished from the mortal participants, and there is a real relation of the supernatural forces to the plot. Yet in his case also the incurable tendency to diffuseness, and the lack of the sense of what constitutes the truly dramatic, prevent his work from producing any unified impression. These adverse tendencies, combined with the circumstances of presentation, must have made it practically impossible for the audience to gain any vivid realization of the basic plan of the whole. Our conclusion must be that the French dramatists of this period, partly as a result of outward circumstances and partly by reason of their own insufficiency, failed to deal adequately with the problem set them by the very nature of the material with which they dealt.

The middle of the sixteenth century marks a decisive break in the course of the development in France. On November 17, 1548, a decree of Parliament forbade the Confrèrie de la Passion, which had had a monopoly of dramatic production in Paris, to give any plays dealing with sacred subjects. This official action merely sanctioned the result of several forces hostile to the sacred drama. The hapless plays were regarded with suspicion on all

sides.   The Protestants despised them as at best undignified, at worst grossly superstitious; the Catholics, on the
contrary, feared they would lead the people to think too
much for themselves in sacred matters; finally, the men of
culture condemned them as crude survivals of an age of
barbarism.   Only a few months after the decree appeared
Du Bellay's *Deffense et Illustration de la Langue française*,
with its explicit advocacy of the substitution of classical
tragedy and comedy for the old native drama.   Du Bellay
had previously [1] written of Greban and his brother as " ces
deux divins esprits ": but his feelings on that point underwent a swift change which only reflected that of the nation
at large.   Paris set the intellectual tone of France; and the
miracle-plays, wholly abandoned by men of letters, slowly
but irrevocably died out.   A lapse of three years brought
Jodelle's *Cleopatre*, and the formal installation of antique
tragedy as the sole model for serious dramatic composition.
This return to antiquity, the first attempt at which, half a
century before, had been received with general suspicion,
and carried out literally behind closed doors,[2] now swept all
before it, and resulted in a decisive breaking with the
immediate past.   This absolute break is the most significant feature of the entire French development, and must be
especially borne in mind because of the complete contrast
which it forms to the corresponding development in England, to which we now turn.

SECTION 3. — THE MIRACLE-PLAY IN ENGLAND

The period of the liturgical drama in England is illustrated
by only a few documents; but we have no reason to suppose

[1] In a dizain prefixed to the *Oeuvres Poetiques* of Jacques Peletier, 1547.

[2] See the amusing accounts of Aubrion and Husson, quoted by Julleville,
i. 445.

that it differed essentially from the corresponding period on the Continent. As early as the tenth century we find the *Quem Quaeritis* provided for in Ethelwold's *Regularis Concordia* (965–75) , which shows that even before the Conquest the dramatic evolution had begun. In the early twelfth century we hear of a play of St. Katharine at Dunstable; and toward the end of the same century William Fitz-stephen mentions the performance at London of " miracles of holy confessors and passions of martyrs." Such references as these suggest a transitional period in which Norman-French was the language of the drama; but the precise extent and nature of this period are not clear. In any case, the extant cycles are thoroughly English in form and treatment, even the Chester, which stands closest to the French plays, diverging from them in many important respects.

Early in the fourteenth century the records of performances on the festival of Corpus Christi testify to the beginning of this independent English development. The characteristic form which it assumed was that of the great cosmic cycle, extending from the Creation to the Day of Judgment. The Old Testament furnished a few striking episodes, chosen, it would appear, largely for their dramatic effectiveness. We find in all the cycles the Creation, the Fall of Man, and the Murder of Abel, followed by the Deluge, the Sacrifice of Isaac, and some part of the story of Moses. Finally, a *Prophetae* in some form is an invariable feature, usually of course as a transition to the New Testament story, which is the portion of the whole that receives the most extended presentation. The life of Christ, from Annunciation to Ascension, is treated in detail, and after a few plays of varying character the cycle fitly concludes with the Last Judgment.

This arrangement shows obvious divergences from the French type. The English cycle is much more an organic whole, with a very fair degree of proportion in its several parts, and a choice of subjects guided, to some extent at least, by purely artistic considerations, and accordingly varying from cycle to cycle. The divergence from the French practice is most marked in the manner of dealing with the Old Testament material. The English plays show none of the elaborate prefiguring of the New Testament in the Old, and none of the scholastic subtlety which makes so dreary a waste of portions of the French pieces. Religious teaching there is, of course; but it consists almost wholly of vigorous and homely moral exhortation, designed to appeal directly to the average auditor. Accordingly there is no such use of fine-spun dialogue or monologue for its own sake, without regard to character or situation, as we find in the French plays, and little diversion of the attention from action to mere discourse. This circumstance favors the growth of a dramatic sense, in so far as it does not direct it toward irrelevant matters; but more positively encouraging factors are not wanting.

The chief of these is to be found in the conditions of presentation. Instead of the vast fixed stage of France, with its tripartite division and its many mansions, the favorite English method was to present each play on a separate pageant-car, the whole cycle thus moving in sequence about the city, and pausing for action at certain appointed places. This method is certainly attested for York and Chester; and it was undoubtedly the prevailing English practice. The result of such a mode of presentation was to throw each individual play into bolder relief; and since the available space did not permit the use of a very large number of performers, the characters were necessarily few, and drawn with firm strokes.   There were of course certain possible extensions of space, and the action might be supposed to shift from one locality to another; but the kernel of the whole remained a single episode presented by a few strongly realized characters.   Hence conditions in England, both general and specific, were wholly favorable to the free development of whatever inherent dramatic skill existed in her people.   The aim of the English playwrights was to make their several pieces as vigorous and lively as possible; grave or gay, as the varying circumstances might demand, but vivid always.

In the issue these playwrights adopted on the whole a distinctly serious attitude toward their material; and such an attitude was favored by the fact that the Saint's play (which, as we have seen, had practically no tragic tendency) seems never to have been a favorite form in England. Though our earliest notice for that country is of such a play, later records of performances of Saints' plays are comparatively scanty, and but three examples are preserved.   One of these is Cornish, and thus outside the general English current, while the other two are the late Digby plays, which belong to a type transitional from the miracle-play to the morality, and are not at all like the French Saints' plays. The *Conversion of St. Paul* is a Scriptural motive, and there is much Scriptural material in the *Mary Magdalen*.   The two plays stand much closer to the Biblical cycles than to the French plays we have examined, and afford no ground for supposing a strong influence of the Saint's play on the English dramatic development.

The state of affairs is well illustrated in the case of London.   There Fitzstephen's notice of Saints' plays in the twelfth century is followed by a petition of the scholars of St. Paul's, in 1378, which begs Richard II to prohibit

certain inexpert persons from representing the history of the
Old Testament, to the prejudice of the petitioners.   (See
Chambers, ii. 380.)   So far as we can make out, the Saints'
plays seem to have been rather local affairs, often connected
with individual churches, and without the hold on the
public that the great Scriptural cycles acquired.   It is
quite natural that they should occur in the transitional
Anglo-Norman period, to which our earliest notices refer;
and they appear sporadically at various times and places,
sometimes as a result of temporary conditions.   In London,
for instance, during the Marian reaction, there was a re-
crudescence of the form, but for a brief period only.   Accordingly we are justified in assigning to such plays only a
very limited part in the formation of a distinctively English
tradition; [1] a fact which involves a corresponding increase
in the possibility of the tragic handling of sacred themes.
The Saint's play in France, so far as martyrdoms became a
favorite sort of ending, acquired a certain aspect of tragedy,
but only superficially.   Such an ending of a Saint's career
was really the seal of his triumph; and the more bloody the
tortures which brought about his end, the greater his glory.
There is occasionally a hint of the vengeance which befalls
the executioners or rulers responsible for his martyrdom;
but such hints come at the very end of the plays in which
they occur, and cannot receive any tragic development,
being in reality only the reverse of the victim's triumph.
The same observation applies, as we shall see, to the Saints'
plays of Italy.

For us, then, the medieval sacred drama of England
centers about the four great cycles — York, Towneley,

---

[1] Hence Professor Gayley's view (*Repr. Eng. Comedies*, p. xxxviii) that
the Saint's play in some measure accounts for " the combination of tragic,
marvellous and comic later noticeable on the Elizabethan stage " is scarcely
supported by the evidence at present available.

Coventry [1] and Chester — that are preserved; and it is now our task to examine the treatment of the supernatural in them. In view of the large mass of material that they offer it will be convenient to begin by discussing certain episodes in which the supernatural figures rather largely, and then to treat more summarily others of less scope and importance. I have chosen the York cycle as the norm, since it best represents the cosmic cycle, reaching from Creation to Judgment; with its plays we shall compare those of the other cycles which present significant divergences. Finally, after this consideration of the various types, we shall endeavor to decide whether we are justified in asserting the existence of a specifically English tradition in the handling of the supernatural.

We begin of course with the Creation, and in York come at once to a nobly imaginative scene. God creates the angels, and makes Lucifer the chief power over them, second only to himself. The angels begin a song of thanksgiving and praise, in which Lucifer joins. From the very first he is conscious of his own glorious brightness, which surpasses that of his fellows, and he rapidly advances in a crescendo of arrogance. His words alternate with the songs in which the loyal angels proclaim their devotion to their Maker, thus producing a splendid effect of choral contrast. Lucifer swings to the pitch of insolence, claiming a seat in the highest of heaven, and a worship equal to that accorded to God himself. At this climax of his pride the divine power suddenly smites him. In the very midst of his boasting the footing fails him and his followers, and they sink to the abyss:

[1] I use Coventry as a convenient term for the *Ludus Coventriae*, without implying any opinion as to the real habitat of that cycle.

Lucifer:
Me nedes noghte of noy for to neven,
All welth in my welde haue I weledande,
Abowne yit sall I be beeldand,
On highte in the hyeste of heauen.

Ther sall I set my selfe, full semely to seyghte,
To ressayve my reuerence thorowe righte of renowne,
I sall be lyke unto hym that is hyeste on heghte;
Owe! what I am derworth and defte. —
                          Owe! dewes! all goes downe!
My mighte and my mayne es all marrande,
Helpe! felawes, in faythe I am fallande.
Sec. Angelus Deficiens:
Fra heuen are we heledande on all hande,
To wo are we weendande, I warande.

Such an effect as this is not the result of chance; it could only have come from a mind wholly master of its material, and able to conceive it under a nobly imaginative aspect.

There follows a brief and vigorous scene in Hell. Lucifer laments the loss of his glory, and is cursed by the other devils, who blame him for their fall. He retorts the charge, and there are savage mutual recriminations, ending in blows. Then the scene shifts back to Heaven; the angels applaud the righteous judgment of God, who declares that he will proceed with the work of creation. First he will give light to the earth, which lies formless and in darkness; for the light " faded when the fiends fell." The day and the night are parted from each other, and God blesses the fruit of the first day's work.

We have then in this first play a series of effects remarkable for their breadth and power. The author works with a sure hand, selecting the chief moments with unerring judgment, and giving them admirable poetical expression. Especially noteworthy is his skill in the use of contrast. The boastful words of Lucifer alternate with the chants of the angels proclaiming the duty of obedience to God, and the fierce quarrel in Hell serves as a foil to the order of Heaven, where the work of creation steadily proceeds. For grandeur of conception this play can challenge comparison with any work of the kind; and the execution is likewise masterly in its degree.

The other cycles cannot match the superiority of York in the higher imaginative qualities; but Chester offers a curious motivation of the fall of the angels. After the Creation God goes on a tour of inspection of his new works, leaving his seat to Lucifer. Thus exalted, Lucifer conceives vain thoughts, and vaunts his worth, while representatives of the celestial orders express their disapproval. God returns, rebukes Lucifer, and casts him with his followers from Heaven. There is a scene in Hell, and then God grieves over the fallen angels, in rather good lines, which contrast with the matter-of-fact words of the *Viel Testament:*

> Ah wicked pryde aye work thee wo!
> My myrth hast thou made amisse.
> I may well suffer; my will is not soe,
> That they shold part thus from my bliss.
> Ah, pride, whi hast thou not burst in two ?
> Why did they that ? why did they this ?
> Behold, my angels: pride is your foe,
> All sorrow shall show wherever it is.

A parallel to the French inadequacy is furnished by Coventry, at the point where God expels the rebellious angels. Lucifer, when he is cursed, calmly remarks,

> At thy bydding thi wil I werke,
> And pas fro joy to peyne smerte;
> Now I am a devyl ful derke
> That was an aungell bryht.

The Towneley play is too fragmentary for purposes of comparison.

The next episode which concerns us is the Temptation and
Fall of Man.   York begins with a speech by Satan, who
expresses his envy that man has been chosen to enjoy the
divine favor which the fallen angels once had, and his
determination to compass the new creature's downfall.   He
assumes the likeness of a serpent, and accosts Eve, his
argument being that she and Adam will win worship through
the forbidden fruit, and be even as God.   She takes the
apple, and offers it to Adam, who at first rebukes her, but
is won over by her plea, only to recognize his sin as soon as
the forbidden morsel passes his lips.   God addresses Adam,
who hears him, but sees him not, and curses the guilty pair,
bidding an angel drive them to " middle-earth."   The
Expulsion forms the subject of the following play, in which
the angel has a prologue, followed by laments of Adam and
Eve.

That Adam should hear God's voice only, not seeing him,
is also a feature of Coventry, which likewise introduces
Satan's envy as the motive of the temptation, though it is
declared after the Fall instead of before it.   God curses
Satan, who retreats in rather comic fashion.   In Chester
Adam is shown us in his earthly life, uttering a prophecy
that salvation will ultimately be granted to man.   This
occurs in the course of a didactic speech to Cain and Abel,
leading to the episode of the latter's murder.

The story of Cain has in the English cycles no such fundamental power as that which we detected in the French
conception; but the treatment of it, especially in Towneley,
is far livelier and more vivid.   In York we have a prologue
spoken by an angel who is sent to bid Cain and Abel offer
tithes to God.   Abel is obedient, but Cain rebellious.   The
part of the piece containing the murder is lost; after the
break we have the angel coming to Cain, and asking where

his brother is.   The question leads to a rather undignified
squabble, in which Cain and the angel actually come to
blows.   This incident, however, is a later addition; and
the end of the play is serious and dignified in tone.

Essentially the same situation, but without the angel, is
presented with vigorous comic strokes in the Towneley
Mactatio Abel.   Here the three characters — Cain, Abel,
and Cain's servant — are set before us with remarkable
vividness and abounding spirit.   The supernatural element
is furnished by God himself, who intervenes twice; once to
rebuke Cain for his attitude toward his brother, and again,
after the murder, to curse him.   In the first case Cain
scoffs at the rebuke with startling freedom:

> Whi, who is that hob-ouer-the-wall ?
> We! who was that that piped so small ?
> Com go we hens, for perels all;
>   God is out of hys wit;

in the second he doggedly realizes that he is hopelessly
accursed.   This serious note, however, gives place to his
decision to bury the body, with his servant's help, and
become an outlaw.   In effectiveness on the stage this piece
of course far surpasses its French counterpart; but in
underlying seriousness the French for once carries off the
palm.   Chester and Coventry contain no variant worthy
of note.

The York *Noah* contains, except for a prologue by God,
no supernatural element, and we may therefore take the
Towneley play as our type.   It begins with a monologue by
Noah, who reflects on the creation of the world, and the
present wickedness of mankind, ending with a prayer that
he and his may receive God's mercy.   God then appears
above, and soliloquizes.   He recalls his love toward men,
which they have so ill requited that he repents that he ever

made them.   He decides to overwhelm the earth with a
flood, drowning all save Noah and his family, who have not
offended.   Addressing Noah directly, he gives him instructions for building the ark.   Noah, amazed at this miraculous voice, asks whence it comes, and is told that God
himself is speaking.   He is overcome that one so humble
as himself should be so highly favored, and craves a blessing.   This is granted, and God withdraws, to play no
further part in the action.

In Chester God's part is more extensive.   He has a prologue, similar in character to his speech in Towneley, but
condensed, and with an immediate turning to Noah.   He
appears after the ark is finished to bid Noah embark, and
again after the subsidence of the waters and Noah's sacrifice
of thanksgiving, to give him instructions for the future, and
a promise that there shall never be another flood.   In
Coventry it is an angel who brings the command to build
the ark, and there is no other supernatural element.

The various plays which deal with the Sacrifice of Isaac
give interesting evidence of how variously even relatively
simple supernatural motives may be employed.   No one of
the six plays on the subject (for beside the cyclical dramas
we have two independent ones) uses the supernatural
participants, God and the angel, in precisely the same way.
In York Abraham has a prologue, in which he reflects on his
blessings; then the angel brings him the command to sacrifice his son.   The angel of course intervenes at the sacrifice,
and returns to utter a blessing as Abraham and Isaac are
on the point of departure.   In Towneley God himself utters
the command, after a soliloquy in which he decides to test
Abraham, but it is the angel who intervenes, though his sending by God is represented.   The end of the play is lost, so
that we cannot tell by whom the blessing was uttered.   In

Coventry the angel alone figures, without any direct inspiration from God, and in rather summary fashion.   In Chester God utters the command; and at the sacrifice two angels appear, one to intervene, and the other to bring the ram, while God delivers the final blessing.   The setting in the two independent plays is rather more elaborate.   In the Dublin play God has a prologue, in which he announces his intention of testing Abraham's devotion to him, and then he sends the angel with his command.   After Abraham has consented the angel declares that he returns to report to God.   In the sacrifice scene the angel intervenes, but God utters the blessing.   Finally, in the Brome play Abraham has the prologue, and then God at once bids the angel visit him.   The angel actually seizes Abraham's sword at the climax, a proceeding indicated in some of the other plays, but here made wholly clear by the rubric.   The blessing is delivered by God, as in the Dublin play.   Accordingly we see that even in this comparatively simple instance each dramatist made his own approach to the material, and shaped it as his individual taste directed.   This diversity is the more striking, since it is obvious that the several writers did not deliberately seek to differ from each other; hence it indicates a noteworthy independence of procedure on the part of the English playwrights.

This may suffice for an account of the Old Testament portion of the cycles, since all the important types have been considered.   The York *Moses* introduces the colloquy of God and Moses at the burning bush, but it so closely resembles the corresponding episode of God and Noah that it does not require separate consideration.   Neither need we linger over the *Prophetae*, except to note that in that case also each cycle handles the motive in its own way, even to varying its place in the cycle as a whole.

In view of the number and variety of the plays that treat the New Testament material we are obliged to adopt a different method in dealing with the points in them which concern us.   To follow, even cursorily, the sequence of events in the cycles would be quite impossible in our present limits; and I shall therefore merely consider certain aspects of the whole mass.   First I shall discuss the four York plays — *Temptation, Transfiguration, Harrowing of Hell* and *Judgment* — which exhibit most perfectly the higher imaginative qualities of which we are in search, and contrast them with the corresponding plays of the other cycles; then I shall discuss the handling of certain minor motives, such as angels and miracles, and finally sum up the conclusions to be drawn from the previously examined material.

The York *Temptation* begins with a ranting speech by Satan, which is, however, not designed to be merely comic. He tells the audience that since his fall he has had little trouble in mustering a goodly following from among mankind; but now he hears rumors of one who shall come to redeem them.   Now that this redeemer has gone alone into the wilderness, Satan is sure that he can bring about his undoing.   Since he has been fasting forty days, hunger is the readiest temptation.   Of course all Satan's wiles are without effect, and at the end he is bidden return to Hell. He recognizes the superior might of his opponent, and slinks off, not daring even to look round.   Angels now appear, and marvel at Christ's patience.   He tells them that he has undergone temptation in order to serve as a mirror to mankind, and prove to them that they can overcome Satan if they will; blessed are they who thus withstand.   He ends with the significant words

> I knawe my tyme is faste command,
> Now will I wende,

which clearly indicate the approaching catastrophe.

Closely connected is the ensuing play of the *Transfigura-tion*. Christ, entering with three disciples, recalls to them the various accounts of himself which men have given, and Peter's declaration that he was God's son. Now, in accord-ance with their wish, the Father is to be revealed to them. They naturally anticipate a marvellous revelation. Forth-with Elias and Moses appear, the one summoned from Paradise, the other from Hell. The disciples are amazed at the sudden brightness, and at the transfiguration of their master, whose raiment is white as snow, while his face shines like the sun. Despite their awe they pluck up courage to question the newcomers, who disclose their identity, and exalt Christ's might. Christ now addresses the disciples, bidding them not fear, since for their sake the marvel is wrought:

> So schall bothe heven and helle
> Be demers of this dede,
> And ye in erthe schall tell
> My name wher it is nede.

The disciples worship in their turn; then clouds descend, with the Father in their midst. The disciples hear a great noise, and are overcome, so that they cannot make out what passes. The Father rebukes their fear, and bears witness to his Son; then the cloud vanishes. Christ bids the disciples tell him what they have seen; but they can hardly find words. They beheld a wondrous light, with three persons in the midst of it; now their lord alone is left. Likewise a cloud descended from heaven; but

> now fares all as fantasye,
> For wote not we how thai are went.

Christ tells them the meaning of what they have seen; the Father has borne witness for his Son, and " a quick man and a dead " have added their testimony. Peter asks why they were not allowed to see the Father's face in all its fairness; but he is told that they have beheld as much as mortals may look on and live. In conclusion Christ bids them return to the others, but tell none of what they have seen till after he has suffered and risen from the dead.

These two plays, in their simple grandeur, have an exalted imaginative quality which makes them akin to the already examined *Creation*. They exhibit an equally skilful use of contrast. The *Temptation* shows us Christ's might in the repulse of Satan; the *Transfiguration* confirms our estimate of that might by the testimony of Elias, Moses, and the Father himself, so that the three kingdoms — the living, the dead, and the heavenly powers — all bear witness to it. The first play refrains from making comic use of the devil, and preserves a sober dignity throughout; the second imparts a deep emotional effect by means of the awe inspired in the disciples by the marvels they behold. This awe is depicted with telling strokes, and with remarkable singleness of impression. There can be no confusion between the awe-struck disciples and the powers which are revealed to them. Finally, there are in both plays incidental touches, such as those just quoted, which widen the imaginative horizon; and each ends with a reference to the coming Passion.

We now proceed to the supreme manifestation of Christ's power in the *Harrowing of Hell*. At the opening we see Christ outside the infernal gates. In a brief monologue he recounts how he has bought mankind with his blood, and now comes to Hell to claim all those who have been his workmen. As a sign of his coming he will send them a light. His body lies in the sepulchre, whither he will return as soon as he has wrought the deliverance of his friends. The light flashes into Limbo, and rouses the prophets to exultant joy. They recall their predictions of the Redeemer's coming; Moses in particular speaks of the wondrous sight he beheld on the mount of Transfiguration. He sees now the same light that he saw then; and it is a sure token of deliverance. Meanwhile the devils are alarmed by the unwonted rejoicing. Beelzebub calls them to a council; but before they can be assembled the voice of Christ is heard, chanting the *Attolite portas*. Satan answers him scornfully, but the other devils are greatly afraid, and prepare to defend the walls. Satan recalls the raising of Lazarus, but declares that he himself inspired the Jews to slay Christ, a sentiment which encourages his followers. At this point the gates are shattered, and Christ enters. All Hell is thrown open, and Limbo lost to the devils, who blame each other for their defeat. Satan stands his ground, and wrangles with his adversary, but gets much the worst of the argument. He is relieved, however, to find that his realm is not to be wholly depopulated, and declares that he will walk east and west, to the confusion of mankind. To his discomfiture he is told that he shall be bound in Hell; Michael promptly accomplishes the task, and Satan sinks into the pit. The ransomed souls rejoice, and praise their deliverer, who leads them forth.

Finally, we have the worthy close of the whole in the *Judgment Day*. It opens with a prologue by God, who recounts the creation of the world, and the fall and redemption of man. Yet this supreme sacrifice has not stirred all men to repentance; therefore their folly must be brought to an end. The angels are bidden to blow their trumpets, and divide the just from the unjust. The souls arise, the good with songs of praise, the wicked with lamentations. The angels divide them, and the Son descends to earth to sit in judgment. The devils, in high glee, make ready to seize the souls that fall to their lot. Christ recounts all that he has suffered for mankind, commending those who have wrought charitable deeds, and rebuking those who have done the opposite. He takes the just to him, and dismisses the wicked to Hell, amid a song of the angels who ascend into Heaven. This play does not attain quite the level of its predecessors, but it surely presents the great theme with fitting sobriety and dignity.

In comparing the treatment of these four motives in the other cycles we may begin by noting that only York treats the *Transfiguration* (a significant fact, to which we shall recur), while Towneley has no *Temptation*, and in the two remaining plays stands close to York, especially in the *Harrowing*, which we may dismiss. The *Judgment*, however, inserts into the framework of the York play two scenes in which the devils figure; scenes, moreover, of a markedly satirical character. The first of them begins with a dialogue of two devils, who have just been loosed from their bonds at the sound of the trumpet, a sound so dreadful that they can scarcely stand. They know it is Doomsday, since Hell has been emptied of all its souls, and they must hasten to give their testimony against the wicked, though they are not eager to come before the grim Judge, who "looks fully grisly." They count up all their stock of sinners, in a long satirical enumeration. Now appears a third devil, Tutivillus, whose account of his various activities on earth has an even stronger satirical turn, especially when he enlarges on the guilefulness of woman:

> When she is thus paynt,
> She makys it so quaynte
> She lookys like a saynt,
> And warse than the deyle.

He ends with a whole catalogue of offenders, which leads the first devil to remark that the great increase of sinners made him sure Doomsday was near; and the second adds that of late they have come so thick to Hell that the porter has had no time to rest. The play now reverts to the York form; after the lost have been turned over to the devils there is another inserted scene depicting their removal, while the devils give them vivid descriptions of the torments that await them. The play ends with a speech by a good soul, praising God's justice.

It is to be noted that the satirical element in these scenes does not make them comic in the sense of being intended merely to provoke laughter. As a recent writer in the *Mercure de France*[1] points out, "Le Jugement dernier, acte final de la vie du monde et sanction suprême de nos actes, est avant tout une critique de moeurs." There is always a serious background behind the satirical touches. Moreover, we must remember that to the medieval mind, very conscious of the intellectual character of sin as an obscuration of the inner light of thought, there was always a certain misshapenness about sinners and devils, especially the latter, which provoked scornful laughter. The distorted moral nature of the devil results in certain physical malformations of body and speech which are an essential part of his nature. Yet if these characteristics move us to laughter, he has others which are ground for fearing him; and so long as he is seriously regarded he cannot become a purely comic figure. Many traits in the medieval devils which may appear wholly amusing to us were so only in part to the spectators of the miracle-plays; and we must beware of overlooking this more serious aspect. In the

---

[1] Camille Enlart, *La Satire des moeurs dans l'iconographie du Moyen-Age*, lxxxii. 620 (16 Décembre, 1909).

occasional instances — chiefly in Chester and Coventry — where a purely comic handling appears, it is so incidental and so trivial that it can be largely neglected in a summary of the whole field.

The three Chester plays with which we are concerned exhibit a marked tendency to substitute dialogue for action, with a consequent loss of dramatic effect. The *Temptation* has little sense of the conflict which the motive involves, and a great loss of dignity, as compared with York. The *Harrowing* begins abruptly with the shining of the miraculous light, and drifts off into an extensive *Prophetae*, followed in turn by a colloquy of the devils, in the course of which Satan bids them prepare for battle against the foe who has wrought so many miracles to their hurt. There is more dialogue after the voice of Christ has been heard outside, but before his entrance, so that the sense of his power which the episode ought to give is largely dissipated.

The tendency to verbosity is most marked in the *Judgment*, where it appears in conjunction with a very conventional structure. We have representative figures of the saved and the lost — Pope, Emperor, King, Queen — each with a long speech. This portion is followed by a speech of Christ, like that in York; the ransomed ascend, and the devils enter, setting forth the pains which the lost are to suffer. Christ reproaches the unfaithful, who are carried off by the devils. In conclusion the four Evangelists appear, declaring that they have recorded the truth, ignorance of which no man may plead in excuse for his sins. This device, original with Chester, is by no means ineffective, setting as it does the seal of authority on all the foregoing New Testament story.

The corresponding Coventry plays show a decided interest in the devils. The *Temptation* begins with a conference between three of them, Satan, Belial and Beelzebub. Satan expresses his suspicion that a redeemer has arisen among mankind, in which case their power cannot last much longer. The other two suggest that the enemy be found out and tempted. Christ's first words are a reference to his sore hunger, which thus affords a clear motive for the manner in which Satan sets about his task. After his repulse angels minister to Christ and sing, and there is a final exhortation to virtue, like that in York.

The Coventry *Harrowing* is exceedingly brief, and without salient characteristics, while the *Judgment* is incomplete. So far as it goes, however, it gives a very fair impression of the confusion that attends the rising of the dead. At the call of the angels the souls come forth with a great clamor, in which the devils join. God welcomes the righteous to his kingdom, and casts off the sinners, who are seized by the devils. The rest of the play is lost; but the whole was seemingly not very extensive.

This brief analysis suffices to show the superiority of York in the treatment of those motives which demand the finest imaginative handling, and also to illustrate the variety of treatment in the several cycles. The best of these plays show a very clear sense of the supernatural as a power expressing itself in action, and perfectly distinct from the mortal participants. The contrast is skilfully wrought by the numerous exclamations of wonder with which the activities of supernatural beings are greeted. We have seen that in the French plays such expressions of wonder are of very secondary importance; in the English cycles they occur with marked frequency, and with decided dramatic aptness. Even Chester and Coventry, which are in general less skilful in the handling of the supernatural, do not lack them; but the instances in these cycles are naturally less fine than those in York and Towneley.   The nature of these speeches ranges from simple expressions of sheer surprise to dialogues which really depict character, as in the Towneley *Prima Pastorum*.   After the angels' song the three shepherds try to explain the marvellous event, each according to his own turn of mind.   The First Shepherd seeks at once for a rationalistic explanation; the Second rejects this, declaring that he heard an intelligible voice, which can only have been that of an angel; while the Third, steering between the two opinions, says that he would have thought it thunder, if he had not heard the miraculous music.   The incident is thus raised from a mere prodigy to an interesting revelation of character, though without any detriment to its awesomeness.

Finally, in the most remarkable scene of its kind in all the cycles, a miraculous incident is made the vehicle of a superb dramatic effect.   I refer to the episode of the bowing banners in the *Second Trial before Pilate*, as it is set forth by York, the only one of the cycles that treats it.   As Christ is brought in by the insulting soldiers, the priests see the banners bow before him, and cry out in wrathful astonishment. Pilate asks the reason for this outcry, and is angry with the bearers when it is told him; but they declare that they were not responsible.   The priests refuse to believe them, and a wrangling argument ensues, till one of the soldiers suggests that the strongest men in the land be employed for the office.   The suggestion strikes Pilate favorably, and two such are found and brought in.   They boast of their prowess, and assert that the banners will not bow in their hands; but the result is the same as before.   At the end Pilate himself is forced to rise against his will and make obeisance to Christ, to his own bewilderment.   He declares

I was past all my powre, thogh I payned me and pynd,
I wrought not as I wolde in no maner of wise.

One could scarcely ask for clearer evidence of the supernatural as a power than these lines reveal.

Naturally this interest in the supernatural becomes at
times conventionalized, resulting in some cases in a purely
spectacular treatment of such motives, without regard to
their relation to the action.   We have already noted an
instance in Chester, in the doubling of the angel at the
Sacrifice of Isaac; a similar doubling occurs in the incident
of the Maries at the Sepulchre.   This doubling is evidently
intended solely for spectacular effect, since it has no influence on the action.   A more extended case is to be found
in the Newcastle *Noah*, which goes rather far in the direction of comic treatment.   It opens with a prologue by God,
who sends his angel to Noah to bid him build the ark.
Noah is asleep, and not pleased at being awakened: " Away
I would thou went," is his salutation to his heavenly visitant.   He comes to a better humor, however, and sets to
work on the ark.   Then enters the Devil, determined to
upset the plan by which Noah and his family are to be
saved; he purposes to do this through the agency of Noah's
wife, whom he calls his friend.   He informs her that her
husband's plan will be little for her good, and gives her a
drink to administer to him, and thus make him disclose his
secret.   Noah returns, weary with his labor, and accepts
the draught, which has the intended effect.   There is an
exchange of abuse between him and his wife, and then he
returns to his task.   The angel briefly encourages him, and
the Devil has a final address to the spectators.

Such a play as this of course shows the supernatural in a
very low estate, with no adequate reason for existence; but
it is by no means representative of the treatment of such
motives in the miracle-plays as a whole.   There is a certain
kind of grim jesting with the supernatural, such as we have

seen in certain of the Towneley plays, which is far removed from the mere foolery of the Newcastle play.   In general we are justified in saying that a purely comic handling of supernatural figures is very infrequent in the English cycles. In the case of Chester it is often hard to decide how far the grotesque effects are intentional, and not merely the result of incompetence; the latter explanation certainly covers several cases.

One point of detail remains to be discussed, because of its significance in relation to the general dramatic development in England — the treatment of death, for which we have two striking examples.   The first of these is the Coventry *Slaughter of the Innocents*, in which Death appears in person. After Herod's command for the massacre has been executed we see him exulting in his deed, and ordering a banquet to celebrate it.   Just as he takes his seat, Death comes in. He has heard Herod's boasts, but they shall come to naught; he is Death, God's minister, sent to slay the guilty monarch.   He has power over all living things, plants as well as animals, and will slay Herod with his spear.   The knights describe the slaughter of the children; Herod orders the minstrels to blow up a merry tune, but scarcely have they begun when Death slays him with two of his knights, and the devil carries them off.   Death ends the play with a moralizing speech, emphasizing his power and his suddenness, in orthodox medieval fashion.   The kinship with the *Danse Macabré* is obvious; and the primary intent of the incident is didactic.   There are, however, touches designed to be effective artistically as well as ethically.   Death thus alludes to his personal appearance:

> Tho I be nakyd and pore of array,
> And wurmys knawe me all abowte;

and he emphasizes this idea in his final words:

> Amonges wormys, as I yow telle,
> Under the erthe xul ye dwelle,
> And thei xul etyn bothe flesche and felle,
>   As thei have don me.

This rather incidental macabre element receives a unique and very powerful development in the Towneley *Lazarus*. The bulk of the play is of a very regular type; but toward the end is interpolated a most striking picture of the corruption of the body.   The following stanzas will give some idea of its peculiar compound of vividness and restraint:

> Ilkon in sich aray with dede thai shall be dight,
> And closid colde in clay wheder he be kyng or knyght,
> Ffor all his garmentes gay that semely were in sight,
> His flesh shall frete away with many a wofull wight.
> Then wofully sich wightys
> Shall gnawe thise gay knyghtys,
> Thare lunges and thare lightys,
>   Thare harte shall frete in sonder;
> Thise masters most of myghtys
>   Thus shall thai be brought under.
>
> Under the erthe ye shall thus carefully then cowche;
> The royfe of youre hall youre nakyd nose shall towche;
> Nawther great ne small to you will knele ne crowche;
> A shete shall be youre pall, sich todys shall be youre nowche;
> Todys shall you dere,
> Ffeyndys will you fere,
> Youre flesh that fare was here
>   Thus rufully shall rote;
> In stede of fare colore
>   Sich bandys shall bynde youre throte.
>
> Youre rud that was so red, youre lyre the lylly lyke,
> Then shall be wan as led and stynke as dog in dyke;
> Wormes shall in you brede as bees dos in the byke,
> And ees out of youre hede thus-gate shall paddokys pyke;
> To pike you ar prest
> Many uncomly beest,
> Thus thai shall make a feste
>   Of youre flesh and of youre blode.
> Ffor you then sorows leste
>   The moste has of youre goode.

Nothing parallel to this can be found in the French plays. We saw how far removed from any such impressiveness was the Lazarus of Greban's *Passion*, whose account of Hell deals chiefly with the topography of its different regions. The Towneley passage belongs in a clearly marked English tradition, which goes as far back as the early Debates of the Body and the Soul.   One of these, indeed, gives us a passage which touches an even higher level than the speech of Lazarus.   The Soul is scornfully upbraiding the Body which it has left.   " From thee cometh a noisome stench," it says.   " There is no fair lady, who was wont to think well of thee, who would lie a night with thee now, for aught that man could offer her.   Thou art unseemly to see, uncomely to kiss; thou hast no friend who would not flee, if thou camest stumbling in the street." [1]   This one detail of the corpse stumbling along without the soul's guidance before its horrified friends really concentrates all the effect which the Towneley passage achieves by accumulation of touches.

My reason for discussing this matter thus at length is that in the Elizabethan period we have precisely this dwelling on the physical consequences of death used as a powerful auxiliary in the handling of the supernatural; and it is interesting to note that it not only goes back to a decidedly early period, but also enters into the drama at a relatively

[1] Ne nis no levedi brut on ble,
  That wel weren i-woned of the to lete,
  That wolde lye a nizht bi the,
  For nozht that men mizte hem bi-hete;
  Thou art unsemly for to se,
  Uncomli for to cussen suwete:
  Thou ne havest frend that ne wolde fle,
  Come thou stertlinde in the strete.
            (Mätzner, *Altenglische Sprachproben*, p. 94.)

early stage, and so could have been felt by the people as a dramatic motive. It is, then, an important constituent of the English tradition.

The preceding discussion has attempted to cover all the various manifestations of the supernatural in the miracle-plays which have a distinct individuality; it has aimed at defining the most important types, not at listing all the existent examples of each type. Accordingly various motives which at first sight seem to offer material for discussion, such as the Chester *Antichrist*, have been passed over, because they are in reality merely variations on motives already treated, and hence without independent value from our standpoint. It has not seemed worth while to make any general statement touching the functions of the angels, since their rôle here is only a development of the fundamental motives which we have already noted in the liturgical drama; but something more explicit has been said of the devils, since they have a greater place in the subsequent development. It is now our task to see whether from this accumulated material any generalization of a distinctly English tradition can be made.

We have seen that the essence of the English miracle-play was a strongly realized situation presented by a few well-drawn and individualized characters, and that these characters, when mortals, had a clear sense of the difference between their own acts and those proceeding from a supernatural power, as is attested by their exclamations of wonder at such occurrences. The supernatural is thus an easily distinguishable element in the drama, its manifestations being made the more striking by reason of the relative simplicity and concreteness of the plot. That is to say, the supernatural is conceived as a power distinct from the mortal participants, and expressing itself in significant

action; a state of affairs wholly consonant with our preliminary definition.

We have found the most perfect exemplification of this in
five plays of the York cycle — the *Fall of the Angels*, the
Temptation of Christ, the *Transfiguration*, the *Harrowing of
Hell*, and the *Judgment*.   These five plays show a marked
kinship of style and conception, and are the consummation
in the English field of the general medieval tendency whose
course we are tracing.   York alone of the English cycles
treats the *Transfiguration*, a theme closely related to the
others, and in some respects the most admirably handled of
them all.   This shows that the authors of these plays pur-
posely selected such themes, with a definite intention and
power of giving them worthy presentation; so that their
achievement is to be praised as a consciously artistic one.
Certain of the Towneley plays supplement this group with a
mocking treatment of some of the motives which is not
vulgarly comic, but the reflex of the awe which the supernatural inspires; we whistle in the dark to keep up our
courage, and make sport of the devil for the same reason.
The other cycles offer no traits of their own to match these
of York and Towneley; but they present numerous divergences of detail which emphasize the vitality and independence of the English playwrights.   Moreover, in almost all
cases they show a sense of the supernatural as a distinct
power; the use of contrast in York differs from theirs in
degree, not in kind.

It is almost unnecessary to point out how utterly this state
of affairs differs from that which prevailed in France.   There
the supernatural is feebly conceived, and slow to set itself
in action; while the general movement of the plot is so
languid that it produces no marked effect when it does
intervene.   On the contrary, it often retards the action, and

destroys the dramatic suspense; and it produces no especial impression on the mortal characters. The difference between the French and the English method of handling the supernatural is fundamental; and the English method is revealed as infinitely more profound and more effective.

We may clinch this demonstration by citing two cases of the treatment of the same motive in the two nations. In the Coventry *Annunciation* the Procès de Paradis is introduced, on the same general lines as in the *Viel Testament*. The episode begins with a prologue by the expository figure of Contemplation, imploring God to descend and redeem his people. The Virtues in Heaven take up the prayer, which God hears favorably. Truth says that the old condemnation may not be revoked; Mercy opposes this view; Justice rebukes her, but she persists. Peace bids them not quarrel, and commends Mercy, but suggests that they leave the decision to God; the others consent. The Son says that one wholly pure man can save the rest; but the Virtues reply that no such man can be found. The Son declares that " a counsel of the Trinité must be had; " the Father tells him that " in his wisdom man was made," and the same wisdom must provide the remedy. The Son sees that only one who is both God and man can accomplish the redemption, and consents to take the task upon himself. The Holy Ghost says he will provide for the incarnation, and Gabriel is despatched to Mary.

The scene is no more to our taste than its French counterpart; but it must be admitted that its treatment here is decidedly more dramatic. We have a distinct sense that the Trinity, if one may so put it, has really arrived at a decision and put it into action. The brevity of the episode preserves its character as a real clash of opposing wills, and we do not wander very far into the mazes of theological disquisition.

Granted that such a theme is to be represented, the English presentation is the more adequate dramatically.

A more interesting case, and one which shows how ingeniously a supernatural motive may be wrought into the dramatic fabric, is the dream of Pilate's wife, Percula, in York. The episode begins with a domestic scene between the lady and her husband, in which they exchange compliments, and drink each other's health; then the lady retires with her son, since it is growing dark, and she must return home. Pilate lies down to rest until it is time for Christ's examination, and the scene shifts to dame Percula's bedchamber. Scarcely has she retired when Satan enters, declaring that if Christ be slain the power of the devils is at an end; he must therefore devise some means of preventing the impending execution. This he does by whispering in Percula's ear that Christ is unjustly accused, and that she must appeal to her husband to intervene. Awaking in terror, she relates what she has dreamed, and sends her son to his father with the news. He delivers his message at the instant that Caiphas and Annas have brought Christ before Pilate, and his story of the dream is met by the accusation that Christ himself has inspired it by witchcraft, in order to save himself from punishment. Pilate, however, refuses to accept this explanation, and declares that he will himself test the prisoner.

The incident of the dream is thus made an integral part of the action. We have a real interest in Percula as a character, and a desire to know what effect her message will have on Pilate; while the whole is given a setting of realistic detail. Greban, on the other hand, limits himself to the mere dream, and is content to show us only Satan whispering to the sleeping woman. She is not characterized, and the message which she sends has no perceptible effect on the action. The English playwright leads up to his incident, and makes it a constituent of a later scene; Greban takes it up when he comes to it, and drops it as soon as he can.

It would thus appear that we are fully justified in asserting that the English writers of miracle-plays have a method of handling the supernatural that is wholly national, reflecting a general attitude toward such matters on the part of the whole people, but utilized by each playwright in a personal way. The real interest of this state of affairs, and at the same time the justification of the preceding lengthy discussion, is the fact that the medieval tradition in England lasted until it was transformed by newer influences, and suffered no such absolute break as in France. The miracle-plays died out, because newer and more interesting forms of drama were devised; but there was no revulsion of feeling against them on the part of the nation at large. They died, in short, a natural death. The Reformation brought about the excision of certain plays, notably such as dealt with the later life of the Virgin; but it did not abolish the cycles as a whole, or in general seek to do so. At York the plays were given up about 1570; but the Chester cycle was still being performed in 1575, and there was even an attempted revival in 1600, frustrated, however, by the mayor. 1580 is possibly the final date at Coventry, though a performance in 1591 may have been of the old plays, and not of such a substitute as we know was given in 1584, when an Oxford scholar was commissioned to write a *Destruction of Jerusalem*, explicitly called a tragedy (Chambers ii. 361). By the end of the century all the chief cycles had ceased to be given, though sporadic plays doubtless lingered in out-of-the-way places. But even if we date the decline of the plays from 1575, it is obvious that they must have exercised an influence in the pre-Shakespearean generation which is by no means negligible, and that memories of them must have survived after the actual performances had ceased. It follows that so long as the tradition which they had established remained vital (and clear traces of it in the Elizabethan period can be found) the supernatural would be treated in a fashion consonant with this native tradition. It was, however, as a result of the influence of ancient tragedy that the supernatural first became prominent in Elizabethan drama; and before we can trace the further workings of the native tradition we must leave the Middle Ages, to follow the fortunes of the tragedy of antiquity as it came to renewed life in Italy, but without forgetting the great background of medieval life and thought which precedes the Renaissance, and in no small degree colors it.

CHAPTER IV

THE RENAISSANCE IN ITALY

SECTION I. — THE SACRED DRAMA IN ITALY

THE drama in Italy, at the period we are considering, exhibits a condition of affairs unique among the literatures of Europe. The Italian sacred drama, parallel with the other medieval developments which we have just been tracing, co-existed with tragedies based on antique models; and so far as extant work is concerned, such classicizing plays are the earlier. The life of Albertino Mussato (1261–1329), the founder of Renaissance tragedy, slightly overlaps that of Dante at either end, and his *Ecerinis* dates from 1314; while the earliest sacred plays preserved, the *Devozioni*, may be dated about 1375, and the first dateable example of the typical Italian form, the sacra rappresentazione, does not occur till 1449. We have notices of dramatic performances as early as 1244; but the scantiness of details leaves little opportunity for the accurate study of the evolution of the liturgical drama in Italy. It is evident that the great religious movement which found expression in the Umbrian *laude* must have affected that evolution; but whether to such an extent as virtually to begin it afresh, as D'Ancona[1] and others hold, seems doubtful. The Umbrian lauds, it is true, did assume a quasi-dramatic form; but of the passage of that form to Florence, and a resulting union with processional dumbshows to create a new dramatic species, there is no real evidence. In any case, Florence,

---

[1] *Origini*, i. 217 ff. For a criticism of this view see Chambers, ii. 91 f.

in the fifteenth century, did produce, in the sacra rappresentazione, a typically Italian form; and we may dismiss
the question of origins, to turn to the plays themselves.   We
shall thus, for convenience of discussion, invert the chronological sequence, in order that our survey of the classicizing
tendency may be continuous.

The earliest dramatic monuments are, as we have seen,
the *Devozioni del Giovedì* and *del Venerdì Santo*, probably to
be connected with the Umbrian school.[1]   They have of
course supernatural elements, but nothing especially noteworthy.   The most striking scene occurs in the second of
the two, in connection with the Crucifixion.   After Christ
has blessed the Good Robber the dead rise from their tombs
and address him, promising him their allegiance, and declaring that the prophets await him in Limbo.   God bids
the angels descend to comfort him; meanwhile the Devil
issues from Hell and threatens vengeance, only to be defied.
The verse of these plays is crude, but they have a certain
rough imaginative power not easily to be paralleled in the
formally more perfect later works.

It is to Florence that we must turn for the flowering of the
medieval drama in Italy; medieval by virtue of its origin
rather than its date.   We have records of dumbshows on
sacred themes as early as 1304, in which year, Villani says,
there was a pantomimic representation of the torments of
Hell; but not until the fifteenth century do examples of a
truly indigenous spoken drama seem to have arisen, chiefly
in connection with the festival of St. John the Baptist,
patron of the city.   Not till 1449 do we find a surely dateable example, Feo Belcari's *Abramo;* so that it is in the age
of the Medici that this development falls.   Belcari, who
became the most noted writer of such plays, was a favorite of

[1] See D'Ancona, i. chap. 14 for an account of them.

Cosimo; and Lorenzo, as is well known, tried his hand at composing one himself.

The sacra rappresentazione is a characteristically Italian form.   It has crystallized into a fairly compact play, complete in itself, unlike the great cycles so favored in the North. There is indeed an example of such a cycle at Ravello; but there French influence is almost certain.[1]   Various forces tended to bring about this compactness.   In the first place, the plays were presented in an elaborate and expensive scenic setting, which tended to make the words less important, and to confine them to points which were really necessary for the dramatic movement; secondly, the metre was not the couplet or the loosely linked lyric measures of the French plays, but the definite octave, which served as a check on exuberance.   Couplets can be strung together as long as the fancy of their writer permits; but when a character has expressed himself in two or three neatly turned octaves, why demand more ?   Longer speeches there are, of course; but in general, especially in comparison with the portentous verbosity of the French plays, the speeches are brief.   This is particularly true of those put in the mouths of supernatural characters, which frequently consist of but a single octave, and are seldom of any great length.

As we turn over the three volumes of rappresentazioni collected by D'Ancona[2] (the most convenient of such collections, to which the ensuing numbers refer), we find that in general the supernatural figures have, as we should expect, much the same functions as in the French and English plays. They are not presented with any overwhelming imaginative force; but they are handled on the whole with a rather

[1] See D'Ancona, i. 301 ff., especially 307–08.
[2] *Sacre Rappresentazioni dei secoli xiv, xv, e xvi, raccolte e illustrate per cura di Alessandro D'Ancona*, Florence, 1872.

satisfying craftsmanship.   In examining the various cases we may first consider them collectively, and then analyze a typical play in which the supernatural figures largely, in order to show the specific traits of the Italian form.

It is to be noted in the first place that God the Father is not brought on to the scene so frequently as in the French plays; and when he does appear it is rather in final tableaux than during the course of the play.   His will is made known by angels, or by mysterious voices from above, as in the *Abramo ed Agar* (i. 29).   Christ and the Virgin, however, appear with greater frequency, and their rôles are substantially those which we have already seen in the French plays; but there are human touches, especially in the portrayal of the Virgin, which recall the freshness of the English plays rather than the doctrinal conventionality of the French.   In the *Annunciation* (i. 178), for instance, after the prophets have proclaimed their message, Mary prays that she may see that Virgin whose glorious destiny is thus foretold, and serve her in some fashion.   She has no suspicion that the Virgin is herself until Gabriel comes to her with his salutation.   The human element outweighs the theological even in the Procès which forms part of a reworking of the piece.

It is in the Saints' plays, naturally, that the intervention of Christ or the Virgin is most usual, often by way of encouraging martyrs who are undergoing persecution.   The Italian Saint's play exhibits a peculiar fondness for bloody martyrdoms, carried out with a singular ingenuity of torture; but we are often consoled by the final spectacle of the victim's reception into Paradise.   At the end of the *Santa Orsola*, for example, (ii. 444), the Saint is revealed to us in Heaven, conversing with God.   The idea of vengeance visited on those responsible for the martyrdom is found in the *Santa Barbara,* where the executioner dies at the end of the play (ii. 90).

When we turn to the minor supernatural personages we find that a very characteristic feature of the Italian plays is the almost constant use of an angel to deliver the prologue, and often the epilogue as well. Such prologues are not especially frequent in England, while in France there seems to be no instance, though twelve plays have introductory *diablerie.*[1] The Italian prologues are usually brief, and concerned only with exposition; but they have a possible connection with the prologue-ghost in " regular " tragedy which we shall later examine.

The Italian angels are in general less bustling than their French counterparts; they appear, execute their mission and depart, without superfluous activity or discourse. In the *Abraham,* for instance, we have one angel to speak the prologue, and another to call Abraham (i. 45); a third to intervene at the sacrifice (53), with a reappearance, it would seem, to reveal to Abraham his future prosperity; while the angel of the prologue returns to utter the *licenza,* or dismissal of the audience. The angel who intervenes in Isaac's behalf seizes Abraham's arm, utters his prohibition in an octave, and vanishes; a measure of the customary brevity of such scenes in Italy.

The function of the angels is thus seen to be largely expository; the devils, on the other hand, have a more important part in shaping the action. They are not treated primarily as comic figures, but preserve their original character as opponents of good. They and the angels are often shown in conflict for the souls of mortals, with varying success, according to the virtue of the soul in question. The

[1] See D. H. Carnahan, *The Prologue in the Old French and Provençal Mystery* (New Haven, 1905), p. 104.

Rappresentazione di un Pellegrino (iii. 424) introduces a
conflict between a devil and St. James for the soul of a follower of the latter, who has been led by the devil to kill
himself. The devil gets possession of the soul, which cries
piteously for mercy, and is encouraged by the Saint, who
prevails over the fiend, binds him with many chains, and
rescues the soul, which returns to its body.

It is in the Saints' plays that the devils are most active;
they employ all their skill in temptation, of course in vain.
In the *Santo Onofrio* (ii. 386) the Saint is accosted by a devil
in the guise of a pilgrim, and is at first deceived; but he soon
recognizes the true nature of his companion, and repulses
him, to be praised by an angel. The same devil later appears to an abbot, but is again repulsed. In the *Santa
Margarita* (ii. 135) the devil appears as a dragon; he is put
to flight, and then resumes his proper shape of a horned
man, only to be cast to earth by the triumphant Saint, who
sets her foot upon his neck. St. Anthony (ii. 34) has a
harder struggle; he is assailed not only by devils but by the
spirits of Licentiousness, Sloth, Gluttony, and Avarice; an
angel encourages him, and he resists their appeals. The
angry devils give him a savage beating, but Christ himself
appears and comforts him. A subplot is furnished by the
adventures of three scoundrels whom Avarice finally leads to
murdering each other; [1] so that the devils have some con-
solation in their defeat.

It will be seen from this brief survey that the Italian plays
have a distinctly individual way of dealing with the supernatural; less nobly imaginative than the English, but much
livelier and less " theological " than the French. They
emphasize the activity of the supernatural personages, and
at the same time preserve their dignity; so that we may say

---

[1] The theme familiar to us in English from Chaucer's *Pardoner's Tale*.

that their achievement, if on a lower plane than the English, is markedly superior to the French. This opinion will be confirmed by an analysis of an entire play, the *Teofilo*, which I select partly for its intrinsic merit and partly for the contrast which it enables us to draw between it and the French *Théophile*.

After the usual prologue by an angel the action of the play begins with the machinations of a devil, who makes the officials of the diocese believe that Teofilo is secretly amassing wealth by unlawful means, with the result that he is dismissed from his office. He at first acquiesces in his dismissal, but is tempted by the devil, who declares that it will be regarded as evidence of guilt if he makes no attempt to regain his office. Won over by this argument, he applies to a Jewish sorcerer, Manovello, for help, which he secures. Lucifer is raised at a cross-road, and tells Teofilo that to attain his end he must become Lucifer's follower; which he promptly does, confirming his action by a written contract. Lucifer sends a devil in the guise of an angel to the Bishop, bidding him restore Teofilo to his former post; the Bishop obeys. The magician advises Teofilo to thank Lucifer for his good fortune, and to ask him for further favors; but he only succeeds in rousing him to repentance. He goes into a church and prays to the Virgin. She appears, but rebukes him sternly, especially for denying her son; for her own part she would pardon him. He implores her to intercede, and pleads his sincere repentance. She makes him recite a brief creed, and then consents to help him, but with no definite promise of pardon as yet. Lucifer, aware of his change of heart, sends a devil to bring him back to allegiance; but the fiend is repulsed, and returns to Lucifer, who sends him to the Jew. The latter tries his persuasive arts on Teofilo, but is likewise repulsed. The Virgin now praises Teofilo for his constancy, and tells him he is pardoned; she bids an angel summon Lucifer before her with the contract, which she compels him to give up. Teofilo makes public confession, and becomes a hermit. Lucifer wreaks his vengeance on the unsuccessful sorcerer, who is beaten and carried off to Hell. There is a final octave by the angel.

It is evident from this analysis that the *Teofilo* is strongest precisely where Rutebeuf is weakest — in the ordering of a well-proportioned and coherent plot; whereas the French play, at least in its earlier portion, is markedly superior in the characterization of the protagonist. Teofilo has but little character, and his submission to Lucifer is not motivated in the least; he is told to worship the fiend, and does so. Théophile, on the other hand, goes through a serious struggle before his lust for vengeance leads him to enter the Devil's service. This, however, is the only detail in the Italian play that can be regarded as unsatisfactory. In the handling of the conversion it is distinctly finer. The Virgin does not grant Teofilo her forgiveness until he has given proof in deed that his repentance is real; he is not finally pardoned till after he has defied the temptations of Lucifer and the sorcerer.[1] In the French play the Virgin is merely a lay figure to whom Teofilo may address his lengthy prayers; in the Italian she is a well-drawn character, divided between compassion for the repentant sinner and indignation that he could ever have brought himself to deny her Son. We thus have a well-proportioned play, with the dramatic suspense preserved throughout, and, in the case of the Virgin, admirable characterization.

Beyond this point, however, the sacra rappresentazione did not go. The example of Lorenzo de' Medici and Poli-

---

[1] This mode of treating the theme is wholly different from the conventional *Miracle of Our Lady*, in which a really ethical element is often wholly lacking.

ziano, who had sought to give the form a finer literary expression, and, in the case of the latter, a new content, was not followed by other writers. The attraction of the antique was too strong, and Poliziano's casting of his *Orfeo* in the mould of the national sacred drama is an isolated phenomenon, unthinkable in France, and without result in Italy. The elaborate enstaging of the sacred plays must have tended to stifle their growth; and the classical tendency begins to appear in them likewise. In the *Santa Uliva*, for instance (iii. 268), we have an interlude depicting the loves of a youth and a nymph, with appropriate song; another interlude in the same play introduces Night and the God of Sleep, with a masque of dancers. But it is in the work of the Florentine Cecchi that we see most clearly the coming in of the new influence, and the definite passing of the sacra rappresentazione into something radically different.

Giovanmaria Cecchi (1518–1587) sought to construct a new dramatic form on the ruins of the old religious drama. He explicitly declares his contempt of the sacra rappresentazione, and his intention of writing farces, which shall be intermediate between comedy and tragedy. In reality he leaned strongly toward the comic side, and enriched his plays by abundant borrowing from Latin comedy, which seemed to him the ideal. He substituted blank verse for the older octave, and made lavish use of the intermezzi which we have already seen even in the Saints' plays. His " spiritual dramas," which give modern versions of the old sacred themes, rely largely on scenic effects, and retain little of the old devotional spirit.[1] The chief interest is in his Roman crew of slaves, parasites, and go-betweens; the

---

[1] See the introduction to the edition of R. Rocchi (Florence, 1895), pp. xcii ff., on survivals of the sacred drama in Cecchi, and on his treatment of the supernatural.

supernatural is relegated to the end, where, even when manifested, it makes little impression on the other characters.
His work in short shows the familiar change of sacred drama
into comedy of manners, but in this case with a strong
classical tinge which proves that we have passed into the
Renaissance.   His innovation, however, like Poliziano's,
attracted no followers; and the drama of Italy went over
bodily to the reproduction of the models left by antiquity.
The Italian sacred drama had not sufficient inherent vitality
to make head against those who despised it for its lack of
culture, or were at best indifferent.   The possibility of any
connection with *belles lettres* passed with Poliziano, whose
Orfeo was soon altered into a semblance of classical form to
suit the new requirements of taste.[1]   Tragedy in Italy is a
creation of the Renaissance, and springs exclusively from
the imitation of ancient models.   This fact justifies the
rather summary treatment of the Italian sacred drama in
this section; a method further justified by the presence in
the Italian plays of many elements common to medieval
drama as a whole, and already sufficiently illustrated by our
survey of the drama of France and England.   We now turn
to this learned tragedy, and proceed to ascertain what use
its authors made of the material which they took over from
antiquity.

Section 2. — Classical Italian Tragedy

As we noted in the previous section, the birth in Italy of
tragedy based on imitation of antique models precedes the
dawn of the Renaissance.   The memory of Seneca had been
recovered by the middle of the thirteenth century, when
Vincent of Beauvais refers to him; and he soon began to

[1] If the *Orfeo* had any influence at all (which I regard as doubtful) it was
only in the direction of the dramatic pastoral.

attract the attention of scholars. One of the earliest of these was the English Dominican Nicolaus Trivet (1259–1329), who wrote a commentary on the tragedies; this, however, can scarcely have become known in Italy. There the first name is Lovato de' Lovati of Padua (died 1309), who seems to have stimulated his fellow-townsman Albertino Mussato to the composition of his *Ecerinis*, the first modern tragedy modelled on the antique.

Mussato, in addition to his activity as a man of letters, had an adventurous and varied career as soldier and statesman. He composed his tragedy with the distinctly practical motive of warning his fellow-citizens against the aggressions of Cangrande by showing them the effects of the previous tyranny of Ezzelino. He preserves the popular tradition that his hero was the son of a fiend, and thus introduces a supernatural motive into his work, though making no especial use of it. In externals—metres, chorus, and division into five acts — he follows Seneca; but he has no conception of the " three unities." The action of the play covers some fifty years, and it is really an epic in tragic form. Mussato himself was quite aware of this fact; in his poetical epistles he compares it to the *Thebais* of Statius (the title *Ecerinis* is an epic one), and speaks of it as *following* tragic measures: " tragicis assimilata metris." Seneca is thus his model only in an external way; and the play was designed for recitation or private reading, not for acting.

A considerable interval separates this play from its immediate successor; but there is a real continuity of literary tradition between them. Coluccio Salutati admired Mussato's Latin, and doubtless called the *Ecerinis* to the attention of his pupil and friend Loschi, whose *Achilles*, written before 1390, is really the first tragedy which successfully copies the antique model. In it the supernatural element is more developed, through the use of a ghost.   Hecuba dreams of the ghost of Hector, who demands revenge, and declares that it will be attained through the death of Achilles at the hand of Paris.   We have thus the type of the revenge-ghost, with the addition of the element of prophecy.   There are also sundry references to the underworld, with attendant argument between Hecuba and Paris on the possibility of the soul's survival of death, Paris taking the skeptical side.   This is a motive which recurs several times in later Italian tragedy.   Loschi, like Mussato, disregards the unities, but follows Seneca's style and thought more closely, thus attaining a greater degree of outward finish.

The family of Loschi had close relations with that of the third author in the sequence, Corraro.[1]   His *Progne* (1428–9) brings the ghost out of a mere narrated vision onto the stage, and thus begins the long line of Renaissance apparitions.   The ghost in question is that of Diomedes, king of Thrace, who delivers the prologue.   He is closely modelled on the Senecan Thyestes, and his chief business is to predict the dreadful deeds which are to be wrought in the house of Tereus.   Corraro attains a certain unity of plot, and rearranges his material with a view to greater dramatic effect; but neither he nor his predecessors are significant except from the historical point of view.   We have in Loschi the ghost in a dream, incidentally eager for revenge, and in Corraro the prologue-ghost, with a primarily expository function; the two types which are to prevail in the Italian tragedy of the Renaissance.

It is not until the very end of the fifteenth century that we find any attempt to compose tragedies in the vernacular.

---

[1] For a detailed account of the lives and works of these three writers, see Cloetta, *Die Anfänge der Renaissancetragödie*, Halle, 1892.

During the period of humanism, indeed, tragedy had attracted much less attention than comedy, even in learned circles; so that it is only natural that a considerable interval should elapse before the attention of vernacular writers was drawn to it.   In 1497, however, translations of the *Phaedra* and the *Agamemnon* of Seneca were published at Venice; and in 1499 appeared the first original tragedy in the vernacular, Cammelli's *Filostrato e Panfila*.   This singular production treats, not a classical myth, but a story from the *Decameron* (iv. 1).   It follows the translations just noted in employing the *terza rima* for the metre of the dialogue, while the classical choruses are replaced by *barzellette*, sung by various mythological personages, after the fashion of interludes.   The prologue is delivered by the ghost of Seneca, who comes from the lower world — " dal cieco tempio," — to which he alludes with some touches borrowed from his own tragedies.   He returns to the light only on sufferance from Pluto, whose power he feels at the end, compelling him to return.   This use of an author's ghost to introduce a drama is of course a purely expository device, designed to secure an impressive opening; the ghost has no relation to the ensuing action, and only incidentally refers to the lower world whence he comes.   There is a reference to that subject later, in the course of a moralizing speech by Panfila:

> Noi siam vittime tutti di Plutone,
>   Mandati insieme alle tartaree sede,
> Dove del mondo si rende ragione.   (p. 288.) [1]

Toward the end of the play there is an allusion to a portent, put into the mouth of a maid-servant, who has heard the ominous song of a bird; she, however, thinks it may portend the death of her own father, who is ill in Athens (p. 344).

[1] I cite the edition of Cappelli and Ferrari, *Rime di Antonio Cammelli*, Leghorn, 1884.

This is one of the earliest modern instances of the use of an omen to produce an effect of awe; and it is something that Cammelli did not find in his source.   On the whole, however, the intrinsic value of his work is small; and his choice of Seneca as a model did not find followers for a considerable period.

The inauguration of strictly regular tragedy in the vernacular is due to Trissino, whose *Sophonisba* (1514) became the norm for all subsequent works.[1]   He reverted to the Greek tràgedians for examples, and to Aristotle for theory. He accepted the three unities, and sought to reproduce the noble simplicity of Greek; but his pedestrian Muse could only inspire him to very juiceless and monotonous blank verse.   Tragedy for him was a purely literary creation, not designed for the stage, and with little or no relation to actuality; he believed that the study of antiquity would furnish him with a formula, by which he could treat satisfactorily any chosen subject.   The form is practically everything, the substance of very minor importance.   It is evident that from premises such as these no vital drama could follow.

The only supernatural feature which the *Sophonisba* displays is an ominous dream, of an allegorical type, in which Sophonisba sees her husband torn in pieces by dogs. The tone of the description recalls Dante rather than any Greek prototype; but it lacks vividness.   In the *Rosmunda* of Trissino's friend Rucellai, however, we have a dream which more concerns us, since it contains a ghost.   At the outset of the drama Rosmunda is eager to find the body of her father, which has been left on the battle-field where he

---

[1] A good general account of this period is M. Biancale, *La Tragedia Italiana nel Cinquecento*, Rome, 1901.   More detailed and erudite is F. Neri, *La Tragedia Italiana del Cinquecento*, Florence, 1904.

was defeated and slain. Her nurse argues against the attempt, but Rosmunda defends her desire, and finally adduces her dream as evidence. She saw her father's ghost, a mournful figure, covered with blood and dust, and so changed in aspect that she could recognize him only by his voice. The type to which this apparition belongs is obviously the Roman, not the Greek. He bade her give his body burial before the next sunrise, and told her where to find it; after warning her of the peril she would incur in the search, he vanished. The narrative of the dream is introduced rather casually, but it suffices to convince the nurse, and the two depart on their dangerous errand. Except for this prelude the supernatural has no part in the drama, which is quite as stiff and uninspired as the contemporary *Sophonisba*, with no picturesqueness of style.

The first visible ghost in Italian tragedy appears in Pazzi's *Didone* (1524), which closely follows the fourth book of the *Aeneid*, and shows the first extensive use of the supernatural in regular tragedy. We begin with a prologue-ghost, in the person of Sichaeus, Dido's first husband. He comes " dall' Abysso profundo," and declares his name and fate. Once before he has returned to the light for the sake of his beloved wife, appearing to her in a dream, and warning her to flee from Tyre to escape his murderers. She might have lived happily in her newly-founded Carthage, were it not for her hapless love for Aeneas, who is about to abandon her. The ghost returns to the light a second time because of his enduring love, and laments the coming disaster. He sees the Furies about to assail the city, and withdraws.

Pazzi does not confine his interest in ghosts to the prologue, but reverts to it at several points later in the play. Dido, for instance, describes the warning dream which she has had,

(p. 64 [1]), and is moved by it to make sacrifices to avert the threatened woe; but her sister Anna is not impressed by it, and scoffs at such presentiments.   In her final speech Dido exults in the thought that

> hor l'ombra mia
> Famosa andrà nel regno di Proserpina   (p. 130.)

and the Goddess of the dead is also referred to in a rather striking invocation, p. 118:

> O notturna Proserpin'a invocata
> Con le urla dolorose ai mesti trivii,
> Voi furie ultrici e tu mal genio mio.

The groundwork of this is of course Virgil's

> Nocturnis Hecate triviis ululata per urbes,
> Et dirae ultrices, et di morientis Elissae,   (*Aen.*, iv. 609.)

but retouched in a manner suggestive of Seneca.

Besides the ghost, Pazzi introduces into his tragedy a divine personage, Mercury, whose appearance on the stage is prepared for by two descriptions by Aeneas (pp. 72 and 79) of similar apparitions to himself.   He comes to introduce into Carthage Iarbas, Dido's lover, who is to defend her from her enemy Pygmalion, and gives him a promise that he shall be successful.   After Aeneas has sailed away, Iarbas is miraculously brought by Mercury into the palace, where he accosts Dido.   She is terrified, and at first thinks him a ghost (a significant allusion!); but he reassures her, and promises to defend her cause.   He eventually kills Pygmalion, but meanwhile Dido has committed suicide, and Iarbas is cheated of the reward of her love.

We have here a more extensive and conscious use of the supernatural than in any previous Italian example.   Pazzi

---

[1] See the edition of Angelo Solerti, *Le Tragedie di Alessandro Pazzi de' Medici*, Bologna, 1887.

leaves his actual ghost in the prologue, but returns to the ghost-idea at intervals, and introduces another supernatural being into the course of his action. It must be admitted that Mercury's power is displayed rather after the manner of a fairy-tale than in any very serious way; and there is so little real action in the tragedy as a whole that he cannot markedly affect it. In comparison with his predecessors, however, Pazzi makes noteworthy innovations in his use of allusions to recall a theme, and in his introduction of a supernatural figure into the actual fabric of his drama.

Seemingly the first author to bring a ghost into the action, following the example set by Pazzi's Mercury, is Lodovico Martelli, whose *Tullia* (1530) is a curious instance of the workings of the tendency to imitate Greek tragedy. It casts in the mould of the Sophoklean *Elektra* the Roman story of the murder of Servius Tullius by his daughter, a procedure which results in a singular mixture of motives and color. The inevitable dream recurs, but without individuality in its treatment. Martelli, however, is not destitute of poetic talent; witness this passage from a speech of Tullia to her mother:

> Questo fia il nuovo sposo, e queste fiane
> Quelle nozze novelle; e i figli nostri
> Saran quei sogni feri, che da noi
> Avran radice, e voi faran paurosi
> Sempre tra'l sonno, [1]

a passage which strikes its own note of dream-created terror. Martelli's ghost, however, is less poetic. He is that of Tullius, appearing without warning to his wife to inform her of his murder, and bid her seek safety in flight. The lack of any preparation for the apparition makes him a purely

---

[1] See *Teatro Italiano Antico*, iii. 64. This convenient collection (10 vols. Milan, 1808–12) contains most of the tragedies here discussed, and will be cited under the abbreviation *TIA*.

decorative figure, and wholly unimportant; but such as he is he remains an almost unique figure in the drama of the time, by virtue of his appearance in the body of the play.

The tragedies which we have thus far examined are based wholly or predominantly on Greek models; but with Giovanbattista Giraldi we have a definite change to imitation of Seneca, and the setting of an example that strongly affected subsequent tragic poets.   Giraldi is no mere closet dramatist, but a writer eager to bring his pieces to the stage, to arouse wonder and gain renown.   He was a native of Ferrara, which had been a centre of dramatic activity ever since the initiation of performances of classical comedy under Duke Ercole I, as early as 1486,[1] and could not fail to conceive of drama as something intimately related to actual production.   His *Orbecche* (1541) restores the Senecan ghost to the stage, and sets the type which practically all his successors are content to follow.   The play has a long prologue, opened by Nemesis with an extensive moralizing monologue; she declares that Sulmone, the chief villain of the ensuing drama, must be punished, and calls up the Furies. Their entrance affects the earth like that of the Senecan Tantalus; the sun is obscured, and   vegetation withers. After they have withdrawn there rises the ghost of Selina, Sulmone's former wife, slain by him because found committing incest with her son.   She asks Nemesis why the Furies are invoked to bring woe upon Sulmone; she herself is Fury enough.   She brings a marriage-torch kindled in Phlegethon for the secret nuptials of her daughter, the disclosure of which is to cause the doom of the whole house.   The model here is obviously the Agrippina of the *Octavia*.   At last she

---

[1] A convenient account of Ferrara as a dramatic centre may be found in the introduction of J. W. Cunliffe's edition of Gascoigne's *Supposes and Jocasta*, in the Belles-Lettres Series, Boston, 1906.

disappears, constrained to return to the lower world; but she awaits the coming thither of her foes before the sun sets on this day.

Giraldi has combined various Senecan elements for this prologue, but without creating anything new. He indulges in imitation of the allusions to the underworld, though with no very forceful result. This, for instance, is a passage of the sort from Selina's tirade:

> Così verranno insieme
> L'avo, la madre, et i figliuoli, e'l padre,
> A l'ombre oscure, a l'infernal regione,
> Ove da Radamante e da Minosse
> Saranno condannati a tai supplizi
> Che avranno invidia a la spietata sete
> Di Tantalo, e parrà lor pena lieve
> Che dia a l'avido augel di sè dur' esca
> Tizio infelice. E l'esser aggirato
> Sempre Ision da la volubil ruota;
> Et il portar del sasso sovr' al monte
> Di Sisifo, e il cader dall 'alta cima;
> E qualunqu' altra pena fia maggiore
> Nel cieco carcer de l'oscuro abisso
> Parrà loro un piacer et un trastullo
> Appo il tormento ch'essi avran tra noi.

It is hard to detect any individual note in this paraphrase, which falls short of the intensity of Seneca's perfervid rhetoric. The supernatural figures of the prologue have no further share in the play; but the decorative allusions crop up again at the beginning of the Messenger's speech describing the fiendish murder of the husband and sons of Orbecche at the hands of Sulmone. The Messenger longs for death after the atrocious sights he has seen:

> E se ciò non si puote, perch' almeno
> Non mi lece passar l'empio Acheronte,
> Poi che indi qua venuti son gli Atrei,
> Gli Atamanti, i Tiesti ? anzi i più feri
> Mostri, che fosser là ne laghi stigi ?   (TIA, iv. 200.)

The place where the crime was committed is described after the fashion of the Theban grove in which the ghost of Laius was invoked:

> Un loco dedicato a sacrifici
> Che soglion farsi da' Re nostri a l'Ombre,
> A Proserpina irata, al fier Plutone;
> Ove non pur la tenebrosa notte
> Ma il più orribil' orrore ha la sua sede.   (Ibid., p. 201.)

Giraldi also gives us the inevitable dream, allegorical, as in the *Sophonisba;* Orbecche sees a dove and her young attacked by an eagle.

In all this Giraldi achieves nothing really significant. He follows the example of Seneca in confining his supernatural beings to the prologue, and his stylistic borrowings, though not thus confined, are mere copyings, without vitality of their own. He is ready to moralize on any pretext, availing himself of his Nemesis for such a use; for the same purpose he introduces the *deus ex machina* into two of his plays, the *Altile* and the *Eufimia*. In act v of the former, Venus appears; she first describes her birth and prerogatives, and then explains that in order to save Norrino, whose life is in jeopardy, she has appeared in a dream to his father Lurcone, bidding him come from Africa to claim his son and clear up matters. She sees that he has just arrived, and therefore departs for Cyprus. In the *Eufimia* it is Juno who intervenes in behalf of Eufimia, whose husband Acharisto is seeking to kill her. Juno has much to say of the sanctity of the marriage-bond, and ends by declaring that she will depart, since she has shown her power. Finally, the *Dido* has a prologue in which divinities figure. There is first a monologue by Juno, modelled on that of the *Hercules Furens*, in which she laments the failure of her attempts to undo Aeneas. Then Venus enters, joyful at the love for Aeneas just aroused in Dido, and engages in a squabble with Juno. They come to terms, however, and Venus has a closing speech, of strongly moralizing cast. In fact, the sole purpose of these divinities seems to be to furnish a vehicle for outdoing the " moral Seneca " in the utterance of maxims. Of any design to use the supernatural in an effectively tragic way Giraldi is guiltless.

A unique type of ghost is that which we encounter in Speroni's *Canace* (1546). The play deals with the incest of Canace with her brother Macareus, and the prologue is delivered by the ghost of their child, who is to be born in the course of the play! The resulting confusion of past and future is not at all cleared up by the poet, whose attempt to justify his procedure by an appeal to the doctrine of pre-existence is far from lucid.[1] The child is endowed by Venus with preternatural knowledge, and predicts what he is to suffer, or (as he seems to say) what he has already suffered:

> Venere a me già morto
> Dona con questo corpo
> Il senno di molt' anni,
> Che mai non numerò la vita mia:
> E seco insieme il senso e l'intelletto
> Di miei passati danni. (TIA, iv. 48.)

Apart from his singular relation of the time-scheme of the play he is merely expository, and significant only as a curiosity.

It is not my purpose to examine all the occurrences of supernatural beings in the tragedies of this period, but merely to select certain characteristic instances. The type is practically uniform; the ghosts, whether alone or associated with allegorical figures, are almost always confined to the prologue, and have no intimate association with the action.

[1] Cf. his *Opere*, Venice, 1740, iv. 88–89.

An attempt at a closer relation, however, is to be found in
Decio da Orte's *Acripanda* (1591), a play which has sufficient individuality to justify examination.   It opens with a
prologue by the ghost of Orselia, first wife of Ussumano, king
of Egypt, who murdered her that he might be free to marry
Acripanda.   She at first cannot see in the unwonted light,
but gradually recovers her sight; a detail which makes her
more human than the majority of the ghosts of the period.
She is moreover distinctly a revenge-ghost:

> A la vendetta, alla vendetta omai
> Ben convien ch' io m' accinga, ombra tradita.

She invokes the Furies to assist her, but they do not actually
appear.   Her first manifestation of herself in the body of
the tragedy is effected through the usual dream, which
Acripanda has.   It is largely allegorical; but ends with
Orselia's ghost, who reproaches Acripanda as the cause of
her death, and declares that they will shortly meet in the
underworld.   Acripanda does not know of the crime committed by Ussumano, and hence does not appreciate the
point of the reproach; but she is naturally much disturbed
by the vision.   At the beginning of ii. 2 she comes terror-
stricken upon the stage, to relate how, as she was sacrificing
in the temple, various portents occurred, followed by the
actual appearance of the wrathful ghost, who drove her
from the sanctuary.   This is perhaps the nearest approach
to a real effect of the ghost on the action which we can find
in Italy at this period; but it really comes to very little, its
chief result being the terror which it arouses in Acripanda.
At the beginning of act iv we have an actual apparition on
the stage; not of Orselia, however, but of Acripanda's two
children, slain in the camp of the enemy.   They appear to
her in a cloud as spirits, before ascending to Heaven, where
they will prepare a place for their mother.   The mixture of

pagan and Christian imagery produces a peculiarly inept effect.   The play is strongly under the influence of Giraldi; it ends in a welter of bloodshed, and the style is very verbose, choked with erudition in true Senecan fashion.

With this play we are close to the end of the century, and in the full decadence of Italian tragedy, which, never very robust, was now yielding the field to pastoral and opera. Early in the next century we encounter in Cappello's *Arcinda* (1614) an indication of the extent of the decline. Here we have a lengthy prologue by the ghost of Sacripante, followed by a council of Pluto, Discord and the Furies, and a monologue by Death, the whole occupying the entire first act.   An earlier instance of the accumulation of supernatural figures in the prologue is to be found in Cresci's *Tullia Feroce* (1591 ?), which has a prologue by Ambition, followed by two ghosts and a Fury.   But the chief interest of Cappello's play lies in its close imitation of Senecan language. Here, for instance, is a speech put into the mouth of the Secretary Frandipardo:

> Ahi Frandipardo misero e infelice;
> Poscia che maggior sete e maggior voglia
> Hai nel tuo cuore, di quella che sente
> Il vagabondo Tantalo a gli abissi;
> E maggior pena gusti, che di quella
> Del misero Ision da l'atra rota
> Agirato d'intorno; e se Sisifo
> Porta gran pena nel portar il sasso
> Sopra la somità del alto monte,
> Quanto maggior dolor sentir debb' io ? [1]

The only possible avenue of originality for the late-coming author is an even closer imitation of Seneca than his predecessors had achieved.   On p. 61 there is a similar description of the infernal rivers, which it is not worth while to

---

[1] See p. 26 of the first edition, Vicenza, 1614.

quote.   Comparison with the passages previously cited from Giraldi will show the closer adherence of Cappello to the letter of his text.   With this play we may fairly consider that the Senecan tradition has sunk to its lowest ebb.

Our study of the dramatic evolution in Italy thus reveals on the one hand a sacred drama of no little merit, but without a firm place in the sympathies of the nation at large, and on the other a learned tragedy based on close imitation of antiquity, and practically unaffected by any native tradition.   The sacra rappresentazione was too feeble to cope with a rival which had behind it the prestige of a firm adherence to the glorious examples of antique tragedy; and its adoption for purely literary purposes by Lorenzo de' Medici's circle came too late to prevent its decline.   There was no such conscious breaking with the immediate past as in France, but the more or less contemptuous indifference with which the native drama was regarded brought about a similar result.   The plays which followed classical models had no vital connection with their age, and lost themselves in a waste of sterile imitation.

The only point at which a continuity between the sacra rappresentazione and the classicizing tragedy can perhaps be traced is in the matter of the prologue-ghost.   The marked expository element in the angels who so frequently open the sacred dramas may have made it more natural to have a ghost perform a similar function; but the later writers can scarcely have been conscious of any influence.   Their action would rather have been an unconscious inheritance of a once prevailing practice.   In any case, the primarily expository function of the supernatural figures in Italian tragedy is undeniable, and it became indeed an article in the artistic creed of the period.   Trissino, in his *Poetics*, enunciates in unmistakeable terms the principle that Gods should have only an expository part; and his words apply equally well to the prevailing practice in regard to ghosts: " Perciò che i Dei non vi si denno introdurre, se non per chiarire le cose, che sono fuori de la favola; cioè, che non si contengono ne la azione, che si imita, e questi tali Dei vi si introducono *per chiarire le cose passate*, e quali gli uomini che sono ne le azioni non possono aver vedute, nè altrimente saperle; et ancora vi si introducono *per predire le cose future*, quando hanno bisogno di essere predette; e cosi *per queste due cause solamente* si introducono i Dei ne la tragedia, che per altro non sarebbe cosa laudabile." [1]   While such principles as these were held by any large number of dramatists, it is obvious that any vital relation of supernatural to action was quite impossible; and our previous survey has shown us how perfectly they sum up the practice of the time.

The handling of the supernatural in Italian tragedy is throughout wholly conventional. Its essential features can be found as far back as Loschi and Corraro — the ghost, the ominous dream, the contrast of belief and skepticism in questions touching the other world — and they are only superficially modified throughout the period of practically a century, from the *Sophonisba* to the *Arcinda*, that we have been considering. It is perfectly evident that the variations of detail which we have been able to detect are after all very slight, and without any real novelty of conception or execution. The attempts of Martelli and Da Orte to introduce ghosts into the action are crude and inept, without any shadow of impressiveness. The Italian ghost is in the majority of cases expository and nothing more; and when he tries to pass beyond the conventional limits it is never with any satisfying result. In short, the Italian development shows us the absolute sterility of the classical

---

[1] *Opere di Trissino*, Verona, 1729, ii. 103. The italics are mine.

(which in this case really means the Senecan) tradition, when it is not fertilized by an independent native attitude toward the supernatural.   Italian tragedy deliberately cut itself off from all connection with the life and beliefs of the time, and contented itself with the obsequious imitation of an antiquity which it after all did not understand.   How different was the case in England we shall immediately have occasion to see.

CHAPTER V

THE ELIZABETHAN AGE IN ENGLAND

Section 1. — Seneca in England

We have seen from our survey of the medieval drama in England that it achieved a serious and artistically satisfying method of dealing with the supernatural; and furthermore, that the tradition thus established lasted until newer forms of drama were definitely replacing the old, and was never brusquely abandoned. In tracing the historical sequence of our subject we are justified in leaving the moralities aside, since by their very nature they lacked the possibility of attaining that contrast necessary to the effective use of the supernatural. The abstractions which take part in the moralities are all on the same plane; and differentiation only leads to the accentuating of the human characters, in other words toward comedy of manners.

Considering, then, the miracle-plays as the source of the native method in the dramatic handling of the supernatural, we have to note that such material as they afforded for treatment was of essentially foreign origin, consisting as it did of the hierarchy of supernatural figures which Christianity had introduced. The method by which such figures are presented may fairly be called native, in view of the contrast it offers to similar methods on the Continent; but the figures themselves are not so. Yet outside the strictly religious circle lay a great body of lore concerning the supernatural which must have largely shaped popular conceptions in such matters, and in time reacted on the drama itself.   We cannot, in the space here available, more than allude to these popular traditions: but a word on their possible relations to the general English attitude is in place.

In the blending of races which ultimately produced the England that is an individual nation, two strains are prominent which imply a definite attitude toward the supernatural; I mean the Celtic and the Scandinavian.   Celtic influence was of course always possible, if for no other reason than that of mere proximity; while Scandinavian blood early became an important constituent of the English stock.   Hence it is inevitable that something of the ideas of these two races should have been reflected in England.

It can hardly be said that the Celtic strain would have contributed markedly to the establishing of a deeply serious view of the supernatural.   The tendency of Celtic thought in such matters seems to be toward a lighter, more fanciful conception of the supernatural, the dramatic counterpart of which would be the *Midsummer Night's Dream*, rather than any tragedy; just as the all-powerful Sidhe themselves have dwindled to the harmless " good people " of current folklore.   Scandinavian thought, on the contrary, was of a sterner cast.   The Eddic lay of *Helgi Hundingsbane* shows how powerfully the Northern imagination could treat the theme of love between the dead and the living; for a presentation of ghosts as perfectly credible participants in ordinary life we may turn to the sober and striking narrative of the hauntings at Fródá in the *Eyrbyggja Saga*.[1]   Such stories are the result of a general Germanic attitude,[2] which finds parallel expression in Anglo-Saxon, from the

---

[1] An English version may be found in Andrew Lang's *The Book of Dreams and Ghosts*, pp. 273 ff.

[2] Cf. E. Mogk in Paul's *Grundriss der germanischen Philologie*, iii. 249; *Der Seelenglaube der alten Germanen*, especially 263 ff.

days of *Beowulf* down. It is easy to see that in medieval England numerous tendencies made for a maintaining of a lively interest in the supernatural, and it is by no means impossible that such an interest should have reacted on the sacred drama, which dealt with foreign material. Certainly this is the simplest explanation of the profound difference between the English and the French dramatic treatment of the supernatural.

The miracle-plays themselves offer, so far as I am aware, no example of that type of supernatural being which became most popular in the Elizabethan period, the ghost. In the third of the Cangé *Miracles of Our Lady* there is a wicked bishop who is transported to Purgatory, but rescued thence and absolved of his sin. This obviously has no connection with ghosts, since the sinner remains corporeal throughout, and hence does not become a departed spirit. In the Towneley *Incredulity of Thomas*, however, we do seem to catch suggestions of the ghost-idea. The word *ghost* is of frequent occurrence in the play, usually of course in its general sense of *spirit*; but as Thomas argues with the other Apostles that what they have seen cannot be Christ himself, but merely some deceiving spirit, he comes close to what we should recognize as specifically the idea of a ghost, notably in lines 234 ff.:

It was a goost before you stod, lyke hym in blood betraced;
His cors that dyed on rood for euer hath deth embraced.

So clear an allusion is scarcely to be paralleled elsewhere in the English cycles; and of the actual appearance of a ghost in a miracle-play there is no hint.

Outside the drama, however, we find an excellent example of a ghost in the alliterative poem of the *Awntyrs ot Arthur*, in which the ghost of Guinevere's mother appears to her in the course of a hunt. As the hunters ride gaily along, the sun is suddenly obscured, and the earth becomes dark as at midnight.   Gawain tries to explain the portent as merely an eclipse, but the explanation evidently does not fit.   The ghost appears, moaning and screaming in fearsome fashion, and horrible to behold:

> Bare was the body, and blake to þe bone,
> Al bi-clagged in clay, uncomly cladde;
> Hit waried, hit waymet as a womane,
> But on hide ne on huwe no heling hit hadde;

a toad sits on her head and picks at it, and her eyes glow like live coals.   The hounds run in terror to the wood and hide there, and the birds are likewise terrified.   Gawain boldly confronts the ghost, and bids her tell her story.   She does so, and then moralizes on the suddenness and impartiality of death, in approved *Danse Macabre* style, with incidental description of the torments which she suffers in Purgatory. Finally she utters a prophecy of the fate of Arthur and his court, and departs.   " With a grisly grete þe goost awey glides," and the sun once more shines forth.[1]

The skill with which the author tempers the mere horror of his ghostly figure is noteworthy.   The effect of the ghost on nature reminds us somewhat of Seneca's absurd descriptions; but here there is no hyperbole, and the episode is well contrasted with the mortal surroundings by ingenious touches.   We have Gawain's attempt at a rationalistic explanation, and the fleeing of the dogs from the apparition. There is also emphasis on the loathsome details of corruption, in the manner of the Towneley *Lazarus*.   If we remember how that impressive passage is really interpolated into a play of ordinary type, we can easily see that if a narrative like that of the *Awntyrs* had similarly been interpolated into some miracle-play, we should have had an

---

[1] See " Scottish Alliterative Poems," *Scottish Text Society*, 1892, pp. 122 ff.

introduction of the ghost into sacred drama parallel to the actual appearance there of the motive of death. As a matter of fact, we find no such passage in the English cycles, and hence are forced to conclude that the Elizabethan ghost, as a dramatic figure, was derived in the first instance from imitation of Seneca. Yet it is interesting to find, in our example from the *Awntyrs*, the union of the ghost with the idea of bodily corruption; a fact which opens the way for a distinctly native conception, when once the Senecan material had been assimilated. For the moment, however, we must turn to the imitators of Seneca, and see what use they made of the motives which they took over.

We saw in our previous discussion of Seneca that the chief characteristics of his use of the supernatural were an abundance of erudite references to the underworld, and a series of detached decorative figures, most prominent among them the ghosts. We further saw how the tragic poets of Italy took over these motives in a spirit of minute imitation, and failed to inform them with any new life. As a consequence of this attitude, they left the supernatural as exterior as it was in their model. When, however, the attention of English writers was drawn toward Seneca, they could hardly be satisfied with such a mode of treatment. Dramatically inept in itself, it also conflicted with all the traditions established by the miracle-plays, which made for a close and vital connection of supernatural and action. As soon as English writers turned to antiquity for inspiration, the example of Seneca made the supernatural an acceptable feature of serious drama; but once it had been adopted, the whole weight of national feeling was against letting it remain a mere detached ornament. Accordingly we should expect to find, even in the plays most strictly imitative of Seneca, a freedom of handling which would tend to even greater independence with the progress of the drama.

It is about 1560 that the first translations of Seneca into English begin to appear;[1] and a striking instance of the immediate and powerful appeal of the ghost to the imaginations of the time is furnished by Heywood's version of the *Troades*, which dates from 1559, and hence is one of the earliest. We recall that the original contained a description of the apparition of the ghost of Achilles. Heywood evidently thought this mere relation of so striking an incident ineffective; and accordingly he brings the ghost onto the stage at the beginning of the second act, and gives him a considerable speech. That he did so with the conscious purpose of improving on his original is made clear by his own words in his preface:

> Forasmuch as this worke seemed unto mee in some places unperfite, whether left so of the author, or parte of it loste, as tyme devoureth all thinges, I wot not, I have (where I thought good) with addition of myne own Penne supplied the want of some thinges, as . . . in the seconde Acte I have added the speache of Achilles Spright, rysing from Hell to require the Sacrifyce of Polyxena.

Evidently the mere description of a ghost seemed to him less effective than his actual appearance, and he revised his text accordingly. That such a liberty could be introduced into a translation shows a remarkable independence of attitude, and a distinct interest in the ghost for his own sake, apart from his classical origin.

There is likewise in these early translations a decided enthusiasm in the reworking of the so numerous underworld allusions which indicates an interest in them not only as a prominent feature of the original, but for themselves. As

---

[1] Cf. Evelyn M. Spearing, The Elizabethan " Tenne Tragedies of Seneca," *Mod. Lang. Review*, iv. 437–461.

an example, chosen at random, take this excerpt from a speech of Deianeira in the *Hercules Oetaeus:*

It will be quit whereas th' infernall fiendes shall·stint the strife
And quit my guilty ghost; my conscience doth my hands condem:
But Pluto Prince of glummy goulph shall purge from slaughter them.
Before thy banks I will appear, forgetful Lethe's lake,
And being then a dolefull ghost my husband will I take.
But thou that wields the sceptre blacke of dark infernall skies,
Apply thy toil: the haynous guilt that none durst enterprise
This ignorance hath overcome; Dame Juno never dare
To take away our Hercules. Thy plunging plagues prepare,
Let Sisiph's stone on my neck force my stouping shoulders shrynke,
And let the fleeting licour from my gaping gums to synke,
Yea let it mock my thyrsty throate whenas I meane to drynke.
And thou that racks Ixion King of Thessayle, o thou Wheele,
My haynous hands deservéd have thy swinging sway to feel,
And let the greedy gripe scratch out these guts on eyther side;
If Danaus' pitchers cease, by me the rome shalbe supplied.
Set open Hell, take me, Medea, as partner of thy guilt.
This hand of mine then both of thine more cruel blood hath spilt,
More then thou did as in respect of mother to thy chyld,
Or looking to thy brother's ghost whose gore hath thee defiled.
Have with thee Lady thou of Thrace for such a cruel wife,
And the Althe that burnt the brand of Meleager's life.[1]

Here we note a systematic heightening, according to the taste of the time, of the striking features of the passage, quite unlike the pallid reflections that we saw in Giraldi, for instance. Such touches, taken over from the translations, soon became a conventional feature in the plays of the period, as we shall shortly have occasion to see.

The independence of attitude on the part of the translators which we have just noted is also evident in the Latin tragedies composed about this time on the Senecan model.[2]

[1] See Seneca, *Hercules Oetaeus,* 934–955. The translation is by John Studley.

[2] For these plays see R. Churchill and W. Keller, " Die lateinische Universitätsdramen in der Zeit der Königin Elisabeth," *Shakespeare-Jahrbuch* xxxiv. 220.

In Goldenham's *Herodes* (1567) we have a prologue-ghost, in the person of Mariamne, Herod's former wife.   She comes of course from the lower world, and is eager for revenge on Herod, which she says she will obtain by making his life so intolerable to him that he will long for death, but be unable to find it.   Later in the play the malign influence of the ghost is alluded to as a contributing cause of Herod's downfall, a trait which is obviously not Senecan.   In Gager's *Dido* (1583) we have, at the beginning of act iii, the ghost of Sichaeus.[1]   He comes from Tartarus, and is indignant at Dido's love for Aeneas, whose treachery he suspects.   At the end he enters the palace, declaring, " Quin intus abeo; stabo et arcebo nefas."   So clear an indication of intention to affect the action is again not Senecan.

The later Latin dramas show an even more marked interest in ghosts; but this is obviously due to the influence of popular drama, which affected the productions of the learned in a way wholly unlike the state of affairs in Italy. Hence such later plays have no independent value as evidence; but they show the wide-spread interest in the ghost characteristic of the time.   In Gwynne's *Nero* (1603), for instance, there are two prologue-ghosts, a chorus of Furies, and a ghost to open each act, with incidental apparitions within the several acts; at the climax the whole company of phantoms watches Nero as he takes poison.   In the *Perfidus Etruscus* Death plays throughout the part of a chorus, and the *Fatum Vortigerni* makes ghosts appear to its hero on the eve of a battle, in a way that recalls *Richard III*.   Even the writers of learned plays are thus not bound to close subservience to Seneca's handling of the ghost.

When we turn to plays in the vernacular we find in the earliest of them, the familiar *Gorboduc* (1562), no overt

[1] Text in Appendix III of Dyce's edition of Marlowe, pp. 391 ff.

supernatural element. The worthy authors are more occupied in developing Seneca's moralizing than in copying his graces of style; such a speech as this of Ferrex:

> The wrekeful gods powre on my cursed head
> Eternall plagues and never-dying woes,
> The hellish prince adjudge my dampned ghost
> To Tantales thirst, or proude Ixions wheele,
> Or cruel gripe to gnaw my growing heart,
> To during tormentes and unquenched flames (ii. 1)

is an isolated instance. At the beginning of act iv, however, we have a dumbshow of Furies and royal sinners which somewhat recalls Seneca:

> There came from under the stage, as though out of hell, three Furies, Alecto, Megera and Ctesiphone, clad in black garmentes sprinkled with bloud and flames, their bodies girt with snakes, their heds spred with serpentes instead of heare; the one bearing in her hand a snake, the other a whip, and the third a burning firebrand; ech driving before them a king and a queene, which, moved by furies, unnaturally had slain their owne children; the names of the kings and queenes were these, Tantalus, Medea, Athamas, Ino, Cambises, Althea.

Though the fact is not explicitly stated, Tantalus and the rest are presumably regarded as ghosts.

The Furies recur in *Tancred and Gismunda* (1568), a play which has a developed supernatural machinery. At the beginning Cupid appears, and exalts his power, with appropriate mythological illustration. In these latter days, he says, his power is not duly reverenced; hence he will manifest it in the ensuing action, the end of which shall be death. He reappears at the beginning of act iii, to announce that his plan is at work, since he has roused Gismunda's passions, and given them an object. "Their ghosts shall give black hell to understand How great and wonderful a God is Love." His purpose being thus accomplished, he ascends to the company of the other Gods, and his place as controller of the action is assumed by the Furies.   At the beginning of act iv Megaera appears with her sisters, who descend after a dance, while she remains to declare her mission:

> Sent from the grisly god, that holds his reign
> In Tartar's ugly realm, where Pelops' sire
> (Who with his own son's flesh whom he had slain,
> Did feast the gods) with famine hath his hire;
> To gape and catch at flying fruits in vain,
> And yielding waters to his gasping throat;
> Where stormy Aeol's son with endless pain
> Rolls up the rock; where Titius hath his lot
> To feed the gripe that gnaws his growing heart;
> Where proud Ixion, whirléd on the wheel,
> Pursues himself; where due deservéd smart
> The damnéd ghosts in burning flame do feel —
> From thence I mount.

She carries a snake, which at the end she throws at Tancred as he enters, thus instilling into him the thought of revenge. In his ensuing monologue he calls on the Furies to aid him; but for the remainder of the play the supernatural is ignored. So far as it is employed, however, it has a real relevancy to the action, and effect on it; while the symbolic device of the snake ingeniously represents the transfer of evil through a physical intermediary, in a fashion which we shall find repeated in some of the plays dealing with witchcraft.

The first strictly Senecan ghost in an English play is Gorlois in the *Misfortunes of Arthur* (1587).   He delivers the prologue, beginning with a description of Hades, and going on to declare his desire for revenge:

> Since thus thro' channels black of Limbo lake
> And deep infernal flood of Stygian pool
> The ghastly Charon's bark transported back
> Thy ghost from Pluto's pits and glooming shade,
> . . . .
> Now, Gorlois, work thy wish, cast here thy gall;
> Glut on revenge! thy wrath abhors delays.

He gives an account of the previous crimes of Arthur's house, and invokes a detailed curse on Arthur and his realm, with a reassuring statement that the curse will have spent its course before his auditors' day. He closes, as Guinevere approaches, with the significant words

> And see where comes one engine of my hate,
> With moods and manners fit for my revenge.

At the end of act i, after the train of tragic events has been set in motion, the Chorus begins, " See here the drifts of Gorlois, Cornish Duke," a touch absolutely foreign to the Senecan manner. At the end of the play Gorlois reappears, and exults in the fulfilment of his vengeance, in consequence of which the effect of his curse is spent; henceforth " Let future age be free from Gorlois' ghost." He predicts the prosperity of Britain, and then reverts to the mood of his opening speech:

> Be 't so; my wrath is wrought. Ye Furies black
> And ugly shapes that howl in holes beneath;
> Thou Orcus dark and deep Avernus nook
> With duskish glens out-gnawn in gulfs below,
> Receive your ghastly charge, Duke Gorlois' ghost!
> Make room! I gladly, thus revenged, return.

His character as a revenge-ghost is thus clearly marked. The insistence on the expiration of his curse is seemingly designed to give us a due sense of his power; an end attained more successfully than in his Senecan prototypes. It is retained in the alternative prologue and epilogue penned by William Fulbecke, which are much more erudite in tone. Such erudition is lacking in the play at large, but the moralizing element is persistent.

We thus see that this ostensibly Senecan ghost is really very different from his models, in virtue of his reappearance at the end, the allusion of the Chorus to his activity, and the accentuation of his desire for revenge. Practically, then, we have in him a distinct advance on the Senecan type. As in the case of the later Latin plays, however, his value as evidence for the stricter imitation of Seneca is impaired by the circumstance that the *Misfortunes of Arthur* was probably not written till after an important event had definitely altered the course of the Senecan tradition, and increased the already existing tendency toward a freer handling of the motives it supplied.

This event was the appearance, in 1586 or thereabouts, of Kyd's *Spanish Tragedy*, followed at no very long interval by that of *Locrine*. Both plays have a marked individual character, and also supernatural elements much more elaborate than in any preceding work. The influence of the *Spanish Tragedy* is the more important in shaping the subsequent development; but *Locrine*, as more ostensibly in the Senecan tradition, at least so far as structure is concerned, may conveniently be discussed first. Its tone is ultra-classical; it outdistances all competitors in abundance of mythological allusion. The structural resemblances to the Senecan method do not much apply to the two ghosts in the play, who are far removed from the rather empty dignity of their Roman prototypes. It is the ghost of Albanact who takes precedence, and a most persistently active spirit he is. In him the type of the revenge-ghost reaches full expression; his sole reason for existence is his compelling desire for revenge on the Scythian king Humber, who slew him in battle. When he first comes upon the stage (iii. 2) he is invisible to Humber and his host, who are preparing for battle. The ghost predicts the impending defeat of his enemy, and exults in the prospect of thus attaining revenge. In scene 6 of the same act he shows himself to the now defeated Humber, and invokes revenge upon him, to be requited with curses.   The brief dialogue may be quoted, to give an idea of the stylistic quality of the play:

> *Hum.*   But why comes Albanacts bloody ghost,
>   To bring a corsive to our miseries ?
>   Is 't not enough to suffer shameful flight,
>   But we must be tormented now with ghosts,
>   With apparitions fearful to behold ?
> *Ghost.*   Revenge! revenge for blood!
> *Hum.*   So naught will satisfy your wandring ghost
>   But dire revenge, nothing but Humbers fall,
>   Because he conquered you in Albany.
>   Now, by my soul, Humber would be condemned
>   To Tantals hunger or Ixions wheel,
>   Or to the vulture of Prometheus,
>   Rather than that this murder were undone.
>   When as I die Ile drag thy cursed ghost
>   Thro' all the rivers of foul Erebus,
>   Thro' burning sulphur of the Limbo-lake,
>   To allay the burning fury of that heat
>   That rageth in mine everlasting soul.
> *Ghost.*   *Vindicta, vindicta!*   (*Exeunt.*)

The cry " Vindicta! " becomes in this period the customary *Leitmotiv* which accompanies the appearance of a ghost, and clearly marks the new character which such figures have assumed.   In act iv we see the consummation of Albanact's revenge.   In scene 2 he intervenes as Humber, worn out with wandering as a fugitive, seeks to obtain food from a rustic, and drives them both in terror from the stage; in scene 4 the ghost-ridden Humber in despair casts himself into a river, and Albanact rejoices in these very Senecan terms:

> Humber is dead! joy heavens! leap earth! dance trees!
> Now maist thou reach thy apples, Tantalus,
> And with them feed thy hunger-bitten limbs!
> Now, Sisiphus, leave tumbling of thy rock,
> And rest thy restless bones upon the same!
> Unbind Ixion, cruel Radamanth,

And lay proud Humber on the whirling wheel.
Back will I post to hell mouth Taenarus,
And pass Cocitus, to the Elysian fields,
And tell my father Brutus of these news.

In v. 4 we have another ghost, that of Corineus, Locrine's uncle, treacherously slain by him.   His rôle is purely expository; he appears amid a thunderstorm to describe the portents which presage Locrine's overthrow.   He is thus of less importance to the action than his fellow; but he takes on something of the color of the revenge-ghost when his daughter Guendoline later declares that her father's ghost still haunts her for revenge.   His excision, however, would not affect the plot.   In addition to the ghosts there is a third supernatural character, Ate, whose function is to expound the meaning of the dumbshows that precede each act.   It is worth noting that such a purely expository function became more and more diverted from the ghost to such abstractions as Ate here.   We shall better appreciate the significance of this fact after we have discussed some further examples of it.

Certainly *Locrine* offers us a case of the connection of supernatural and plot; but we can hardly say that its effect is proportionate to its extent.   The ghost of Albanact is not a dignified figure, and his frequent appearances, though evidently very seriously intended, are devoid of impressiveness.   Corineus is more restrained, but, as we saw, quite superfluous.   Neither apparition has the slightest atmosphere of mystery; the underworld allusions, numerous though they are, are too learned to create any dramatic effect.   *Locrine* has taken the important step of bringing the ghost into the action, and making him affect the mortal characters; but on the stylistic side it remains fettered to the classical commonplaces, and fails to attain the level of original art.

In the *Spanish Tragedy*, on the other hand, we have a genuinely artistic product. The supernatural beings, the ghost of Andrea and Revenge, remain indeed outside the action, " to serve as Chorus in this tragedie," but the action is conceived as under the guidance of Revenge, who predicts to the impatient Andrea the doom which will eventually befall his enemies. The ghost is thus intimately concerned in the action, though he does not actually participate in it. Kyd's originality is seen in the opening speech of Andrea, who describes his fortunes in the underworld. On the conventional Senecan type of such descriptions is grafted the Vergilian account of the descent to Pluto's realm, thus producing a composite of genuine literary merit. The outworn details take on a new life from their presence in the fluent narrative of Andrea's fortunes at the judgment-seat of Hades, to which a human interest is given by the discussion of the judges as to what place in their realm befits him. At the end he tells how he was escorted by Revenge to the upper world, there to behold the undoing of Balthazar, the cause of his own death. Though he and his guide sit outside the action as Chorus, his interest is more keenly excited as he finds the turn of events at first contrary to his wishes, and upbraids Revenge in consequence. This gives considerable variety to the dialogues between the two which serve as interludes between the several acts, leading up to a climax at the end of act iii, when Andrea summons Revenge to awake, and reproaches him for his seeming indifference. After the accumulated murders of the finale, the ghost exults in the downfall of his enemies, and declares that in the underworld he will recompense his friends and continue his revenge on his foes, who shall replace the famous criminals of antiquity:

Then, sweet Revenge, do this at my request;
Let me be judge and doom them to unrest;
Let loose poor Titius from the vultures gripe,
And let Don Ciprian supply his roome;
Place Don Lorenzo on Ixions wheel,
And let the lovers endless pains surcease,
Juno forget old wrath and grant him ease;
Hang Balthazar about Chimeras neck,
And let him there bewail his bloody love,
Repining at our joys that are above;
Let Serberine go roll the fatal stone
And take from Siciphus his endless moan;
False Pedringano, for his treachery,
Let him be dragged thro' boiling Acheron,
And ther live dying still in endless flames,
Blaspheming gods and all their holy names.

One might see in these closing words a symbol of the fate of
the Senecan tradition in England; the malefactors of antiquity are to be supplanted by those of a new world.

Andrea thus clearly belongs to the type of the revenge-
ghost, though we are not, as in *Locrine*, shown any act of his
which helps to bring his revenge about.   We are, however,
repeatedly told that the course of events is under the direction of the incarnate Spirit of revenge, and must be satisfied
with that as representing the relation of supernatural to
plot; it is a postulate, and nothing more.   As an instance
of the supernatural in action the *Spanish Tragedy* is thus
imperfect; but as a decided step toward the creation of an
appropriate setting it deserves high praise.   Andrea is the
first ghost on the modern stage who derives his dignity not
from mere imitation of a tradition but from the artistic
power of his creator.   The detailed commentary on the
action, which never descends to mere exposition, is far
removed from the Senecan ideal of detachment; and the
final declaration of a purpose of continuing revenge even
in the underworld is a novel idea, which found prompt favor

with the writers of the time. But the value of the *Spanish Tragedy* lies less in any novelty of structure than in the fact that it contains a supernatural atmosphere of real illusiveness, even though it lacks the final virtue of contrast with mortal surroundings. It thus supplies precisely what *Locrine* lacked, and the problem of the later dramatists was to combine the contributions of the two plays — to make the supernatural share intimately in the action, and at the same time to preserve its inherent and peculiar impressiveness.

With the *Spanish Tragedy* the imitation of Seneca has taken a decisive turn in the direction of freer handling; and later instances must either depart more or less radically from the Senecan type, as we have seen that the *Misfortunes of Arthur* does, or else be mere learned survivals, consciously archaic. Certain examples of the latter type, occurring in the neighborhood of 1600, may be conveniently disposed of now, since they have little relation to the time in which they were written. Just after the turn of the century we have Greville's *Alaham* and Alexander's *Alexandraean Tragedy*, in both of which the prologue-ghost assumes a strangely hypertrophied form. The prologues of both plays have a composite character, essentially expository, but with a good share of underworld description. In the former the element of exposition is subordinate; the ghost comes to bring vengeance on his degenerate descendants, and delivers the usual catalogue of infernal torments, though with some attempt to refine their crudities. The exposition takes the odd shape of a description of the qualities of the different characters, in considerable detail. At the end, various plagues are invoked to wreak their worst on the devoted kingdom. In the second play we have an even longer but much less varied prologue, covering some nine pages, in which the ghost of Alexander describes his earlier career, with a plentiful sprinkling of allusions to the underworld. This is of course the *reductio ad absurdum* of the Senecan prologue; and Jonson's procedure in his *Catiline* naturally shows a revulsion from such an extreme. His ghost of Sylla is no mere purveyor of information, but the incarnation, as it were, of all the past iniquity of Rome that comes to a head in Catiline. The apparition thus becomes an appropriate decorative figure, all the more imbued with the classical spirit because there is no slavish adherence to the letter. He is a more truly Roman ghost than any of Seneca's.

With *Catiline* the strictly Senecan tradition in England reaches a sober close; and we may briefly summarize its contribution to the development. First, and most important, it made the ghost, in virtue of his classical origin, an accepted stage figure. Once he had been introduced, however, the inherent lack of vitality in the Senecan conception left him free to be acted on by the general interest in the supernatural which we saw was characteristic of the English nation. As a result, the English playwrights did not adhere closely to the Senecan norm, even when they were consciously following it; and after *Locrine* and the *Spanish Tragedy* no minute imitation of Seneca was possible, except as a consciously learned procedure. The English writers were thus delivered from the pitfalls which engulfed their brethren of Italy. The erudite allusions to the underworld which were the second contribution of the Senecan influence soon lost their connection with the supernatural and became a common decorative device, promiscuously employed, their place being eventually taken, with relation to the supernatural, by something of native growth, namely, allusions to death and its attendant circumstances. It is now our task to study the further contributions of the native tradition to the handling of the supernatural.

SECTION 2. — THE GROWTH OF NATIVE TRADITION

In turning to the plays that disclose traits which we may fairly ascribe to native tradition, we must not expect to find this tradition clearly marked at the outset. The plays which aimed at a consciously tragic effect followed in general the classical tendency, and it was only by degrees that native motives and methods were turned to purposes of tragedy. We shall thus have to find our earlier indications in plays which are often far removed from tragedy, but which nevertheless furnish us material of no little significance.

We may begin with a play which shows the persistence of the tradition established by the miracle-plays, the *Looking-Glass for London and England* by Greene and Lodge, in which the old didactic machinery, now somewhat the worse for wear, is used to enforce a modern lesson. We have the prophet Hosea, " brought in by an angel, and let down over a stage in a throne," who comments on the action, and draws the appropriate morals; we likewise have Jonah, in discourse with another angel. A Usurer is tempted to suicide by a devil, and a mock devil furnishes grotesque sport. In addition, sundry allusions to ghosts enliven the text. In one instance they serve merely as portentous figures:

> Behold, amidst the adyts of our Gods,
> Our mighty Gods, the patrons of our war,
> The ghosts of dead men howling walk about,
> Crying, " Vae, vae, woe to this city, woe! " (iv. 3)

but they also become revenge-ghosts.

> My curses still shall haunt thy hateful head,
> And, being dead, my ghost shall thee pursue,

says a father to his unnatural son (iii. 2); and the Usurer mentioned above is tormented in his remorse by the thought of his victims:

Tread where I list, methinks the bleeding ghosts
Of those whom my corruption brought to naught
Do serve for stumbling-blocks before my steps.   (v. 2.)

These allusions are of course rather slight, but they are not
adorned with classical trappings, and seem to represent
native conceptions.   To this same category of survivals
from the miracle-plays belong, it may be noted, the Good
and Evil Angels in Marlowe's *Faustus*.

The plays which Greene wrote unassisted are in general
of a romantic cast, and the supernatural, though it appears
in a variety of shapes, is but a single strand in the whole
fabric of wonder and prodigy.   In *Alphonsus* (iii. 2) we have
a scene of necromancy, in which the ghost of Calchas is
evoked to reveal the issue of Amurack's wars.   Here the
tone is more classical, as these lines of the invocation show:

I conjure thee by Pluto's loathsome lake,
By all the hags which harbour in the same,
By stinking Styx, and filthy Phlegethon,
To come with speed, and truly to fulfil
That which Medea to thee straight shall will!

It is, however, classical with a strong Elizabethan infusion.
The ghost is angry at the summons, but consents to disclose
the future to Amurack in a dream.   The prediction is
uttered by Amurack himself, who describes what he sees
in his vision.   Venus, like Ate in *Locrine*, performs the duties
of a chorus, and at the beginning of act iv oracles are given
by a Brazen Head.   There is also (ii. 1) an allusion to " the
ghosts that wander round about the Stygian fields," which
shows how the idea of the ghost fluctuates between the two
traditions.

In *Friar Bacon* we find a considerable use of magic, but not
with any very serious intent.   Even though Bacon's magic
arts lead to fatal consequences in the duel between two

youths who have beheld their fathers' fatal quarrel in a magic mirror, this is but a momentary shadow on the action, chiefly useful as motivating Bacon's repentance and his abandoning of his enchantments. We may fairly say that in Greene's work the supernatural has no other office than to excite wonder and surprise, and that it has not freed itself from the classical tendency.

The varied literary activities of George Peele give his work a greater value in illustrating the course of events in this early experimental period. In *The Old Wives Tale* we have something resembling Greene's romantic plays, but with a greater realism in its treatment of a theme derived from folklore, the gratitude of a ghost for the rites of burial. The virtuous knight Eumenides comes, in the course of his wanderings, on the body of a ne'er-do-well whom his parish declines to bury, despite the remonstrances of his boon companions. The knight gives all his money to defray the expenses of burial, and the grateful ghost serves him in the guise of a mortal, his true character not being detected until the very end, when, after slaying the enchanter Sacripant, he vanishes into the ground. The fact that he is not recognized as a ghost until after he has vanished rather takes him out of our categories, but he remains an interesting instance of a really native theme.

Peele's essays in the chronicle-play afford further illustrations of the overlapping of the two traditions. In *Edward I* we find a marvellous occurrence, Queen Elinor's sinking into the earth at Charing Green and her rising again at Potter's Hive, taken over directly from Peele's ballad source, with almost no attempt at any other effect than that of mere surprise, though the storm which precedes her vanishing, and the mention of witchcraft just before her reappearance, seem to be rudimentary devices for suggest-

ing an atmosphere of mystery.   It is such a crude transfer
of the marvellous, with little effort to weave it into the
dramatic fabric, that must have been a general mark of the
early use of the supernatural in chronicle-plays.

In *The Battle of Alcazar* we have a very singular jumble of
assorted motives, predominantly classical in tone.   At the
beginning of act ii appear " three ghosts crying ' Vindicta! ' ", followed by a long description of the infernal
regions, in which Nemesis, assisted by a ghost eager for
revenge, drums up the Furies, and they all form an infernal
council.   The Kydian idea of vengeance even in Hades
finds expression in this imprecation on an enemy:

> Then let the earth discover to his ghost
> Such tortures as usurpers feel below;
> Rack'd let him be in proud Ixion's wheel,
> Pined let him be with Tantalus' endless thirst,
> Prey let him be to Tityus' greedy bird,
> Wearied with Sisyphus' immortal toil,"   (iv. 2)

in which we should note the unusually close copy of the
Senecan list of sinners.   But the play also shows a touch of
native feeling, though in a rather unpromising place, the
lines so often quoted as a specimen of Elizabethan bombast
at its worst:

> Are we successors to the great Abdallas,
> Descended from th' Arabian Muly Xarif,
> And shall we be afraid of Bassas and of bugs,
> Raw-head and Bloody-bone ?   (1. 2)

Whatever we may think of these bugbears, they are at least
not classical.   On the whole Peele follows the tendencies
initiated by Kyd, though he lacks Kyd's intellectual force
and restraint.   In his use of motives he is indiscriminate:
now prevailingly classical, as in *The Battle of Alcazar*, now
inclining to the native side, as in *Edward I*, and still more in
The Old Wives Tale.   In virtue of these latter plays he may

be called the first conspicuous exponent of the native tradition.

Such crude transfers of the marvellous into a chronicle-play as we have just seen in Peele are also to be found in Shakespeare's first essays in the form. In his work, however, it is more interesting to note the way in which allusions to the supernatural occur incidentally, evidently because they are a perfectly normal part of their author's thought. The absence of classical tags shows that such allusions are not forced in as adventitious ornaments, but are natural results of the native habit of mind. Let us look at a few examples. The ghost-idea appears in *Richard II* (iii. 2), in Richard's self-commiserating speech:

> For heaven's sake, let us sit upon the ground,
> And tell sad stories of the death of kings: —
> How some have been deposed, some slain in war,
> Some haunted by the ghosts they have deposed.

In *2 Henry VI* (iii. 3) the dying Cardinal Beaufort thinks himself haunted by the ghost of Humphrey, Duke of Gloster, whom he caused to be put to death. There are also incidental comparisons of men to ghosts: " And he will look as hollow as a ghost," says Constance of Arthur (*King John* iii. 4). In *Henry V* the English before Agincourt are thus compared:

> Their gesture sad,
> Investing lank-lean cheeks, and war-worn coats,
> Presenteth them unto the gazing moon
> So many horrid ghosts. (Chorus, act iv.)

Earlier in the same passage the night " like a foul and ugly witch doth limp so tediously away; " and in *1 Henry VI* we have " the famished English, like pale ghosts " (1. 2). For magic, we have in *King John* (v. 4) an allusion to the practice of melting wax images; while in *2 Henry VI* we have a

considerable necromantic scene (i. 4), in which the Duchess
of Gloster elicits from a spirit ambiguous prophecies, at the
time of night

> when screech-owls cry, and ban-dogs howl,
> And spirits walk, and ghosts break up their graves.

Even a classical theme may be used in such a way as to show
that it has become so familiar that the sense of its origin is
lost, as when the Queen-Mother in *King John* is called " an
Ate, stirring him to blood and strife " (ii. 1). All these
show how natural were such references for a writer of the
time, and are also evidence of the progress of the native
tradition, which now comes to its first fulfilment in two
important plays — the anonymous *Woodstock*, or *First Part
of Richard II*, and Shakespeare's *Richard III*.

Structurally *Woodstock* retains certain Senecan affili-
ations; but its supernatural is practically free from any
classical influence.[1] At the opening of act v, Woodstock is
in captivity, and about to be done to death. Lapoole and
two murderers enter and discuss their plans, after which the
curtain is drawn and their slumbering victim revealed. A
thunderstorm breaks, and the ghost of the Black Prince
enters, coming, not from the gloomy shores of Acheron, but
from his actual tomb at Canterbury:

> Night, horror, and th' eternal shrieks of death,
> Intended to be done this dismal night,
> Hath shook fair England's great cathedral,
> And from my tomb elate at Canterbury
> The ghost of Edward the Black Prince is come
> To stay king Richard's rage, my wanton son.

Unable to rouse Woodstock, he wishes for the strength he
had when alive, and again implores him to wake, since if he
is slain the guilt of his blood will fall on the ghost's own son

---

[1] See the edition, with introduction, by W. Keller, in the *Shakespeare-
Jahrbuch*, xxxv. 3 ff.

Richard. The ghost vanishes; the storm breaks out anew, and a second phantom enters, that of Edward III, likewise from his grave. He is, however, less effective than his predecessor, being over-eager to talk of himself and his own exploits. Immediately on his disappearance Woodstock awakes in great agitation, and recounts his vision; he implores the ghost to return, and hurriedly tries all the doors of the room. Finding them all made fast, he decides that the whole affair is merely a dream:

> The doors are all made fast; 'twas but my fancy.
> All 's whist and still, and nothing here appears,
> But the vast circuit of this empty room.

At that moment Lapoole and the murderers enter, and the deed is soon accomplished.

The complete abandoning of the classical tradition in this episode is manifest. Not a single allusion to the ancient underworld occurs in it, while there are constant references to events of English history. The ghosts come from their actual tombs, and have no knowledge of Tartarus or the four notorious sinners. The second ghost has not the value of the first; he imparts too much information, and reminds us of the unnecessary Corineus of *Locrine*. The ghost of the Black Prince, however, is the most commendable apparition we have yet encountered. He is distinctly concerned in the action, since he wishes to save Woodstock, and thus keep his own son from incurring blood-guilt. The effect of his entrance is heightened by the usual storm, and by the novel device of Woodstock's trying the doors when he awakes. The scene may be called the first in which the native tradition alone achieves an extended and impressive effect.

The appearance of ghosts in a dream is repeated in the familiar scene of *Richard III*, which also gives us our

first opportunity to examine the treatment of the same
theme by two different writers.   The earlier *True Tragedy of
Richard III* makes but a superficial use of the supernatural.
At the beginning the ghost of Clarence crosses the stage,
uttering a Latin couplet, which of course ends with " Vindicta ! "   He is the only visible ghost in the play, for the
phantoms which beset Richard on his last night of life are
merely described, in a fashion little more developed than
the bare statement in the chronicle that he beheld " divers
images like terrible devils," though it does give them the
added concreteness of ghosts eager for revenge:

> Sleep I, wake I, or whatsoever I do,
> Methinks their ghosts come gaping for revenge,
> Whom I have slain in reaching for a crown.

Beyond its portrayal of disordered emotion the scene has no
especial value; while the momentary appearance of the
ghost of Clarence is too conventional to have any merit of
its own.

In Shakespeare, on the contrary, the ghosts are brought
actually before us, and the scene has a distinct individuality.
Its most noteworthy feature is the use of repetition to
create and enhance an appropriate mood.   The grim
refrains " Let me sit heavy on thy soul to-morrow! " and
" Despair and die! " relentlessly force home the conviction
of the undying wrath of Richard's victims.   He awakes in
terror, to find that the lights burn blue — a proof of the
reality of his uncanny visitants.   His ensuing speech is a
remarkable portrayal of his bewildered state of mind, and
carries on the mood until Ratcliff enters, and the startled
monarch cries " Who 's there ? "   The entire episode has
passed over into the domain of the psychological; our
interest is no longer solely in the ghosts and their words, but
also in the result of their apparition on the mind of Richard.

The representation of his terror secures the contrast that has been lacking in most of our previous examples, and raises the present one to an artistically satisfying and wholly relevant decorative episode. Moreover, it is prepared for by the recital (i. 4) of the dream in which the hapless Clarence thinks himself dead, and is confronted by the angry spirits of those whom his treachery has undone. The idea which is so prominent at the end of the play is thus introduced almost at its beginning.

We thus see that the chronicle-plays, naturally the best embodiments of the native tradition, have brought us, in *Woodstock* and *Richard III*, to genuinely artistic results. Before summarizing the contribution of the formative period which they close we must examine, in the work of Marlowe, something not clearly ascribable to either of the two traditions we have been tracing, but rather one of those inexplicable achievements which spring from high genius. The second part of *Tamburlaine* is really akin to the spirit of Aischylean tragedy, depicting as it does the unsuccessful struggle of its hero with forces beyond his control, to which he finally succumbs. The play lies outside the general currents of its time, and in striking fashion recalls both former and future masterpieces. We begin very simply on the human plane; Tamburlaine's beloved Xenocrate is stricken by disease, and all the remedies that his affection and power can command are of no avail. In his wrath he would descend into Hell or assault Heaven to win back his love; but all that he can do is to embalm her corpse, and destroy the town in which she died. He seeks to forget his grief in battle, and a new opposition confronts him; one of his sons wearies of the continual carnage which accompanies his father's progress, and declares that he will no longer engage in the work of conquest. This incompre-

hensible revolt Tamburlaine can crush, and he strikes, with
the blind instinctiveness of a wounded animal; but the
problem which his son has raised is not thus easily disposed
of.   Hitherto the assaults of Fortune have been external,
in the loss of wife and son; but now the conqueror is assailed
in his own person.   Death, so long his slave, comes to claim
him as a victim.   He would wreak himself on this new foe,
as he has done in the past on his mortal opponents; but
strength fails him:

> Techelles and the rest, come, take your swords,
> And threaten him whose hand afflicts my soul.
> Come, let us march against the powers of Heaven,
> And set black streamers in the firmament,
> To signify the slaughter of the gods. —
> Ah, friends, what shall I do ?   I cannot stand.

In his frenzy he beholds Death himself, shrinking from
before his glance, but inexorably creeping on when it is
turned away:

> See where my slave, the ugly monster Death,
> Shaking and quivering, pale and wan for fear,
> Stands aiming at me with his murdering dart,
> Who flies away at every glance I give,
> And, when I look away, comes stealing on.
> Villain, away, and hie thee to the field!
> I and my army come to load thy back
> With souls of thousand mangled carcasses.
> Look, where he goes; but see, he comes again,
> Because I stay; Techelles, let us march
> And weary Death with bearing souls to hell.

He summons all his powers for an attack on the rebel Cal-
lapine, whose troops he scatters; but the effort is his last,
and he recognizes the fact — " Tamburlaine, the scourge
of God, must die."   No tragedy, from the days of Athens
to Marlowe's own, can match this portrayal of the overthrow of a conqueror by the forces which lie beyond his
control, and in the end bring him to naught.

In *Faustus* — so far as we can recognize its original plan through the sadly garbled state in which it has come down to us — we find an equally amazing performance. Superficially it seems to have some kinship with the romantic plays in which magic figures; but the gulf between them is abysmal. For Greene and Peele magic is one more convenient means of satisfying a simple thirst for wonders; for Marlowe its fascination is essentially intellectual, through the promise of boundless vistas of knowledge and undreamt-of power which it seems to offer. The finest passages of the play attain a wonderful breadth and intensity, too familiar to all readers to need illustration here. The conception of Hell has passed from the medieval grotesqueness, with its mingled crudity and terror, to a great imaginative height. The paraphernalia of magic are kept in the background, except so far as they offer scope for sounding enumerations; and the appalling final scene is wholly concerned with Faustus' emotions until the very end, when the cry " Ah, Mephistophilis! " marks the entrance of the fiends. Yet the medieval strain is not wholly abandoned; we have the Good and Evil Angels, embodiments indeed of the impulses which divide the will of Faustus, but quite in the manner of the older sacred drama; we have likewise the masque of the Seven Deadly Sins. These, however, are but slight details; the bulk of the play springs directly from Marlowe's own creative power. Once more he gives us a curious parallel to a Greek tragedy. Just as we saw that the *Prometheus* fell short of the finest treatment of the supernatural, so *Faustus* loses somewhat in effect by reason of insufficient contrast. Its hero is drawn on too superhuman a scale, and the conceptions of the play are too vast, to give it an exact relation to ordinary human life; even Tamburlaine is kept closer to our level by reason of his passion for Xenocrate.   This is merely to appraise *Faustus* from our particular standpoint, in no way to depreciate its lofty and peculiar merits.   That Marlowe should have produced, in an age like his, tragedies which for inherent excellence can be compared with the highest achievements of the Greeks, is surely ground for high praise of his extraordinary genius.

So far as details are concerned, Marlowe unquestionably belongs in the native tradition.   He uses classical touches, it is true; but that is a mere superficial trait, borrowed from the general practice of his time.   That classical allusions had in his eyes no peculiar value is shown by this passage from the second part of *Tamburlaine*, which combines classical, Christian and Mohammedan motives, with the sole aim of producing a resonant speech:

> Now scalds his soul in the Tartarian streams,
> And feeds upon the baneful tree of hell,
> That Zoacum, that fruit of bitterness,
> That in the midst of fire is engraffed,
> Yet flourishes as Flora in her pride,
> With apples like the heads of damnéd fiends,
> The devils there, in chains of quenchless flame,
> Shall lead his soul thro' Orcus' burning gulf,
> From pain to pain, whose change shall never end.   (ii. 3)

He does not use the ghost in any of his extant plays, but a significant passage from *The Jew of Malta* shows what he can accomplish in the way of eerie suggestion.   At the opening of act ii Barabas, prowling about the house of which he has been dispossessed, likens himself to one of the spirits that haunt the places where treasure has been buried:

> Now I remember those old women's words,
> Who in my wealth would tell me winter's tales,
> And speak of spirits and ghosts that glide by night
> About the place where treasure hath been hid:

And now methinks that I am one of those:
For whilst I live, here lives my soul's sole hope,
And when I die, here shall my spirit walk.

The conception here set forth is clearly native, and places
Marlowe definitely on the more vital side of tradition,
though his wonderful individuality sets him apart from
and above his fellows.

We may now sum up the progress made in this experimental period, which we may regard as ending in the early
nineties. We have seen that the influence of Seneca brought
the ghost onto the English stage, but that from the very
outset the native interest in the supernatural made him a
figure of much greater significance than his classical prototype.   Even where he remains confined to the prologue
(which he seldom is) his malign power is subsequently referred to; and in the majority of cases he has a real relation
to the plot.   The desire for revenge which appeared sporadically in the classical ghosts becomes the dominant
trait of their English successors, to such a degree that
we may fairly say that the developed revenge-ghost
is the creation of the Elizabethan age.   Naturally
this eagerness for revenge involves a close connection of
the ghost with the plot; he either actually sets in motion
a train of events which will bring about the downfall of
his enemies, or is deeply interested in the action, even if
he does not personally affect its course.   With so interesting a function to perform, it is natural that he should spend
but little time in that mere exposition which was so conspicuous a feature in the Senecan ghosts.   The Elizabethan
dramatists, when they give supernatural figures such purely
expository functions, tend to put them into the mouths of
abstractions, like Ate in *Locrine*, or Venus in *Alphonsus*.
The ghost is thus left free to express himself in action, and is

not obliged to waste time in superfluous discourse.   Dr. Fischer [1] maintains that the increased use of such supernatural figures, especially allegorical ones, by the Elizabethans, is due merely to the striving of imitators to surpass a prominent feature of their model; and further, that the giving of expository functions to such figures betrays unskilful imitation of the worst side of that model.   As a matter of fact, the Elizabethan dramatists could not have derived from Seneca this discrimination of functions, for the simple reason that it was not there.   The Senecan ghost, as we saw, is essentially expository, and has no effect on the action;   the Elizabethan ghost, on the contrary, is not primarily expository, and does affect the action.   So sharp a contrast can hardly be the result of imitation of non-existent features of the original.   One need not hold that the Elizabethans were wholly conscious of the advantages which they would derive from freeing their ghosts of mere exposition; but the result undeniably was to give the ghosts much more scope for expressing themselves in action, and it was a result not derivable from anything in Seneca.

The independence of attitude thus evident from the beginning led to a steadily increasing divergence from Seneca, until in the *Spanish Tragedy* and *Locrine* the supernatural had practically worked free of his influence, retaining only classical tags for decorative purposes.   Meanwhile the native tradition had slowly been permeating romantic drama and chronicle-play, at first in conjunction with the classical, from which it is finally liberated, to reach its first fruition in *Woodstock* and *Richard III*.   Even before this the transcendent genius of Marlowe had given, in *Tamburlaine* and *Faustus*, the first successful examples of the use of the intrinsic supernatural in entire plays, and not merely in

---

[1] *Zur Kunstentwicklung der englischen Tragödie*, pp. 56, 57.

more or less incidental fashion. We thus see how varied are the products of the English dramatic impulse, even in this experimental period, and how strongly their abundance contrasts with the sterility of Italy in the same field, even where both peoples have a common source of inspiration. As we turn to the period of final achievement we shall find the contrast even more marked.

SECTION 3. — THE PERIOD OF ACHIEVEMENT

The middle of the last decade of the sixteenth century seems to mark a loss of interest in the supernatural on the part of both playwrights and public. Older plays that dealt with such themes were no longer performed, and newer ones seem scarcely to have been written; two examples in Heywood (in *The Iron Age* and *Edward IV*), if indeed they belong to this period, are isolated, and in any case unsuccessful. Toward the end of the decade, however, a change set in. The *Spanish Tragedy*, unacted since 1593, was revived with great success in 1597, and revivals of similar older plays may also have been made, as well as productions of new ones attempted.[1] This return of popularity was enthusiastic and long-continued. The familiar prologue of the *Warning to Fair Women* (1599), with its sarcastic description of the revenge-ghost:

> Then, too, a filthy whining ghost,
> Lapt in some foul sheet, or a leather pilch,
> Comes screaming like a pig half-stick'd,
> And cries, Vindicta! — Revenge, revenge!
> With that a little rosin flasheth forth,
> Like smoke out of a tobacco-pipe, or a boy's squib,

[1] For this period see the valuable study of A. T. Thorndike, "The Relations of *Hamlet* to Contemporary Revenge-Plays," *Publ. Mod. Lang. Assoc.*, xvii. 125.

is an unregarded protest rather than a proclamation of a new order of things.

It was apparently the exuberant genius of John Marston that first discerned in these revived plays the opportunity to make a new and significant departure in the treatment of the supernatural.   He brought to the task a highly colored poetical style, often bombastic but seldom commonplace, and a skill in the manipulation of theatrical effects which leads him to striking results.   In his *Antonio's Revenge* he produces a modern counterpart of *Locrine*, much more plausible than its predecessor, even if not wholly satisfactory as a work of art, and undoubtedly very effective on the stage.

The note of surprise and terror is struck at the very opening, when Duke Piero and his accomplice enter with the corpse of Feliche, Antonio's friend, whom they have just murdered.   Piero's words,

> 'Tis yet dead night, yet all the earth is clutch'd
> In the dull leaden hand of snoring sleep;
> No breath disturbs the quiet of the air,
> No spirit moves upon the breast of earth,
> Save howling dogs, night-crows, and screeching owls,
> Save meager ghosts, Piero, and black thoughts,

in Marston's characteristic style, serve well as a prelude to the ensuing scenes of horror.   The supernatural is more clearly hinted at in the second scene, in which Antonio recounts a dream which he has had in the night just passed. He beheld two ghosts, one of them his father's; and as usual " both cried ' Revenge! ' "   He sought to clasp them, after the example of Aeneas, but with equal failure.   On awaking he was appalled by the portentous aspect of the sky, in which a comet shone balefully.   The clown Balurdo parodies his narrative, but he remains convinced that something dreadful impends.   His foreboding is soon realized;

Piero falsely declares that his daughter Mellida, to whom Antonio is betrothed, was found by him lying with Feliche, and that he slew the offender. Antonio's happiness thus crumbles at a blow, with the death of his father Andrugio, through poison administered by Piero, as an added affliction. A remarkable tragic complication is thus initiated.

The real entrance of the ghost into the action occurs in the first scene of act iii, when Antonio visits the church in which his father lies buried, in an effort to obtain from him guidance for his future course. His prayers prevail, and the ghost rises:

> Thy pangs of anguish rip my cerecloth up,
> And lo! the ghost of old Andrugio
> Forsakes his coffin. Antonio, revenge!

He reveals the fashion of his murder, and the treachery of Piero. His widow Maria is, unwittingly, about to marry the murderer; but the ghost declares that he will visit her before his return to rest. An interesting feature of this scene is its free use of Senecan allusion, and even of direct quotation, while maintaining a distinctive character of its own. Antonio has an interview with his distraught mother; then Piero enters, followed by his little son Julio, whose sleep has been disturbed by dreams of spirits. This introduction of a person more sensitive than the rest to the presence of the supernatural is a most significant innovation; it at once looks back to the Greek use of the chorus and forward to certain modern devices for attaining a similar end, such as the Grandfather in Maeterlinck's *L'Intruse*, or the blind Anna in D'Annunzio's *Città Morta*, later to be discussed. Antonio determines to kill the child as an offering to his father's spirit, but hesitates when Julio pleads for mercy in Mellida's name. The resolution is confirmed by the reappearance of the ghost, and the deed is committed.

Another innovation, this time one of style, appears in the speech which precedes the act:

> Now barks the wolf against the full-cheek'd moon;
> Now lions' half-clamm'd entrails roar for food;
> Now croaks the toad, and night-crows screech aloud,
> Fluttering 'bout casements of departed souls;
> Now gape the graves, and thro' their yawns let loose
> Imprison'd spirits to revisit earth;
> And now, swart night, to swell thy hour out,
> Behold I spurt warm blood in thy black eyes.

These allusions to blood and the charnel-house mark a departure from the Senecan reminiscences which served a like purpose in the older plays, and in their turn establish a current practice.   In the second scene of the act Maria is shown on the point of retiring; when she draws the curtains of her bed the ghost, in fulfilment of his promise, is seen seated upon it.   He forgives his wife for her unwitting offence, and bids her join Antonio in procuring revenge; forthwith Antonio enters, dripping with Julio's blood, and is praised for his deed by the ghost.   Act v is preceded by a dumbshow, in which the ghost shares; he remains after the departure of the other personages, and delivers a monologue, largely expository in character.   In the final scene of the play he is present to watch the torture and death of Piero, but does not speak.

This summary sufficiently shows the variety of supernatural incidents which Marston's fertile imagination has brought into his tragedy.   He accomplishes what the author of *Locrine* crudely attempted; and if his achievement is not, according to our standards, wholly convincing, it is assuredly ingenious, and well adapted to the stage.   The frequent Latin reminiscences are not merely transferred, but are combined to produce a novel result, in a way that recalls Kyd's procedure.   Several of the novelties which Marston introduced were taken up by his successors, notably the device of making the ghosts speak from above and below the stage, when, in the church scene, Antonio happens to end a speech with the word " murder," and the ghosts take it up. On the stylistic side we have the substitution of the charnel-house for Tartarus as a source of decorative imagery. Such allusions were of course not unknown in English drama before Marston's day; witness Constance's rhapsody over the charms of death in *King John*. Marston, however, appears to have been the first to bring such allusions into direct connection with the supernatural, in order to heighten the impressiveness of the latter. He uses it most extensively in the later *Sophonisba*, where the witch Erichtho appears. She is directly borrowed from Lucan; but it is highly significant that in the lines descriptive of her unholy art Marston entirely omits the mythological allusions which are plentiful in his original, and which he himself uses liberally in *Antonio's Revenge*. This certainly suggests that he felt himself to be employing something which did not need classical trappings to enhance its effectiveness. Consciously or not, he is reverting to the old English tradition which we saw so remarkably exemplified in the Towneley *Lazarus*. The lines in which Erichtho's dwelling is described, and those in which she herself gives an account of her dealings with corpses, may fairly be called unparalleled in the explicitness with which they detail the loathsomeness of corruption, as the following excerpt will testify:

> She bursts up tombs,
> From half-rot sear-cloths then she scrapes dry gums
> For her black rites; but when she finds a corpse
> But newly graved, whose entrails are not turn'd
> To slimy filth, with greedy havock then
> She makes fierce spoil, and swells with wicked triumph

To bury her lean knuckles in his eyes;
Then doth she gnaw the pale and o'er-grown nails
From his dry hand; but if she find some life
Yet lurking close, she bites his gelid lips,
And, sticking her black tongue in his dry throat,
She breathes dire murmurs, which enforce him bear
Her baneful secrets to the spirits of horror. (iv. 1)

The opening scene of act v introduces a novel conception of
the ghost.   Syphax has lain with Erichtho, in the belief
that she is Sophonisba; on awaking he discovers the deception, and is mocked by the witch, who vanishes into the
ground when he threatens her.   He curses his fate; the
ghost of his father Hasdrubal rises, tells of the defeat of the
Carthaginians, and confesses the power of the Gods. Syphax
asks what his own fate is to be; but the ghost vanishes
without deigning to respond.

The favor with which these innovations were evidently
received seems to have attracted the attention of Chapman,
ever eager to detect the features in the work of his fellows
which would appeal to the public, and to have combined
with his own moralizing tendency to produce curious results.
I need not detail here the various bits of evidence [1] which
suggest that *Bussy D'Ambois* came into being about 1600,
just as Marston was restoring the ghost to the stage.   *Bussy*
contains a double supernatural machinery, consisting of
spirits and a ghost.   The Friar who acts as go-between for
Bussy and Tamyra controls the former, and himself becomes the latter, taking a prominent part in the catastrophe.
In act iv Bussy suspects that Mountsurry, Tamyra's
husband, has been informed of their intrigue, and entreats
the Friar to use his magical skill to ascertain the truth.

---

[1] See the introduction to the edition by F. S. Boas in the Belles-Lettres
series, and also E. E. Stoll in *Mod. Lang. Notes*, xx. 206.

Tamyra enters and confirms Bussy's suspicion, saying that his enemy Monsieur has revealed the secret by a paper. The Friar invokes Behemoth and his train, one of whom is sent to fetch the paper; he fails, but Behemoth reveals to the Friar and his companions the colloquy of Bussy's foes, which is taking place at a distance. This recalls Greene's magic mirror in *Friar Bacon*, but is both more developed and more relevant to the plot. Behemoth ends the scene with an enigmatic prophecy, and a promise to reappear to Bussy, with a clearer message, when invoked. Thus far we have a sufficiently close relation of supernatural to plot; but now a new motive appears, and is treated in singular fashion. In the first scene of act v the Friar mysteriously dies, as he is endeavoring to intervene between Tamyra and her husband, who is about to take vengeance on her for her infidelity; in scene 3 his ghost makes a brief appearance to Bussy and promises to meet him in Tamyra's chamber. Bussy in perplexity invokes Behemoth, in a magnificently poetical outburst:

> Methought the Spirit
> Threw his chang'd countenance headlong into clouds;
> His forehead bent, as it would hide his face,
> He knockt his chin against his darkned breast,
> And struck a churlish silence thro' his powers.
> Terror of darkness! O thou King of flames!
> That with thy musique-footed horse dost strike
> The clear light out of crystal on dark earth,
> And hurlst instructive fire about the world,
> Wake, wake the drowsy and enchanted night
> That sleeps with dead eyes in this heavy riddle!

The spirit informs him of the Friar's death, and warns him that his own will ensue if he answers Tamyra's next summons. Chapman's solution of the problem of bringing Bussy, thus warned, into the power of his murderers is ingenious. Montsurry, disguised as the Friar, enters with the fatal letter, and convinces Bussy that the spirit's report of the Friar's death was false.   Bussy accordingly dismisses the prophecy of his own fate, and obeys Tamyra's call.   In the scene of the murder the ghost plays a large but curious part, in which his ghostliness is far from evident.   He shines, however as a moralist, exhorting Bussy to forgive his murderers, and striving to reconcile husband and wife at the end.

The contrast between Chapman's management of the ghost and that of the spirits certainly rouses a suspicion that the former has been rather awkwardly brought into the play, and did not form a part of the original conception. There is absolutely no reason why the Friar should die as he does, and his brief appearance to Bussy is not at all necessary to the progress of events, since Bussy was sufficiently perplexed to have called up Behemoth in any case.   It is not, I think, incredible that Chapman should have wished to introduce into his play so popular a figure as the ghost, and he therefore kills off the Friar in order to obtain one.   He had, we may conceive, planned his finale with the Friar participating as a mortal; but his untimely demise made it necessary for him to appear in the later version as a ghost, if he were to be retained at all.   To secure some semblance of ghostliness Chapman introduces such a detail as the fright of the hired ruffians at the Friar's appearance in the last scene; but this could easily have been added later, and is not paralleled in the conclusion of the scene, where the Friar says and does nothing which might not with equal, or even greater, propriety have been accomplished by a mortal.   It is significant that at the beginning of the scene, where Tamyra and the Friar are conversing, the lines which most clearly allude to the latter as a ghost are not found in the earlier group of quartos, but only in the later ones which give Chapman's revised text.[1]

In view of these facts it seems to me a plausible inference that Chapman followed Marston's lead, inserting into his play a ghost to catch the fancy of the multitude. The introduction of the ghost is unskilfully managed, and is glorified by no such outburst of poetry as that which is aroused by the invocation of Behemoth. The picture of the spirit with his changed countenance cast headlong into cloud recalls some audacious vision of Blake's; but the ghost is as unspectral as could be imagined.

We may perhaps be confirmed in the view that Chapman here fell in with a movement initiated by one of his fellow-dramatists by the fact that in the sequel to *Bussy* he shows the influence of Shakespeare's handling of the ghost in *Hamlet*. In the *Revenge of Bussy D'Ambois* Clermont D'Ambois has been charged by his brother's ghost to avenge his death; but he hesitates to act on such an incitement. This appeal of the ghost to him is at first disclosed to us only by narration; but at the beginning of act v, after Clermont has determined to execute the unwelcome command, the ghost appears on the stage. He declares that he comes to urge on the work of revenge, and bids men avoid evil and cleave to good. Clermont enters, in conversation with the Guise; the ghost returns, seen only by Clermont, and bids him right his wrongs. The Guise, astonished at Clermont's demeanor, asks the cause, and is inclined to be skeptical when it is told him. The incident is obviously modelled on

---

[1] See the Boas edition, p. 132. The revised lines are these:

> *Tam.* But, my dearest father,
> Why will you not appear to him yourself,
> And see that none of these deceits annoy him ?
> *Umbra.* My power is limited; alas! I cannot.
> All that I can do — See! the cave opens.

the scene between Hamlet and his mother.   The length of
the ghost's speech impairs the effect; but the Guise is sufficiently impressed to declare at the end:

> But this thy brother's spirit startles me,
> These spirits seld or never haunting men,
> But some mishap ensues.

For the rest of the play Chapman reverts to his own manner.
In scene 3 the ghost briefly appears to Tamyra, who would
embrace him.   He declares it impossible, and bids her
watch the impending vengeance.   After Clermont has
slain Montsurry the ghost enters leading four other phantoms, who dance about the body, and depart.

The moralizing trend of Chapman's ghosts may well be
his own contribution; even a ghost could hardly fail to become Senecal and sententious under his hands.   So far as
his ghosts really affect the action, however, they merely follow established types, and have little independent value,
though they do illustrate the avidity with which audiences of
the time accepted such supernatural figures, whatever their
artistic merit.

Still another variety of the moralizing ghost is presented
by Montferrers in Tourneur's *Atheist's Tragedy*.   Treacherously murdered by his brother D'Amville, he appears
in a dream to his son Charlemont, who is in Belgium on
military service.   At the opening of the scene (ii. 6) Charlemont is overcome by drowsiness, and beholds the ghost, who
delivers the following remarkably succinct message:

> Return to France, for thy old father's dead,
> And thou by murder disinherited.
> Attend with patience the success of things,
> But leave revenge unto the King of kings.

Charlemont awakes in amazement, and proceeds to reflect
on the causes of dreams; he can scarcely credit this one, and

as the soldier who shares his watch saw nothing, he decides that it was a mere idle vision. At this the ghost promptly reappears, to be challenged and vainly shot at by the soldier. Charlemont, convinced by this second apparition, begs the ghost's forgiveness.

We have in this case a distinct change in the conception of the revenge-ghost, and one which, however praiseworthy from a moral standpoint, is dramatically inept. The ghost's sole reason for return is to secure vengeance; and if he is satisfied to leave the task to a higher power, he may as well not appear at all, since he does nothing but exhort. In a subsequent scene (iii. 2) the returned Charlemont fights with his uncle's son Sebastian, and is about to kill him as a sacrifice to his father's memory; but the ghost again intervenes:

> Let him avenge my murder and thy wrongs
> To whom the justice of revenge belongs.

Finally, in v. 1, he appears while D'Amville is brooding over his nefarious schemes, and tells him they shall come to naught. His appearances are thus episodic, and their chief interest lies in the moral exhortations that he utters. Tourneur adds a new emphasis to the type; but his conception of the ghost is not one which has any real dramatic value.

In addition to his innovations with regard to the ghost, Tourneur shows himself an apt pupil of Marston in dealing with sepulchral material. The third scene of act iv passes in a churchyard. Charlemont, dogged by his uncle's creature Borachio, kills his assailant, and utilizes a disguise brought by another character (with very different intent) to appear as a ghost and frighten his uncle, who has foul designs on his niece Castabella. D'Amville returns alone, in a state of abject terror which contrasts strongly with his former

atheistic views, and yet is psychologically correct.   He
imagines that he sees the ghost of his victim —

> Yonder's the ghost of old Montferrers, in
> A long white sheet, climbing yon lofty mountain
> To complain to Heaven of me. —
> Montferrers! Pox o' fearfulness! 'Tis nothing
> But a fair white cloud —

and at the cry of " Murder! " within, as Borachio's body is
discovered, he thinks his sin has found him out.   Incidentally Tourneur's fancy supplies him with variations on
the theme of corruption which are not mere echoes of
Marston, as when the disguised Charlemont seeks refuge
among the tombs:

> I fear I am pursued.   For more assurance,
> I'll hide me here i' th' charnel-house,
> This convocation-house of dead men's skulls.

In getting into the charnel-house he takes hold of a skull,
which slips and almost makes him fall; at which he exclaims

> Death's head, deceivest my hold ?
> Such is the trust to all mortality.

While Tourneur's novelties cannot be unreservedly praised,
they at least prove that he was no servile imitator, and
make his work an important stage on the road that leads
from Marston to Webster; he virtually creates a new species
of drama, which we may call the sepulchral tragedy.

In turning from the plays just discussed to the work of
Shakespeare during the same period we come into a new
world.   Old devices take on new life under his hands, and
crudities are marvellously subtilized.   *Julius Caesar*, the
first in his series of tragedies, shows a wholly novel handling
of the revenge-ghost, the more remarkable in that it precedes many of the plays we have just been studying.   The

living Caesar dominates the first part of the play; his angry
ghost controls the second; and the thought of the latter finds
expression in the former. Brutus, when the conspirators
are laying their plans in his orchard, observes

> We all stand up against the spirit of Caesar,
> And in the spirit of men there is no blood;
> O that we then could come by Caesar's spirit,
> And not dismember Caesar! But, alas,
> Caesar must bleed for it,

in serene unconsciousness of the irony of his words. It is of
course only after the murder that the idea can receive its full
development. Antony, as he soliloquizes beside Caesar's
corpse, predicts the woes that will befall Italy in consequence of the deed; and to crown all

> Caesar's spirit, ranging for revenge,
> With Ate by his side come hot from hell,
> Shall in these confines with a monarch's voice
> Cry " Havock," and let slip the dogs of war. (iii. 1)

Before long the ghost is actually revealed to us, in brief but
effective fashion. The brevity of the episode is indeed its
most striking feature. Brutus, as he sits quietly reading in
his tent at Sardis, notices that the light has grown dim; the
ghost enters, declares his fatal errand, and vanishes, before
Brutus can collect his naturally startled senses. He is
vexed that " now he has plucked up heart," and would learn
more, the ghost has not remained to be questioned. He
does not at this point say that he recognizes the apparition
as Caesar's ghost; but we know that he is aware of its
identity from his speech as he stands beside the body of
Cassius:

> O Julius Caesar, thou art mighty yet!
> Thy spirit walks abroad, and turns our swords
> In our own proper entrails,

and even more clearly from his words to Volumnius just before his own death:

> The ghost of Caesar hath appeared to me
> Two several times at night; at Sardis, once;
> And, this last night, here in Philippi fields.
> I know my hour is come.

We are thus assured by the conspirators themselves that the wrath of the ghost has been the dominant agent in their downfall.

This parsimonious use of the ghost, in such striking contrast with the practice of other dramatists of the time, seems to be intentional.   Shakespeare has realized that in the majority of cases the supernatural is best presented in brief episodes, reenforced by fitting allusion.   He lets us conceive the ghost as an existent hostile power, gives us an actual glimpse of it, and confirms our belief by the testimony of those whom it has undone.   The revenge-ghost is thus the unifying principle of the tragedy, to which Julius Caesar, dominating the first part by his presence, actual or divined, and the second by his survival as a spirit eager for revenge, has rightly given his name.   The ghost is thus intimately associated with the plot; he is not, it is true, absolutely necessary to its progress, but his excision would remove one of the chief factors that makes for its continuity.

We can further appreciate Shakespeare's parsimony in the use of the ghost by comparison with a more conventional play on the same subject, the so-called " academic tragedy " of *Caesar and Pompey*, which seems to date from 1606.[1] This play is a very orthodox example of Kydian tradition; we have Discord as an expository figure, in the prologue and

[1] See T. M. Parrott, " The Academic Tragedy of Caesar and Pompey," *Mod. Lang. Review*, v. 435.

at the beginning of the several acts. The ghost of Caesar has a considerable part, delivering a monologue, reconciling Antony and Octavian that they may undertake his revenge, and appearing to Brutus on the day of Pharsalia to tell him he shall die that day by his own hand, which he later does, in the ghost's presence. The play concludes with a dialogue between the ghost and Discord, quite in the manner of the *Spanish Tragedy*. We see in this instance the amount of space which the ghost would naturally occupy in a tragedy of ordinary type; and the contrast with Shakespeare's procedure is obvious.

In *Hamlet* a further advance brings the supreme treatment of the ghost in Elizabethan drama. The revenge-ghost becomes the instrument by which the train of events is set in motion; and he is depicted with a skill that defies competition. The elaboration with which he is treated contrasts strongly with the method of his employment in *Julius Caesar;* but the difficulties are handled in a way that only heightens the effect. The first allusion to the ghost is wholly vague; " What, has this thing appeared again to-night ? " asks Horatio of the guardsmen. Bernardo answers that it has not, and proceeds to relate the manner of the previous apparition; but his story is abruptly cut short by the entrance of the ghost, " in the same figure, like the king that's dead," as Bernardo says. We are thus assured of his identity; but he does not speak himself, vouchsafing no answer to Horatio's questions. Horatio, the somewhat skeptical scholar, is left in a state of considerable awe. The exposition is now resumed, and we are informed of the conditions in Denmark which make an apparition no incredible thing at this juncture. We are thus led to think that the ghost may merely portend the troubled state of the times; but his prompt return once more rouses our curiosity.   Horatio again attempts to learn his errand; but the cock crows, and he vanishes, despite the efforts of the guard to seize him.   " We do it wrong, being so majestical, to offer it the show of violence," says the awed Marcellus.   He and Horatio exchange some of the traditional lore on the subject of ghosts which their strange experience has quickened in their memories, and decide to inform Hamlet of the apparition.   We have thus twice beheld the ghost, and seen the striking effect which he produces on Horatio and his companions, and yet have no idea of why he comes.   A more complete contrast with the usual revenge-ghost, who announces his errand as soon as he appears, could not be imagined.   Moreover, the effect of the apparition on us is heightened by its effect on Horatio, whose cool mind is entirely convinced of the ghost's reality, though he has no personal interest in the matter.   His testimony is thus wholly unprejudiced, and in consequence very weighty.

The scene in which Hamlet is informed of the strange occurrence is handled with equal subtlety.   He himself prepares the way for the disclosure by calling up in his mind's eye the image of his dead father: " Methinks I see my father."   Horatio's prompt and startled question, " Where, my lord ? " reveals what is passing in *his* mind; a suspicion, namely, that the ghost has appeared to Hamlet, or is even actually present.   He is undeceived, however, and can go on quietly, " I saw him once, he was a goodly king."   Hamlet's reflective " He was a man, take him for all in all, I shall not look upon his like again," now brings the startling disclosure, " My lord, I think I saw him yesternight; " and Hamlet's " Saw! who ? " records with inimitable brevity the effect that the news produces on him.   We now have the detailed narrative, and Hamlet's decision to visit the haunted spot himself.   After his friends have gone out he lingers, to express the suspicion that the news has at once roused in him:

> My father's spirit in arms! all is not well.
> I doubt some foul play: would the night were come!
> Till then, sit still, my soul. Foul deeds will rise,
> Tho' all the earth o'erwhelm them, to men's eyes.

We are thus assured that the ghost's errand is the customary one of demanding revenge; but the full confirmation is again delayed. A scene in the house of Polonius intervenes before we are transported to the ramparts; and even there Hamlet's account of the wassail customs draws our thoughts away from the ghost, who recalls himself to us by an unheralded entrance. Hamlet's impassioned appeal is utterly different from the older addresses to returning spirits; but it wins from the ghost only a beckoning to a remoter part of the platform. Hamlet would follow; his friends remonstrate, but a moment of swift action frees him from their grasp, and he departs. Now, after all this preparation, we are permitted to hear the ghost's message; and the delay imparts to the familiar theme a singular novelty, in addition to which it is given a remarkably imaginative expression. The ghost cannot describe the torments which he suffers in Purgatory; they are too awful for mortal ears. The murder, too, which he recounts, is peculiarly atrocious; he was done to death " with all his imperfections on his head." But he is not wantonly savage in his demand for revenge:

> But, howsoever thou pursu'st this act,
> Taint not thy mind, nor let thy soul contrive
> Against thy mother aught.

The dawn comes on, and he is constrained to depart; and the tension is broken by the entrance of Horatio and the rest. When Hamlet swears them to secrecy, the voice of the ghost is heard from beneath; and Hamlet's overwrought nerves

find relief in grim jests — " You hear this fellow in the cel-
larage," " Well said, old mole! can 'st work i' the earth so
fast ? " — which are a natural revulsion from the terrific
experience through which he has just passed, and afford him
the only relief possible under the circumstances.

We have previously noted that in general the supernatural
is effective in direct proportion to the brevity of its actual
appearances; but *Hamlet* clearly shows that this principle is
not to be treated as absolute.   A greater elaboration of
structure could scarcely be devised; but the impressiveness
of the result is only enhanced by the accumulated scenes.
We see the ghost once before we know who he is, and see him
again without discovering the cause of his appearance; we
are not even sure that his desire is for personal revenge,
though that is the natural assumption in the Elizabethan
age.   Shakespeare, however, carefully diverts us from this
aspect of the ghost's coming; when Horatio, in an effort to
make the ghost speak, enumerates the possible motives of his
unrest, he omits that of revenge altogether:

> If there be any good thing to be done,
> That may to thee do ease, and grace to me . . .
> If thou art privy to thy country's fate,
> Which, happily, foreknowing may avoid . . .
> Or if thou hast uphoarded in thy life
> Extorted treasure in the womb of earth,
> For which, they say, you spirits oft walk in death,
> Speak of it: stay, and speak.

leaving it for Hamlet, from whom it comes with greater
appropriateness, to suggest.   When the expected truth is
at last fully revealed, the suspense has been so well sustained
that the revelation loses nothing of its force; and we are led
gradually back to our familiar world by the incident of the
oath of secrecy.

Besides these novelties of structure, the ghost shows novel traits of character.[1] His demand is not merely for personal revenge; he would save his realm from the clutches of the unworthy Claudius, and at the same time preserve his misguided widow from the consequences of her unlawful second marriage. Hence the significance of his warning to Hamlet, " Taint not thy mind," which distinctly bids him regard the work of revenge as the execution of impartial justice. It is the ghost's misfortune that his chosen instrument cannot maintain himself at this height, but surrenders to the lust for a wholly personal vengeance. It is to recall him to the nobler course that the ghost reappears in the scene between him and his mother (iii. 4); to whet his purpose indeed, but also to bid him spare his mother, " to step between her and her fighting soul." The scene is as remarkable for its brevity as was the earlier part of the play for its complexity. We have Hamlet's excitement, the Queen's bewilderment at his conduct, the ghost's solicitude for his wife, and the vivid conception of the ghost's aspect evoked by Hamlet's words, all in the compass of some thirty lines. After this we see nothing more of the ghost, and naturally so. The vengeance that he desires is not attained: the play ends in general slaughter, in which the death of the King is but an incident, and Hamlet himself perishes, leaving to Fortinbras the kingdom which he could not himself secure.

The effect of the supernatural in *Hamlet*, though it presents obvious correspondences with the practice of the time, is thus absolutely different from anything to be found in the work of Shakespeare's contemporaries. The elaboration of

[1] In the ensuing paragraph I accept the interpretation of the play proposed by M. F. Egan, in his able and suggestive essay, *The Ghost in Hamlet*, (Chicago, 1906).

treatment shows an almost defiant disregard of difficulties; a single slip would mar all, but each detail only adds to the total achievement.   The information which the ghost gives his son could not be conveyed through any other channel; the ghost is therefore absolutely necessary to the play as it stands.   We have already noted the skill with which his appearances are led up to; and the accompanying allusions are wholly native in tone, the traditional lore concerning the conduct of perturbed spirits.   Shakespeare seems to have derived from Marston the use of sepulchral allusions, but he manages them with far greater skill and delicacy.   He does not use them as merely horrible details, but deliberately employs them to secure contrast by making them the vehicle of a sinister humor.   The graveyard scene is too familiar to need more than mention in this connection; the same quality is displayed in Hamlet's replies when he is questioned by the King as to the whereabouts of the corpse of Polonius:

> *King.* Now, Hamlet, where's Polonius ?
> *Ham.* At supper.
> *King.* At supper ?   Where ?
> *Ham.* Not where he eats, but where he is eaten; a certain con-vocation of politic worms are e'en at him.   Your worm is your only emperor for diet; we fat all creatures else, to fat us; and we fat our-selves for maggots.
>
>   . .   . .
> *King.* Where is Polonius ?
> *Ham.* In heaven; send thither to see; if your messenger find him not there, seek him i' the other place yourself.   But indeed, if you find him not within this month, you shall nose him as you go up the stairs into the lobby.
> *King.* Go seek him there.   (*To some Attendants.*)
> *Ham.* He will stay till you come.

This is very far from the rhetoric of Marston, or the cal-culated horrors of Tourneur.

Still another detail which Shakespeare seems to have borrowed from Marston is the device of making the ghost speak from below the stage. This is less likely to have been taken over from the old *Hamlet*, for the ghosts in the older plays are chiefly interesting for what they say or do when actually on the stage; there is as yet little attempt to use subsidiary devices for heightening their impressiveness. We have seen the device in Marston, and noted imitation of it on the part of Tourneur; and it is something which we should naturally associate with Marston's method of procedure. Shakespeare, however, turns it to his own uses; in his hands it becomes the means by which the scene of the oath of secrecy, which leads us back to the world of ordinary life, retains a supernatural tinge which enhances its effect. Hamlet could not joke as he does if the ghost were actually present; yet we need some reminder of the ghost, to prevent the transition from seeming too abrupt. The voice from beneath satisfies both these requirements.

In *Hamlet*, then, the native tradition reaches its most perfect expression, and the revenge-ghost his full development. In *Macbeth* we have a different approach to the supernatural, and one which results in an even finer achievement, involving as it does a profounder conception of the forces in question. Shakespeare desires to bring before us the supernatural powers which call into action the sinister impulses of Macbeth's nature. He has, however, no store of generally known mythology from which to derive such figures. A hint in Holinshed supplies him with the concept of the Weird Sisters, Goddesses of destiny, who met Macbeth on his day of triumph; but these are not creatures familiar to the general public of his time. He is thus confronted by a difficulty similar to that which Aischylos faced in the *Eumenides*; he must approach these unfamiliar beings

through something of common knowledge. Now the
obvious channel through which every Elizabethan believed
that the power of evil spirits could be exercised against
mortals was that of witchcraft. Accordingly Shakespeare
avails himself of this universally held belief, and presents
his Weird Sisters at first under the guise of witches. As
such the audience could readily accept them, and by this
acceptance they were led to Shakespeare's deeper conception. The element of witchcraft is thus as superficial in the
Weird Sisters as were the touches of physical horror in the
Aischylean Furies. All that the Sisters are represented as
doing at the outset of the play is perfectly suited to the idea
that they are witches and nothing more. We soon perceive,
however, that important constituents of the real idea of
witchcraft are lacking. The Sisters do not derive their
might from any covenant with powers of evil, but are themselves such powers, owing their sinister capacities only to
themselves. Neither do they demand anything of Macbeth,
or seek to attach him to their service; they merely reveal
the future to him in such a way as to bring to expression that
restless ambition which is really a capacity for crime, as
soon as opportunity is presented. The prompt fulfilment of
their first prediction leads him to take the readiest way to
accomplish the rest; and once he is started on the path of
bloodshed he cannot turn back. He thinks he can dominate
the forces of which he is really the sport; and they revenge
themselves on him with unsparing irony. This same irony
also colors the apparition of the ghost which is so striking a
feature of the play. Macbeth invites Banquo to the feast,
and insists on his presence, when he has already set on foot
the plan for his murder; but the ghost keeps the engagement
which the mortal man cannot fulfil. It is essential for the
due appreciation of the episode that the ghost be conceived

as actual, and not as a hallucination of Macbeth's. Macbeth has indeed a peculiar power of visualization, clearly seen in the incident of the air-drawn dagger before Duncan's murder. He recognizes that as a figment of his imagination, saying himself, " There 's no such thing." When he is confronted by the ghost, however, such arguments have no effect on him, because he knows their futility. Yet his physical courage remains unbroken; even after the ghost has once appeared and vanished he can drink to Banquo's health, and wish him present. This defiance may be partly due to a desire not to arouse the suspicions of the guests, but it is also sincere. " What man dare, I dare," he truly says; let the ghost assume the shape of some beast, however terrible, or return to life and confront him in an actual body, and he will deal with it, but before this horrible figure, " with twenty mortal murders on his crown," he feels himself powerless. It is in vain that Lady Macbeth tries to recall him from his fit, and even cites the air-drawn dagger as proof that this is another delusion of the same sort. The argument, though it is one that Macbeth might well have caught at, does not touch him in the least. That the ghost should appear to him alone is perfectly explicable; he is merely using the power of " selective apparition " to present himself to the person with whom he is most concerned. He does not need to be a revenge-ghost, for the very powers that raised Macbeth are about to cause his downfall, and Banquo will be revenged without the necessity of taking any action himself. After the departure of the guests, Macbeth does argue himself into accepting the unreality of the ghost, and speaks of his " strange and self abuse; " but this is only a passing mood, without real conviction. The apparition drives him to consult the Weird Sisters, and gain from them the predictions in which he trusts, only to be involved in ruin; while his insistence forces them to reveal to him the line of kings which will spring from Banquo, and assure himself of what he least desires — a revelation which is vicarious vengeance for Banquo.   We all know how the predictions which seemed impossible of fulfilment are in fact realized, and how Macbeth falls, fighting to the last, with that stubborn courage which he has always shown in the face of physical danger.

The tragedy of *Macbeth* thus lies in the attempt of a mortal to control the baleful powers to which he has yielded himself, and in the irony with which they turn their own promises to his undoing.   This central idea is presented in a way which brings out the fearful strain under which the protagonists labor.   The tense, close-packed lines give us a marvellous sense of that strain, a sense that culminates in Lady Macbeth's words

> These deeds must not be thought
> After these ways; so, it will make us mad.

She perceives the danger, but cannot succeed in distracting herself from that way of thought, with the result which we know from the sleepwalking scene.   Macbeth, after all better able to support the strain, is not the agent of his own death, which comes to him from outside; but his wife is her own executioner.   Macbeth's very helplessness in the face of supernatural assaults acts as a safeguard for his sanity.

One of the most noteworthy traits of *Macbeth* is the skill with which sound is used to play on our nerves.   In the absolute silence which accompanies the murder of Duncan, the faintest sounds are audible; " I heard the owl scream, and the crickets cry," says Lady Macbeth, in answer to her husband's question, " Didst thou not hear a noise ? " Macbeth hears a mysterious voice while he is about the deed; and at the close of the scene the knocking at the gate reveals the presence outside of something which must lead to the disclosure of the crime. In the same scene the porter's monologue supplies a relief such as was gained in *Hamlet* by playing with the thought of death; but here it is the idea of Hell, with its satirical implications, which furnishes the contrast. *Macbeth* thus offers analogues to *Hamlet* in certain details; but the cruel irony which pervades it has no counterpart in the earlier play, and the supernatural characters which guide the action are entirely extrahuman. Even the ghost, who has but a decorative function, is without those reminiscences of humanity which generally cling to such figures, and which are so conspicuous and so moving in the ghost of Hamlet's father. In virtue of these traits the play stands on a height of its own, and is the most deeply and essentially tragic of its author's works.

In the work of Webster, who closes the period of achievement, we have tragedies of a different type. He takes over the sepulchral tragedy from Marston and Tourneur, because it suits his habit of mind; but he transforms it into something peculiarly his own. In his treatment of the supernatural he aims less at arousing terror by the exhibition of actual figures than at the evoking of an atmosphere of tense abnormal horror, in which the most trivial events are portentously magnified. He attains his most characteristic effects by revealing the sinister implications which lie in the combination of commonplace occurrences. In the earlier of his two masterpieces, *The White Devil*, we do have actual ghosts; but they are of a type far removed from that of their predecessors. Duke Francisco (iii. 2), as he sits brooding over the memory of his dead sister, forms so strong a mental image of her that she seems to stand before him.

She may, even though actually represented, be regarded merely as the coinage of his brain, as he himself declares:

How strong
Imagination works! how she can frame
Things which are not! Methinks she stands afore me,
And by the quick idea of my mind,
Were my skill pregnant, I could draw her picture.
Thought, as a subtle juggler, makes us deem
Things supernatural, which yet have cause
Common as sickness.   'Tis my melancholy. —

*   *   *   *

Remove this object;
Out of my brain with 't; what have I to do
With tombs or death-beds, funerals or tears,
That have to meditate upon revenge ?

It is quite conceivable that a subjective vision should be thus represented for the benefit of the audience, without involving any opinion as to the vision's reality.   In this case Francisco deliberately rids himself of the image because he needs all his faculties to meditate upon revenge; he does not require a ghost to rouse him to action.   Later, however, we have an actual ghost, that of Brachiano, who appears to the villain Flamineo.   He makes no answer to Flamineo's half-ironical questions, but throws earth upon him, and shows him a skull in a pot of flowers that he carries. Flamineo naturally interprets this as an omen of evil, and determines to do his uttermost to escape it.

In *The Duchess of Malfi* Webster achieves the most characteristic expression of his genius.   By a masterly accumulation of significant details he produces effects of poignant and almost disembodied intensity.   The scene (iii. 3) in which Antonio, with the paper on which is written the nativity of the Duchess' new-born son, encounters the villain Bosola is typical of Webster's method.   Antonio's nose suddenly bleeds, and this is his comment on the incident:

> My nose bleeds.
> One that were superstitious would count
> This ominous, when it merely comes by chance:
> Two letters, that are writ here for my name,
> Are drowned in blood!
> Mere accident.

Mere chance it may be; but it is none the less ominous. In act iv we see the Duchess, imprisoned by her brother Ferdinand's command, and the tortures which result in her death — the severed hand, the effigies of Antonio and their children, the masque of madmen — in all of which the agony is spiritual, and set in bolder relief by the utter humanity with which the noble victim is depicted. " I am Duchess of Malfi still," she tells the disguised Bosola; and her last care is for her children. After the deed is accomplished Ferdinand repents; and he and his brother the Cardinal pay dearly for it. Ferdinand is seized by a horrible form of madness, in which he imagines himself turned to a wolf; and he enters (v. 2) in terror of his own shadow, which seems to his disordered mind to be something pursuing him. The Cardinal has stronger nerves; but even he sees in his fish-pond " a thing armed with a rake That seems to strike at me " — a significant medieval survival! Before the climax Antonio and his friend Delio walk near a ruin. There is an echo there, which returns ominous answers to Antonio; and he, as he muses, is crossed by a sudden vision of " a face folded in sorrow." Bosola, turned repentant, accomplishes his revenge on the two brothers, but unwittingly slays Antonio also, and himself perishes.

It is easy to see how far Webster has travelled from the material horrors of Tourneur, though the kinship between the two is equally obvious. Webster, however, owes to none but himself the peculiar cast of his imagination, which provides him with an amazing store of sinister and uncanny

metaphors. He has likewise a lyric gift unknown to Tourneur or Marston, which finds expression, just before the
climax of each of his two tragedies, in two wonderful dirges.
In both cases he evidently feels the need of lyrical expression
to temper the horror of his scenes; and the dirge is the
nearest approach to a Greek choral ode that is possible for
him. The dirge in *The Duchess of Malfi* is the finer of the
two, being both more fitted to the situation and more perfect
in expression. It shows the fashion in which Webster suddenly illuminates and fuses a mass of details by some flash of
transfiguring insight; a quality which makes his two great
tragedies unique in their time, if not in all time.

The period of achievement which closes with Webster is
clearly a natural product of the growth of the native tradition, which now stands wholly free of classical influence, and
brings its qualities to full expression. Marston initiates the
new tendency, and powerfully affects it; even Shakespeare
is not free from his influence. But Shakespeare turns his
borrowings to his own use, and owes his merits to none but
himself. In *Hamlet* and *Macbeth* he makes the supernatural
an indispensable part of the drama, and depicts it with
unsurpassed power; though Webster, with his own peculiar
achievement, almost rivals him. We have likewise Chapman and Tourneur, to show the favor which such motives
enjoyed, and the zeal of dramatists in discovering fresh
variations on them. As a whole, the period is a glorious
realization of the promise which we detected in the English
drama, even at the outset.

Section 4. — Devil-Plays and Witch-Plays

The Elizabethan dramas which deal primarily with devils and witches form a distinct class; and though they are not in general of a really tragic cast, certain of them do attain the status of genuine tragedy. The proper appreciation of these demands a discussion of all the cases, which are indeed not very numerous, though they cover practically the whole period we are considering.

The devil-plays are the earlier of occurrence, and also the less tragic. We saw that even in the miracle-plays the devil had a distinctly comic side, though it was often subordinated to his more awesome aspects. In the course of time, and with the changes of belief, this comic aspect became the predominant one; and by the Elizabethan period not much of the original serious conception survives. We do find it, somewhat sporadically, in *Faustus*; but even there the added comic elements which overlie the deeper motive sufficiently show the customary trend of thought. The first instance of a devil-motive in the period is the farcical mock conjuration in *Gammer Gurton's Needle;* and the running allusions to such matters in later comedies do not suggest an attitude of real dread. Shakespeare uses Joan of Arc's supposed relations with the fiends in *1 Henry VI*, but not in a very striking way, and with emphasis on the trivial and unpleasant aspects of the legend. We find plays which fluctuate between the semi-serious and the wholly comic, such as Rowley's *Birth of Merlin*, where matter which does not lack a serious side, and which indeed occasionally compels the dramatist to a certain sobriety, is for the most part made an excuse for foolery of a rather vulgar sort. Likewise the prologue of *The Merry Devil of Edmonton*, in which the enchanter Fabell tricks the fiend who has come to demand fulfilment of his contract into granting him a seven years' respite, is serious at the beginning, but soon passes into the comic, and has no bearing on the rest of the play.

We may say that Barnes' *Devil's Charter* (1607) is the first attempt after *Faustus* to make a devil-motive the basis of a serious drama.[1] The seriousness of the dramatist's intentions is unmistakable, and his plot does not lack opportunities for effective situations; but he is hampered by a want of reticence at critical points, and by a sense of humor more remarkable for its pervasiveness than for its merit.   The play deals with the crimes of the Borgias, particularly with those of Pope Alexander VI, whose success is ascribed to a contract with the Devil.   The outward trappings of the black arts occupy a very conspicuous place, and give rise to many passages of sheer nonsense.   The supernatural elements become more pronounced as we near the climax. In iv. 1 Alexander summons the devils in order to learn the identity of the murderer of his son, the Duke of Candia. The devil " bringeth in the ghost of Candia gastly haunted by Caesar persuing and stabing it; " a similar vision reveals Lucretia's murder of her former husband Viselli.   Alexander decides that his only safety lies in a new accumulation of crimes, by which he and his son Caesar may retain their power.   The devils, however, delude his expectation.   At a banquet, at which the Pope intends to poison certain of his foes, a devil changes the wine-bottles, and Alexander and Caesar are caught in their own toils.   Alexander retires to his chamber, and a brief scene shows us the rejoicing of the devils at his approaching doom.   We can see that the old

[1] The play is edited by R. B. McKerrow in Bang's *Materialien*, vi, Louvain, 1904.

classical allusions have not yet lost their charm from this speech of Astaroth's:

> Let Orcus, Erebus and Acheron,
> And all those ghosts which haunt the pitchy vaults
> Of cole-black darkness in Cimerian shades
> Muster themselves in numbers numberless
> To dance about the ghost of Alexander.

The climax which follows is in itself a fine one. Alexander, feeling his end draw near, opens the curtains of his study, and beholds the Devil, arrayed in the pontifical vestments, and come to demand the fulfilment of his contract, which has been drawn up in such fashion that Alexander is defrauded of seven years that he thought were his. This is a splendid moment; but Barnes must wring the last drop of terror from the scene, and its power accordingly evaporates. Alexander's part here is that of Herod of the miracle-plays brought up to date, and his ravings must have satisfied the most exacting groundling. The Devil carefully explains the trickery of the contract, while Alexander writhes in agony; ghosts are introduced again, to reveal to him the crimes and fates of his son and daughter; at the close " a devil like a post " enters with a horn to summon him. Here Barnes inserts a stroke of genuine power; Alexander thinks of his doom as typified in the loss of his pontifical vestments:

> My robes, my robes, he robs me of my robes;
> Bring me my robes, or take away my life;
> My robes, my life, my soul and all is gone.

But Barnes cannot maintain this level, and Alexander shrieks out mere gibberish as the devils drag him away. The merits of this final scene are largely obscured by the trash which Barnes has inserted to tickle the groundlings; yet at the bottom of the mass there does lie an impressive conception, which we wish that he had treated with greater restraint.

In Dekker's *If This be not a Good Play the Devil is in It*, we have another example of a conception that surpasses the material.   The play is planned on a large scale, and certain of the details are vividly executed; but we do not feel that it has a real structure, or is really thought out.   It opens with a prologue in Hell, from which we learn that the Devil's kingdom has fallen into a decline; accordingly three lesser fiends, Ruffman, Lurchall, and Shackle-soul, are despatched to Naples to restore their master's power.   The three sub-plots which set forth their schemes naturally give much scope for satirical detail, especially that connected with Shackle-soul, who enters a monastery, and in the disguise of a cook entirely upsets its discipline by his seductive dainties.   Ruffman meanwhile applies himself to the corruption of the young King, and Lurchall gets a Usurer into his toils; but in the end the Sub-prior of the monastery, who alone has resisted the devices of Shackle-soul, brings about the confusion of the devils.   They do not, however, return empty-handed; and the final scene is a realistic presentation of the torments of Hell, given added point by the presence of such contemporary malefactors as Ravillac and Guy Fawkes, and ending with the reception of the ghost of a Puritan.   The satire is after all not very subtle or penetrating, and the devils are not treated with any real seriousness. The play is really a development of that tendency to a purely spectacular handling of the supernatural which we noted as early as the work of Greene and Peele.

We thus see that the devil-plays after *Faustus* progress steadily in the direction of comedy, a movement which reaches its logical conclusion in the monumental humors of Jonson's *The Devil is an Ass*.   This comic handling contrasts strongly with the treatment of ghosts during the same period. Wherever we have comedy brought into connection with a ghost, it is always a mock ghost which furnishes the occasion, as for instance in *The Atheist's Tragedy;* while the humor in such cases is usually rather grim, not at all like the frank sport which is made of the devils. No *bona fide* ghost is ever subjected to such indignities as Jonson's Pug, who is only accepted on sufferance, is bamboozled by most of the mortal characters, and at the end wholly fails to convince his master that he is really a devil, and is ignominiously dragged off to Newgate. The devil seems to have exhausted all his capacity to awe; the satirical aspect, which, as we saw, was already present in the medieval period, now entirely absorbs the more serious elements. The ghost, on the contrary, seems always to have commanded respect. This cannot fully be explained as a consequence of his classical origin; a writer like Tourneur would scarcely have been deterred from making sport of a ghost by any respect for antiquity. It is difficult to escape the conclusion that the ghost inspired in the Elizabethan mind a respect based on genuine dread; so that, while the devil-plays passed wholly into the domain of comedy, plays in which ghosts participated were always, in intention at least, serious.

With the plays that deal with witchcraft we come upon a motive which has distinct tragic possibilities, and one which corresponds to nothing in antiquity. The ancient belief in sorcery of course involved no idea of damnation; the sorcerer might be a person to be execrated, and was probably destined to a violent end, but the specific element by which Christianity added the final horror to the conception was lacking. To the Middle Ages is due the belief that a mortal could, by compact with the powers of evil, win the

ability to torment others at the price of his own soul; and
this conception passed over into the Renaissance, almost
unaltered, if not in some degree actually encouraged, by the
progress of science.   In the Elizabethan age it was an accepted article of belief for practically everyone; and the
persecutions which ever and again broke out gave it an
immediate appeal when brought upon the stage.   The
various extant plays which employ it as a motive show, in
very interesting fashion, the variety of treatment which was
possible.

We have already seen that *Macbeth*, which may be
regarded as the starting-point of the series, is not really a
witch-play at all, since it uses witchcraft merely as a means
of approach to the profounder conception of the Weird
Sisters.   Shakespeare would probably have adopted the
same method if James had never become king of England;
belief in witchcraft was the only universal tenet to which he
could, for his purposes, appeal.   He treats the theme
realistically, but subordinates it to his deeper plan, and gives
it a certain breadth which keeps it above the merely sordid.
It is, however, not an inherent part of *Macbeth*, and is not at
all the element which gives the play its peculiar character.

In Middleton's *Witch* we have the least relevant treatment of the motive.   It has little to do with the main plot,
which is the old story of Rosamund Queen of the Lom-
bards decked out with a romantic " happy ending."   The
play emphasizes the intercourse of the witches with their
familiars which is to us the most repugnant feature of the
whole matter; and the mortals who resort to the witches
do so because of slighted love.   Middleton's treatment
fluctuates between occasional seriousness and decidedly
vulgar buffoonery, to the detriment of any unified effect.
He does show, however, as does no other writer of the time, a

sense of what may be called the poetry of witchcraft — the joy of the midnight journeys through the sky, when the witches

> transfer
> Our 'nointed flesh into the air
> In moonlight nights, on steeple-tops,
> Mountains and pine-trees, that like pricks or stops
> Seem to our height. (I. 2)

This poetical aspect finds its best expression in the familiar song of act iv, where all that is coarse and trivial seems left behind on earth, and only a disembodied delight in the flight through the air remains:

> O what a dainty pleasure 'tis
> To ride in the air
> When the moon shines fair,
> And sing and dance and toy and kiss.
> Over woods and over mountains,
> Over seas, our mistress' fountains,
> Over steeples, towers and turrets,
> We fly by night, 'mongst troops of spirits;
> No ring of bells to our ears sounds,
> No howls of wolves, no yelps of hounds;
> No, nor the noise of water's breach,
> Or cannon's throat our height can reach.

In Heywood's *Late Lancashire Witches* we have a contemporary document, set forth quite impersonally and with no moral bias; an unflinching portrayal of the pettiness of current beliefs, carried out with a passionless intellectual curiosity which to a modern taste becomes ghastly.   The crudity with which the narratives of the Lancashire outbreaks are transferred to the stage is almost incredible. The witches play the customary tricks — in the shape of dogs they mislead hunters; at a wedding-feast the cake is turned into bran and the other viands to various objects, while the musicians are made to play different tunes at once; and there are comic episodes in a haunted mill.   At the climax the transformation of the leader of the witches, Mistress Generous, from a mare to a woman, is all but represented on the stage. The servant Robin bids his master look in the stable for the gelding which he suspects has been used for unholy nocturnal rides; he finds an old mare, and at Robin's advice removes her bridle, to find that she is his own wife, transformed by Robin, who had previously been changed into a horse by her, and thus acquired his acquaintance with the magic implement. Generous enters with his wife, who hypocritically pleads repentance, but soon returns to her old courses. She is at last detected by the cutting off of her hand during one of her escapades; her accomplices are also discovered, and the whole band is handed over to justice, with the full approval of their relatives and friends. There is little artistry here, but an unmatched picture of witchcraft as an actuality in the life of the time — not merely confined to the lower orders of society, but with sinister possibilities of intrusion into its higher classes, and displaying unashamed all the coarseness and triviality of the conception.

Finally, we have the real tragedy of witchcraft in *The Witch of Edmonton*, chiefly, it would appear, the work of Dekker and Ford. A realistically portrayed English village is the scene of an intrigue which combines with a traffic with the powers of evil to produce fatal results. Frank Thorney has seduced Winifred, a maid in his master's house, but has sufficient manliness to marry her. His character, however, is at bottom unstable; and his father, whose property is in a precarious state, plans for him a marriage with Susan, daughter of Carter, a well-to-do neighbor. Old Thorney taxes his son with the secret marriage, but Frank denies it, and consents to wed Susan. He has thus involved himself in an untenable situation, and decides to fly with Winifred. His inherent cowardice, however, makes him think of murder as another possible refuge; but he lacks courage, and needs some external impulse to bring him to the act. This impulse is supplied by the second strand of the plot, the motive of witchcraft. Mother Sawyer, an old crone of the village, has been driven to desperation by a brutal neighbor, Banks; he declares that she is a witch, and his persecutions at length make her one indeed. She longs for the power to avenge herself on her enemies, until that desire wholly overmasters her. In one of her fits of cursing she is surprised by the devil in the shape of a black dog, and easily yields to his promises. The devil, thus given a footing in the community, works for his own ends, as well as those of his mistress. Thorney, as he prepares for flight, is accompanied by Winifred in disguise, and by Susan, who is to turn back after they have reached a certain point on the way. She of course thinks that he is going on some matter of business. At this moment the black dog enters, rubs against him, and rouses his murderous impulse to action. He kills Susan, after avowing his treachery to her, ties himself to a tree, and accuses two innocent men of the crime. His duplicity is at last discovered; Mother Sawyer, who of course has no direct share in his deed, is accused of witchcraft, and the two are brought to execution.

The play derives a singular interest from the fact that in it we perceive a witch as it were in process. Whereas in the previously examined plays we have witches who remain such throughout, and have no claim on our sympathies, we observe in this instance the compulsion which drives a mortal woman into her compact with the powers of Hell. Mother Sawyer is really the victim of the prejudices of the village; and though her nefarious compact is regarded as

actual enough, we feel that she receives in this world sufficient punishment for her offence, the responsibility for which
does not rest upon herself alone.   The authors show a
detached but very genuine sympathy for her, and carefully
avoid dwelling on the merely grotesque or repulsive aspects
of witchcraft.   The understanding and restraint which
mark the play set it apart from its fellows just considered,
and raise it to the level of genuine tragedy.   It might be
objected that Mother Sawyer's language is more poetic than
we should expect from one in her circumstances;   but
nothing excludes the supposition that she may once have had
a better station in life, and her eloquence is perhaps in part a
contribution from her familiar.   In any case, the lines in
which she expresses her thirst for vengeance are splendidly
vigorous, and lead up to a superb climax in her cry when the
dog appears to her no longer black but white, in sign that he
is about to desert her:

> Why to mine eyes art thou a flag of truce ?
> I am at peace with none; 'tis the black color,
> Or none, which I fight under.

The tragic possibilities which Middleton and Heywood were
content to pass over in favor of what would appeal to the
prejudices and passions of the multitude here find admirable
expression.

We thus see that *The Witch of Edmonton* is the only play
of those dealing strictly with devils or witches which attains
throughout the status of genuine tragedy.   In *Faustus*
the emphasis is on Faustus himself, not on the fiends; and in
Macbeth the element of witchcraft is subordinate, almost
accidental.   *The Devil's Charter* does touch tragedy in its
final scene, but Barnes cannot refrain from loading down his
fine conception with mere rubbish.   Otherwise the devil-
plays pass over definitely into comedy and satire; while the

witch-plays remain either crudely romantic, as in Middleton, or trivially realistic, as in Heywood. Yet the two classes do illustrate the variety of interest which the Elizabethans found in supernatural themes, and do result, in at least one instance, in a genuine tragedy, whose sober realism and restraint set it among the masterpieces of the period.

SECTION 5. — THE PERIOD OF DECLINE

As often happens in an extensive artistic movement, symptoms of decline are visible in the Elizabethan treatment of the supernatural well before the dramatic impulse has exhausted its strength. We saw that even Tourneur's conception of the ghost might be regarded as a step in the direction of an inferior method; but his contribution to the type of the sepulchral tragedy keeps him a significant figure, and makes it impossible to regard him as marking a real subsidence. Not long after his day, however, definite evidences of decline appear; and we may perhaps date the real beginning of the process with the *Second Maiden's Tragedy*, licensed in 1611. The play may be regarded as a variation of the sepulchral tragedy, dealing as it does with the unhallowed love of a Tyrant for the corpse of a Lady who has killed herself rather than submit to his passion. He has her tomb opened, and the body removed to his palace, where he lavishes adornments and caresses upon it. In consequence of this deed the Lady's ghost appears (iv. 4) to her lover Govianus, and bids him avenge the outrage. Her appearance is thus elaborately described in the stage-directions:

On a sudden, in a kind of noise like a wind, the doors clattering, the tombstone flies open, and a great light appears in the midst of the tomb; his lady as went out standing before him, all in white, stuck with jewels, and a great crucifix on her breast.

She has a curious way of speaking of the body as her real
self —

I am now at court
In his own private chamber —

which makes us wonder just how her existence as a ghost is
to be conceived.   Govianus swears to avenge her wrong, and
does so by entering the palace in disguise and poisoning the
lips of the corpse.   The Tyrant kisses it, and is poisoned
thereby; in his death agony he beholds the ghost, in the
exact semblance of the body.   At the very close the ghost
returns and accompanies the body as it is carried out for
reburial, but does not speak in either case.

The play moves with sustained dignity, but has a curiously petrified effect; there is no life-blood in it.   The apparition of the ghost is more spectacular than impressive,
and scarcely attains any real eeriness.   The theme of the
play is distinctly unpleasant, even though the treatment is
not designedly repellant; and we feel in reading it that we
are on the verge of a period of convention and decline.

In Massinger the ghost becomes a purely conventional
figure, with no dramatic reason for existence.   In *The
Unnatural Combat* (1621) the atheist Malefort is at the end
confronted by the ghosts of his victims, who appear amid a
storm.   He questions them, but they reply only with gestures, and shortly after their disappearance he is killed by
a flash of lightning.   In *The Roman Actor* (1626) we have
ghosts in a dream, in the first scene of act v.   While the
emperor Domitian is asleep the ghosts of two of his victims,
Rusticus and Sura, rise " with bloody swords in their hands;
they wave them over the head of Caesar, who seems troubled
in his sleep, and as if praying to the image of Minerva,
which they scornfully seize, and then disappear with it."
Domitian awakes and finds that the statue has actually

vanished, a somewhat inexplicable result of the apparition of ghosts in a dream merely.   The two, when executed (iii. 2), had threatened to appear to Domitian before his fall, so that the element of revenge is still present; but Massinger's ghosts are obviously of little dramatic value.   In neither play do they speak, or affect the fortunes of the other characters by their apparition.

The lowest point in the Elizabethan treatment of the ghost is touched in Fisher's *True Trojans* (1625), a poor play dealing with Caesar's expedition to Britain.   In the prologue Mercury leads in the ghosts of Brennus and Camillus, who are respectively to excite Britons and Romans in the impending war.   Mercury's speech contains a conventional description of the underworld, and the two ghosts engage in an exchange of taunts.   In ii. 7 they are seen at work on Caesar and Nennius, leaders of the opposing armies; and a last flicker of the dominant thought of revenge appears when Camillus bids Caesar regard the invasion of Britain as an exacting of vengeance for the sack of Rome by the Gauls.   The ghosts are thereafter ignored until the end, when they reappear and vaunt the prowess of their respective sides, after which Mercury reconciles them. More unnecessary and unimpressive ghosts than these of Fisher's never trod the stage.

A more interesting play, and one which, if it had come earlier, might have had genuine merit, is the little known *Vow Breaker*, by William Sampson.   It was published in 1636, though doubtless written somewhat earlier, since the title-page says, " As it hath been divers times acted by several companies with great applause."   The story, stripped of a sub-plot of the siege of Leith in Scotland and some irrelevant matter, is one of domestic intrigue.   Young Bateman is betrothed to Anne, but leaves her to go to the

wars; in his absence she is plighted to another and wealthier
suitor.   At the beginning of act ii Bateman returns to find
her married; she repulses him; he will not curse her, but
swears " Alive or dead I will enjoy thee yet," so that Anne
is somewhat disturbed by his demeanor.   He hangs himself,
declaring

> My airy ghoast shall find her where she lyes,
> And to her face divulge her perjuries,

and his father discovers the body.   Anne mocks at the old
man's grief, but her cousin Ursula is touched by it, and is
also afraid of the possible coming of the ghost.   Anne, however, scoffs at the idea: " He swore he would have me quick
or dead.   Let him ly still in's grave, I will in my bed, and
let consequents prove the rest."   Her scorn is promptly
requited; at the beginning of the next act she enters in
terror, following Ursula, and declaring that she is haunted
by the ghost, in the exact semblance of the living Bateman.
Ursula, who does not seem to take the matter very seriously,
reminds her of her previous doubts, and goes out.   The
ghost enters and claims Anne as his own, declaring that he
comes from the classical Hades.   Ursula returns with
Boote, Anne's father, but neither of them can see the ghost.
Anne tries to approach him, but he repulses her, and the
others cannot even hear his voice.   Boote, in one of the few
speeches of the play that has a note of its own, asserts that
the phantom must be the work of witchcraft:

> If it be so, 'tis done by sorcery;
> The father has combinéd with some witch
> To vex thy quiet patience, and gain credit
> That he would haunt thee dead, as oft he said.
> Hell can put life into a senseless body,
> And raise it from the dead, and make it speake;
> Use all the faculties alive it did,
> To work the Devil's hellish stratagems!
> If I but find he deals in exorcimes
> I 'le make him burn to pacify the witch.

Anne decides to visit Bateman's father, in order to test the ghost's reality; the ghost duly appears, but does not speak, and vanishes when his father, in response to Anne's supplications, forgives her. In act iv we see Anne after the birth of her child; she is disturbed in consequence of a dream which seems to portend her death, and bids her attendants not fall asleep, lest she be carried off. They do succumb to drowsiness, however, and the ghost enters, summoning Anne to awake, and declaring that he will take her to Hades:

> The ferryman attends thee at the verge
> Of Cocitus, and sooty Acheron,
> And he shall waft thee into Tartary,
> Where perjury and falsehood finds reward.

His power to pass through natural obstacles is described in hyperbolical terms. Anne leaves her bed and goes out, to be brought back drowned. The two fathers quarrel over her body, but are reconciled, and this strand of the plot ends.

Even such a summary as this indicates some of the reminiscences of former works which color that of Sampson's. The influence of the *Spanish Tragedy* is writ large over it, and that not merely in connection with the ghost; Shakespeare, and to some extent Webster, also affect it. As a result, there is less " smack of the soil " than might have been expected, except in Boote's speech on witchcraft, already noted. The play, however, does associate a ghost with a story drawn from contemporary life, and the ghost is for the most part unquestioningly accepted by the other participants. Sampson clings fondly to the outworn classical trappings, though his indifference to quantities shows that they are hardly native to his genius. Had the play come earlier, and had its author had a greater individual endowment, it might have been, if not a counterpart of the *Witch of Edmonton*, at least a parallel to the *Lancashire Witches*, and given us a picture of the ghost-lore current in the popular mind at this period.   Even as it stands it is by no means devoid of interest, especially as showing how long the tradition established by Kyd persisted.

This later period is not without one example of a ghost which is excellent in itself, and also curiously indicative of modern practice; I mean the ghost of Alonzo in Middleton's *Changeling*.   In the first scene of act v Beatrice is in an agony of fear over the success of her stratagem to keep herself from her husband's arms; and as the danger of failure increases, De Flores hits on the fiendish device of ensuring their safety by the murder of the maid who is serving as Beatrice's substitute.   At the moment that he has finished detailing his scheme he notices something strange:

> Ha! what art thou that tak 'st away the light
> Betwixt that star and me ?

Then, with a swift regaining of his courage,

> I dread thee not;
> Twas' but a mist of conscience; all's clear again.

He goes out, and Beatrice turns in sudden terror:

> Who 's that, De Flores ? bless me, it slides by!
> Some ill thing haunts the house; 't has left behind it
> A shivering sweat upon me; I' m afraid now.

The phantom is immaterial, almost symbolical; but he gives the incident a thrill of the supernatural which is conveyed in masterly fashion by the differentiation of the effect on the two characters.   It is decorative, but a bit of decoration which is absolutely in its place.

On the whole it is clear that just as the early Elizabethan drama attained maturity by freeing itself of classical conventions, so the great plays of the period of achievement created their own conventions, which imposed themselves on later and inferior playwrights, and led to futile imitation. Yet the pieces which show positive signs of decay are not numerous; and even at a late date such a play as the *Changeling* testifies to the survival of the better attitude, and even points forward to a new method. The interest in the supernatural gradually fades, as the general dramatic impulse grows weaker; but only in a comparatively few cases does it end in absolute failure, and it shows a vitality that proves its inherent strength, and also the hold which it had gained on the public. It is undeniably one of the elements to which Elizabethan drama owes its power and its depth.

Section 6. — The Elizabethan Contribution

Our previous survey has covered a considerable period of time, and a large number of works; and it will be convenient to preface an attempt to summarize its contribution to our subject by a recapitulation of the historical development. We have seen that the medieval drama of England produced an original method of handling the supernatural, and passed on this method as a distinct native tradition. Under classical influence the supernatural became an accepted feature of the newer serious drama; but the established tradition made it impossible for dramatists to take over classical motives as they stood, and compelled them to treat them freely. Meanwhile the purely native interest in the supernatural made its way in romantic drama and chronicle-play, until it became strong enough to absorb the classical tradition and reduce it to a mere decorative survival.   This period of conflict and absorption ends in the early nineties.   After a few years of comparative indifference a revival of certain of the older plays leads to a renewal of interest, and prepares the way for a splendid period of achievement, culminating in Shakespeare and Webster. This period, however, creates conventions of its own, which careless writers can be content to copy; and so a period of decline sets in, which carries us nearly to the Closing of the Theatres, and the end of the epoch.

In this long sequence of works the most enduring supernatural type is obviously the ghost.   He enters the drama early, and his classical extraction makes him readily acceptable.   The traits which he derives from Seneca, however, are not of a dramatic cast; and he must obtain new ones if he is really to survive.   This he does by becoming frankly a revenge-ghost, in which capacity he soon attains independent existence.   We saw that the ancient ghost, especially in Greek tragedy, occasionally showed a keen desire for revenge; but in Seneca this aspect was largely obscured, and the imitators of Seneca could hardly derive it from him, though we did see a few essays in that direction in the Renaissance tragedy of Italy.   Practically, however, the revenge-ghost as a developed dramatic type is the creation of the Elizabethan age.   We see this element strongly marked in even the earliest examples, and the desire to make the supernatural express itself in action led to its steady accentuation.   We do not have the developed revenge-ghost until a train of events is shown us which the ghost actually sets in motion with the aim of causing the downfall of his enemies.   The first play to reach this stage is *Locrine*, though in it the revenge-ghost is still mechanical and subordinate.   But he steadily increases in importance, until in *Julius Caesar* he becomes the unifying element of the tragedy, and in *Hamlet* the impelling force which initiates the entire action.

Much ingenuity has been expended in the classification of the Elizabethan ghosts; but a detailed scheme seems hardly necessary. In general they fall into two great classes, based on the ancient antithesis of saying and doing. We have the ghost who merely expounds, and the ghost who actually affects events; and the prevalence of the revenge-ghost makes the latter class by far the more numerous. The Elizabethan dramatists instinctively avoid the ineptitude of a ghost who merely talks; they know that " it needs no ghost brought from the grave " to inform us of facts which might perfectly well be brought to our notice by other means. Such information as the ghost in *Hamlet* gives is on another plane entirely; from no source but his murdered father can Hamlet be assured of the truth of his vague suspicions, and the return of the ghost is thus demanded by the logic of the play. But the wearisome Senecan ghost who can only discourse of his ancestry and his torments in Hades enjoys little favor on the Elizabethan stage; the Elizabethan desires to see his ghosts in action, conformably to the essence of the supernatural as a power.

It must be evident to any open-minded person who surveys our accumulation of cases that the average Elizabethan ghost is as real as any other participant in the drama. This has been sufficiently demonstrated by Dr. Stoll in his paper on *The Objectivity of the Ghosts in Shakespere*, (see bibliography), which brings in most of the examples which the period affords; and though one may dissent from him in some minor details, as I do with regard to the ghost of Isabella in *The White Devil*, his general conclusion is unassailable. This at once disposes of certain ingenious and unnecessary attempts to subtilize and explain away the ghosts as subjective hallucinations, even when, as in the scene between Hamlet and his mother, the ghost actually speaks.   These relics of an outworn attitude toward the subject have, it is to be hoped, lost their appeal.   There is one argument against them, however, which has perhaps not yet been stated with sufficient force.   It has been customary to assert that the more or less skeptical remarks of persons to whom ghosts have appeared — Brutus' " Now that I pluck up heart thou vanishest," for example — are proof that the dramatist intends us to regard the ghosts as after all unreal.   Now no person is anxious to encourage in his mind a belief that a ghost may actually appear to him; least of all is a murderer anxious to believe that the ghost of his victim may return and reveal the crime, or at best haunt his slayer to madness.   Accordingly, when such a fearsome event does occur, the murderer must, in self-defence, do all he can to convince himself that the apparition is unreal; but all his efforts are, in the Elizabethan view, vain, as we saw clearly in the very case of Brutus.   Another argument against the reality of ghosts, that of the power of selective apparition, is merely the result of ignorance of the subject on the part of those who propound it.   The idea that a supernatural being can appear to whom he will, even amid a crowd, is as old as Homer.   When Athena comes to the hut of Eumaios " Telemachos saw her not coming toward him, for the Gods indeed do not appear manifest to all; but Odysseus and the dogs saw her."   Those who cannot accept Elizabethan ghosts as actual participants in the several plays had better confine their attention to other periods.

Not all the ghosts, however, have an equal dramatic necessity for existence; and they may be divided under the two heads of intrinsic and decorative.   Of the former the ghost in *Hamlet* is the unsurpassable example; of the latter we have several types. The ghost, in fact, by reason of his half-way character of a mortal who has become supernatural by death, is better suited to decorative treatment, and can less well become the motive force of a whole play than such beings as the Furies or the Weird Sisters, who are supernatural and nothing else. But a decorative ghost may be good or bad, relevant or irrelevant. The ghost may be used to typify and intensify the idea of revenge, without actually bringing about the downfall of his foe, as do the ghosts in *Richard III* and *Macbeth*. He may also be merely a token of such downfall, like the flitting ghost of the *Changeling*, or the similar phantom of Susan that appears to Frank Thorney in *The Witch of Edmonton*. Such decorative use is legitimate and impressive; it enhances the underlying trend of the tragedy. On the other side we have the purely expository ghost (relatively infrequent, as we noted, in Elizabethan drama), and the silent phantoms which, as in Massinger, appear without any fitness to the occasion. It is obvious that the cases of unsuccessful treatment are far fewer than those which really have a reason for being.

In almost all the cases, good and bad alike, the idea of revenge persists, though it may be feebly expressed. The normal Elizabethan ghost returns for the purpose of securing a personal revenge; and even where the motive is ennobled, as in *Hamlet*, it is by no means weakened. Perhaps as a consequence of this insistence the coming of a ghost very seldom calls forth any expression of tenderness from the living; in *Hamlet*, when the Prince exclaims "Alas, poor ghost!" the phantom at once replies "Pity me not," and elsewhere such bursts of compassion are almost unknown. It would seem that the Elizabethans felt so keenly the inherently awesome character of the supernatural that they did not care to dilute its effect by any of the concessions to human pity which are natural enough in the case of the returning dead.

The incidental allusions which increase the effect of the actual apparitions are, as we saw, derived from two main sources — classical imitation and the charnel-house.   The former are a natural consequence of the classical *provenance* of the ghost himself; but they represent no vital conceptions in their source, Seneca, and can be but lifeless fragments if merely reproduced at second hand.   As a consequence of the general vitality of the Elizabethan drama they soon fall into a very subordinate position, to be replaced by images drawn from the phenomena of bodily dissolution.   Such images belong to a well-established native tradition, doubtless reaching back to primitive times, and practically untouched by classical influence.   As a result, a whole series of motives is evolved which corresponds to nothing in classical tragedy, and at length produces what is really a distinct form, the sepulchral tragedy, which lends hints to Shakespeare, and is glorified by Webster.

The two writers who are most closely identified with these two classes of allusion — Kyd and Marston — are also those who exercise most influence on the external course of the drama, for obvious reasons.   Kyd reshaped the classical trappings into something that had real literary beauty, but which presented definite traits susceptible of imitation, in the retention of mythological details, and the idea of vengeance pursued even in the underworld.   We have seen how the tradition which he established crops up in later plays, notably in the " academic " *Caesar and Pompey* for a school drama, and in the much later *Vow Breaker* for a piece from the popular stage — two productions sufficiently diverse in spirit and circumstances to make their close reproduction of a definite type decidedly striking.

The influence of Marston was of a more extended sort, including not only the stylistic side of charnel-house allusions, but also the whole theatrical apparatus by which he enhanced the effectiveness of his ghosts on the actual stage. This influence has been sufficiently illustrated in the previously cited examples; and it is an even more important one than Kyd's, involving as it does, whether consciously or not, a resumption of a distinctly native line of tradition, and also an increased attention to the enstaging of the supernatural.

For the best instances of the intrinsic supernatural we turn of course to Marlowe and Shakespeare. In *Tamburlaine* we have the futile struggle of a conqueror against forces which lie beyond his control, and in their own good time remove him from the scene of his triumphs. In *Faustus* we have a scholar who desires all possible material satisfactions, and willingly sacrifices his soul for them, only to realize that he has lost himself by the surrender. *Tamburlaine* attains a higher level by reason of the skill with which Marlowe emphasizes the humanity of his hero; he will end the rhapsody in which Tamburlaine imagines the triumphal reception of Xenocrate into Heaven with the simple line " Physicians, will no physic do her good ? " and the mad speech which announces a determination to fight hand to hand against the Gods with the piteous avowal, " Ah, friends, what shall I do ? I cannot stand." *Tamburlaine* is thus the closest spiritual approach to Greek tragedy which any literature can display up to Marlowe's own time.

In Shakespeare the achievement is of course more varied. He begins with a simple perception of the value of the supernatural as a decorative adjunct, and progresses to such a skilful use of the ghost as we find in *Julius Caesar*, and to the incomparable ingenuity of *Hamlet*. He cannot advance farther in that direction; in *Macbeth* he changes his method, and pushes his tragic exploration to the very verge of the mortal world. Macbeth and his wife suffer the extremest passions which mankind can survive; she, indeed, less yielding than her husband, succumbs to them. The action is controlled by the Weird Sisters, elemental powers who have no links with humanity, and who exalt and crush Macbeth with equal unconcern, not even openly mocking the failure of his attempt to dominate them. *Macbeth* is the most appallingly tragic play since the *Oresteia*, and does not even close on such a note of hope as does the *Eumenides*; it pushes on relentlessly into an unescapable abyss.

Shakespeare too has left some impress on plays later than his own; but in the nature of the case his influence could not be one of detail. The imagination which shaped Hamlet's father and the Weird Sisters was beyond the reach of imitation; and even the stylistic side of his work was of an essentially different quality from that of his competitors. We saw one clear instance of imitation, in Chapman's *Revenge of Bussy D'Ambois*, which of course chooses for imitation precisely the most imitable part of *Hamlet*. In view of the general nature of Chapman's ghosts we may be grateful that he did not attempt to rival the complexities of the opening of that play.

On the purely technical side, we perceive in the work of the period various efforts, doubtless unconscious, to attain some of the advantages which the Greeks derived from the chorus. Marston's boy Julio in *Antonio's Revenge* is an instrument sensitive to the approach of the supernatural, as we saw that the chorus might be; and Webster's magnificent dirges show his desire to secure such an imaginative expansion and relief in moments of supreme horror as the chorus could compass by its purely lyrical expression. Plays in which the ghost is the chief supernatural factor naturally have less need of such means; and Shakespeare in *Macbeth* replaces the chorus by the sustained intensity of the language in which he clothes the speech of his characters. We may note that if he had had the services of a chorus in *Julius Caesar*, the idea of Caesar's spirit eager for revenge might have been made more salient, and clearer to even a casual survey; but the existing allusions doubtless satisfied the requirements of the time, quicker than we to kindle at such hints. We thus perceive how similar problems lead to analogous solutions, even where no direct influence is traceable, and where the respective fields lie as far apart in space and time as the Attic and Elizabethan theatres.

The final impression, as one surveys the whole field of the Elizabethan treatment of the supernatural, is that of variety and independence. All possible forms of the supernatural are represented, and handled with remarkable ingenuity of detail. The developed type of the revenge-ghost is, as we saw, practically the creation of this age, and the examples of it which we find there are equalled nowhere else. Instead of being satisfied, like the Italians, with a meaningless imitation of a bloodless original, the Elizabethans, though utilizing the same original, made him but a pretext for approaching their own wealth of native traditions, initiating a movement which culminates in Shakespeare. Even after the culmination is passed, the decline is not rapid, and in some cases barely perceptible, especially in Webster, who maintains the level of previous achievement. Beside the more important manifestations we have such subordinate but interesting types as the use of folklore in Peele's *Old*

Wives Tale, and the plays which deal with devils and witches, these latter too, at their best, penetrating into the domain of tragedy.   So amazing a variety, coupled with the grandeur of the highest achievements, gives the supernatural in the Elizabethan theatre a place such as it had not held in any dramatic literature since the days of Aischylos.

PART III

SOME MODERN ASPECTS

CHAPTER VI

THE PERIOD OF SUBSIDENCE

Section i. — Restoration Tragedy.

The close of the Commonwealth in England brings us to the beginning of what we may regard as the modern world; and with the Restoration begins a new stage of dramatic development. It is a stage which shows a curious mingling of two traditions, in no case more marked than in the treatment of the supernatural. The dominating influence, for serious drama, was that of French classical tragedy, which had little interest in such themes. Yet the Restoration dramatists were the heirs of the Elizabethans, and felt their kinship; and Elizabethan drama was full of the supernatural. The joint result of these two tendencies was a retention of the supernatural in a form and in a period unsuited to its proper expression, and consequently an unsatisfactory use of it. Yet the study of instances of the employment of the supernatural in a purely conventional way is not without its interest; especially in this case, where it shows the persistence of the Elizabethan tradition even under unfavorable circumstances.

I have said that French classical tragedy had little interest in the supernatural. The earliest Renaissance tragedies provide us with a few instances of the prologue-ghost; the first of them, Jodelle's *Cléopatre* (1552) is introduced by the ghost of Antony, who has a long speech, obviously modelled on similar discourses in the Italian tragedies of the period. It begins with the customary allusion to Hades:

Dans le val tenebreux où les nuicts éternelles
Font éternelle peine aux ombres criminelles,
Cedant à mon destin, je suis volé naguère,

and then becomes expository, describing the baneful effects
on Antony of his love for Cleopatra.   Toward the end there
is the inevitable reference to the four great sinners, and the
statement that the ghost has just appeared to Cleopatra in
a dream, and bidden her slay herself rather than yield to
the Romans.   We have here a mere rehash of elements
taken over from the Italian prologue-ghost, with no originality of treatment.

Similar conventional prologues open Garnier's two earliest
tragedies.   His *Porcie* (1568) is introduced by the Fury
Megère, whose discourse is long, expository, and erudite.   A
similar discourse, placed in the mouth of the ghost of Aegeus,
opens the *Hippolyte* (1573).   It begins with a description of
Hades, which, however, the ghost prefers to Athens, his
abode in life; it goes on to narrate the career of Theseus,
and to predict the woes which are to befall him, and finds
occasion to bring in the four sinners once more.   Neither
speech has the slightest originality.   There is also a prologue-
ghost in Hardy's *Mort d'Alexandre* (1621 ?), again purely
expository.

It is thus clear that the French tragic poets had little real
interest in the ghost; and the writers on the theory of
tragedy pronounced against the use of supernatural figures
in very explicit language.   We saw that Trissino was willing
to sanction such use, if it were confined strictly to exposition;
but the French theorists were more rigid.   Thus Jean de la
Taille, in the discourse " De l'art de la tragédie " prefixed
to his *Saul le Furieux*,[1] declares that one ought not to introduce persons who are called feigned, and who never existed,

---

[1] See the reprint of the play by A. Werner, Leipzig, 1908, p. 11.

such as Death, Truth, or Avarice, since only creatures equally unreal could take pleasure in such representations. The great aim of Renaissance criticism was to secure verisimilitude in works of art; this desire is most marked in connection with the drama, and in drama it is France which seeks it most unremittingly. In a later writer, Laudun (1598), we have a definite pronouncement on the subject of ghosts, almost contemporary, it will be seen, with the beginning of the period of achievement in England. " If the ghosts appear before the action begins," he says, " they are permissible; but if they appear during the course of the action, and speak to the actors themselves, they are entirely faulty and reprehensible." [1] In other words, if they do nothing of importance, and have no effect on the action — in short, if they utterly belie their character as supernatural beings — they may be tolerated; otherwise they are out of keeping with tragedy, which must be real and historical. It is not hard to see why the ghost is not a favorite on the French stage of this period, or why classical French tragedy should exhibit very little interest in the supernatural at large.

In view of these facts it is obvious that the supernatural elements in Restoration tragedy did not come from France, but were a direct heritage from the Elizabethans. The method of their treatment, however, is not very suggestive of their Elizabethan prototypes. The ghost is the principal variety, though there is some use of spirits; but the only aim is to produce a spectacular effect. This aim combines with bombastic attempts at the " grand style " to produce a remarkable series of ineptitudes, in which ghosts stalk across the stage to no purpose, and portents are described

---

[1] Quoted by J. E. Spingarn, *Literary Criticism in the Renaissance*, p. 205. Cf. the general discussion, pp. 202 ff.

with a vehemence which passes the borders of absurdity. A convenient example with which to begin our survey, and one which has rather more individuality than its fellows, is the *Oedipus* of Dryden and Lee, produced in 1678.

Here the superposition on the consummate simplicity of Sophokles of a romantic sub-plot in the manner of Corneille and a ghost-raising in the manner of Seneca produces a sufficiently extraordinary composite.   It is interesting to find that in their treatment of the ghost the authors unconsciously follow the procedure of Heywood in his translation of the *Troades:* they seek to gain a greater effect by actually representing a narrated episode, the raising of the ghost of Laius.   The words of the preface to the play are instructive in this regard: " All we could gather out of Corneille was, that an Episode must be, but not his way; and Seneca supplied us with no new Hint, but only a Relation which he makes of his Tiresias raising the ghost of Laius; which is here performed in view of the Audience."   This is not the only Elizabethan reminiscence in the piece.   Creon is transformed into a misshapen monster, on the model of Richard III; and Oedipus, tormented by visions, walks in his sleep like Lady Macbeth.   The plague and its accompanying portents are strongly emphasized, as preparation for the necromantic scene of act iii.   The ritual of evocation is couched in a lyric style which is occasionally effective, but for the most part trivial.   Thunder is heard, and groans come from beneath the stage, poetically explained by Tiresias as

> the Groans of Ghosts, that cleave the Earth with Pain,
> And heave it up; they pant and stick half way.

At last the ghost rises, in his chariot as he was slain; he begs to be sent back to Hell, which he prefers to Thebes, but is compelled to disclose the identity of his slayer, Oedipus, whom he curses. Oedipus enters just after the ghost has vanished, and is of course righteously indignant when he learns of the accusation. The dénouement is substantially that of the Greek until the end, which brings a welter of slaughter in the worst Elizabethan manner, utterly opposed to the true spirit of the legend.

This ghost of Laius is as successful a specimen as Restoration tragedy affords; and it is obvious that his artistic value is not great. The songs which supposedly adorn the scene have no lyric merit, and create no appropriate atmosphere of dread. The portents are emphasized in so mechanical a manner that their impressiveness is lost. It is clear that the ghost represents a mere spectacular survival, with no appeal to the deeper sentiments of authors or spectators, and with no skill in handling to justify his introduction. He does, however, deliver a message which affects the action, and so has greater reason for existence than most of his fellows of the time, who are, as we shall see, almost wholly superfluous decorative figures.

Lee, Dryden's collaborator in this instance, also employs ghosts in the plays which he wrote independently. Thus, in his *Nero* there is a brief warning apparition of a ghost, followed in the next scene by that of Caligula's ghost to Nero, in a fashion somewhat reminiscent of Jonson's *Catiline*. The ghost declares that he will obtain revenge on the Romans by inciting Nero to renewed crimes. A slight tinge of classicism permeates the scene. Nero, presumably on awaking, remarks

> Where have I been ? Thou daemon of the night,
> Return; I 'm racked with this appalling sight.

Otherwise Lee's ghosts are non-speaking decorative figures. In act i of *The Rival Queens* the ghost of Philip appears to a group of conspirators who are plotting against his son Alexander; he walks across the stage, shaking a truncheon, but does not speak, and produces only a momentary effect on the conspirators.   At the beginning of act iv of *Mithridates* we see Mithridates " encompassed with the ghosts of his sons, who set daggers to his breast, and vanish." In the same play we have a passage descriptive of portents which perhaps deserves quotation as a specimen of Lee's style:

> Strange doleful Voices shrilly echo'd thro'
> The darken'd Fane; the Monuments did open,
> And all the Marble-Tombs, like Spunges squeez'd,
> Spouted big Sweat; the Curtain was consumed
> With wondrous Flame; and every shining Altar
> Dissolv'd to yellow Puddle, which anon
> A Flash of thirsty Lightning quite lick'd up;
> While thro' the Streets your murder'd Brothers rode,
> Arathias, Mithridates, and Machares,
> And madded all the screaming Multitude.   (v. 2.)

In *Caesar Borgia* he narrates the famous vision of the Pope and Caesar as corpses before their actual death; and at the opening of *Constantine the Great* we see two angels, addressing the emperor in a dream.

The two types of ghosts, those who speak and those who do not, are also represented in the work of John Crowne. To the former belongs the ghost of Herod in *The Destruction of Jerusalem*, who exults in his former crimes, and predicts the impending woes, having thus a definite expository function.   Most of Crowne's ghosts, however, belong to the second class.   One appears twice in his *Regulus*, another in his *Darius*.   A re-working of Seneca's *Thyestes* offers us a somewhat retouched version of the scene between Tantalos and the Fury, without anything really new.   In *Charles the Eighth* a ghost is raised by a magician, and returns just before the end of the play to indicate the approach of the catastrophe.   Crowne's ghosts may be dismissed as absolutely conventional, and the same is true of the specimens which we find in Elkanah Settle.   In his *Cambyses* we have two visions, one (iv. 1) of spirits, the other, (v. 3) with ghosts added.   An episode in *The Female Prelate* (1680) clearly shows the spectacular intent.   The ghost of the Duke of Saxony's father appears to his son, who is imprisoned, and lights a train of fire on the dungeon wall, which spells MURDER! — a last feeble flicker of the revenge-ghost.

A more ambitious attempt at the use of the supernatural, but without any better result, is to be found in Shadwell's *Libertine*, a version of the Don Juan story.   At the end of act ii the ghost of Don Juan's father, who was murdered by his son, rises and bids him repent; but the incident is not impressive.   At the end of act iv the statue accepts the Don's invitation to dinner, and offers one of his own, which is depicted in the last scene of act v.   The church is filled with the ghosts of the Don's victims, who call for vengeance. The statue gives him and his companions blood to drink; devils appear and sing a song; and at the end the villain is engulfed, defiant to the last.   Shadwell mars the effect of the scenes with the statue by introducing a buffoonish servant, whose terror does not add to the impressiveness of the incidents; but they are so lacking in poetry and illusion that the farcical details are really of little moment.

It is clear from this brief survey that the ghosts in Restoration tragedy are mere Elizabethan survivals, shorn of all their power to excite awe, and used solely as spectacular stage figures.   Often they do not speak; and when they do it is with no added effect.   Another Elizabethan survival is the devil-motive, which occurs in *The Duke of Guise*, also by Dryden and Lee, in the form of a sub-plot which embodies the familiar theme of the delusive contract.   Shadwell reworked the *Lancashire Witches*, but the resulting piece is not significant. Some incidental allusions to ghosts occur in the plays of the period, but the specimens above quoted suffice to give an idea of their character, as well as of that of the numerous portents, of which we may fairly say, in the opening words of *All for Love:*

> Portents and Prodigies are grown so frequent
> That they have lost their Name.

Non-speaking ghosts, it may be noted, also occur at the end of Otway's *Venice Preserved* (1682).

The supernatural in the Restoration period, then, is a meaningless survival from a better time, with no real relation to the new age, and with no merit in its treatment. It does show how strong was the tradition which brought ghosts into a drama dominated by ideals hostile to them, and written in an age which had no real interest in such subjects. Any other value than this purely indicative one is not easily discoverable in it; and an examination of the cases in question fails to disclose in them any artistic traits which have independent value, or even the merit of satisfactory copying of a great original.

SECTION 2. — THE EIGHTEENTH CENTURY

The opening of the eighteenth century marks no especial change in the dramatic development, except that the growing desire for correctness of taste and adherence to accepted models gradually relegates the ghosts to mere narrative, instead of actual representation. The change is of course gradual, and by no means complete; but there is an evident decline in the number of actually visible apparitions. This period may accordingly be passed over rather briefly, with note merely of a few typical cases.

The work of Nicholas Rowe, who was active in the first years of the century, shows how feeble the Elizabethan tradition had become, though he does not abandon it altogether.   In *The Fair Penitent* (1703) the last act contains various macabre elements, but no actual ghost.   The scene is " a room hung with black; on one side Lothario's Body on a Bier; on the other a Table, with a Scull and other Bones."   This speech from *Ulysses* (1705) is a sample of what the age regarded as the Elizabethan manner:

> The fatal Moment comes, ev'n that dread Time
> When Witches meet to gather Herbs on Graves,
> When discontented Ghosts forsake their Tombs,
> And ghastly roam about, and doleful grone;
> And hark! the Screech-Owl screams, and beats the Window
> With deadly Wings.

An apparition of Pallas in the clouds also adorns this act.

Similar ghostly narratives occur in the work of Aaron Hill. His *Elfrid* (1710) contains a description by Athelwold of the appearance of his father's ghost.   As he was riding in a storm he was thrown from his horse; as he rose he felt the touch of a dead hand, and beheld

> The shrowded ghost of my dear ancient father,
> In the sad posture of a man who mourns! . . .
> And while my knocking knees bent to the earth,
> That in the posture of an aweful duty
> I might desire to know the mighty cause
> Which broke the peaceful marble he was laid in
> To send him back to earth in this strange form,
> Ev'n while the half-born words dy'd on my tongue,
> He seem'd to weep, groaned thrice, and vanish'd from me.

In *The Roman Revenge* (1753) Calphurnia tells Caesar how Portia in a dream

> Saw her father's entering shadow
> Glide thro' her chamber, in a dusky ray;
> Stopping, it fix'd a pale and empty eye,

Spoke, in a thin, faint, death-denoting voice,
And pierced her to the soul. — *Portia, thou'rt mine*,
Th'embodied phantom cry'd. — It said, and pass'd,
And melted into air, and flow'd away.   (i. 4.)

In such cases as these the supernatural is obviously at a very low ebb indeed, and has become the most negligible of decorative survivals.   A real interest in the supernatural was of course alien to the spirit of the age; and though various writers engaged in the discussion of its proper artistic use, it was with little effect on the actual treatment of it, especially in dramatic form.

Interesting evidence of the failure of the age to comprehend the true spirit in which the supernatural should be employed is furnished by two Shakespearean adaptations of this period in which the ghosts of the original are retained, but all their impressiveness is lost.   The first of these is Colley Cibber's *Richard III* (1700).   The skill with which he avoids conveying any of the merits of the original into his reworking is remarkable.   The scene begins with a monologue by Richard; at the end of it he hears a groan, which he explains as due to the wind, or else to his fancy.   He sleeps, and the ghosts rise, all at once, and only four in number, those of King Henry, Anne, and the young Princes.   They harangue and moralize, with no trace of the refrains which added so much to the force of the original scene; and Richard's monologue after their disappearance is much docked, and inept.   " O Catesby, I have had such horrid dreams! " he remarks, after the other has entered; but his horror is scarcely shared by the reader.

In 1722 John Sheffield, Duke of Buckingham, published a reworking of *Julius Caesar*, which he reduced to the classic norm by dividing it into two plays.   It is in the second of them, *Marcus Brutus*, that the ghost appears.   In iii. 5

we have the visit of the ghost to Brutus. "Enter a spirit in the shape of Caesar, full of wounds," with whom Brutus has a considerable dialogue, of a rather quibbling kind. The impressiveness of the original is of course wholly lost. When Brutus kills himself, the ghost momentarily appears and vanishes, not speaking. The reference to "a spirit in the shape of Caesar," and the impersonal way in which Caesar is referred to by the phantom, suggest that the reviser has ceased to regard the ghost as actual. As a result, all the other allusions to the ghost, so important in Shakespeare, are omitted, and the subtlety by which the revenge-ghost is made the unifying principle of the original is wholly abandoned. The two adaptations show how utterly unable were their authors to enter into the spirit of their model, or even to reproduce him with fidelity.

An interesting backwater of the English tradition occurs, curiously enough, in France, where Voltaire's study of Shakespeare led him to try his hand at introducing ghosts into tragedy. He makes his experiment in two plays with practically identical plots, *Eriphyle* (1732) and *Semiramis* (1748). In the former the ghost of Amphiaraus appears (iv. 3) to Alcmeon, who is unwittingly about to marry his mother, Eriphyle, and demands vengeance on her as responsible for his death. The incident is absolutely unimpressive, but Voltaire claims to rival Aischylos! In the *Dissertation sur la Tragédie* prefixed to *Semiramis* he expounds his theory of ghosts, approving of their use only with reservations. "Je ne voudrais pas," he says, "comme Shakespeare, faire apparaître à Brutus son mauvais génie." He clings to the old Renaissance doctrine that supernatural figures must be used only for decoration, though he does admit that they should arouse terror. What he does not see is that his method is absolutely incapable of attaining any

such end.   The ghost in *Semiramis* has precisely the same
function as Amphiaraus, except that he is made more
incredible by appearing without warning in the midst of an
assembly.   One can fairly say that Voltaire as a competitor
of Shakespeare or Aischylos in the use of the supernatural
cuts a rather poor figure.

The remainder of the century brings no new life into the
field of the dramatic supernatural in England.   The dawning romantic impulse expressed itself most readily in other
forms, and found but a pale and tardy reflex in the drama.
John Home's *Fatal Discovery* (1769) shows the influence of
the Ossianic poems in the narrative put into the mouth of
Orellan in act iii.   In his youth he unwittingly slew his
betrothed and her brother; he has spent the rest of his life
in expiation, as a hermit, and once every year

> From the skies
> Descend the shadows of the murder'd pair,
> Pale as the colors of the lunar bow.
> Hov'ring before the cavern's mouth they spread
> Their arms; they fix on me their pitying eyes,
> And with a shriek they vanish into air.

No really new element is discernible in this speech.

Even the rise of the " terrific school " of fiction produced
but little effect on the drama, and resulted in nothing really
novel.   Horace Walpole's *Mysterious Mother* (1768) plays
with all the materials of horror, including ghostly narratives,
but contains no presented ghost.   The opening lines, in the
new Gothic manner

> What awful silence! how these antique towers
> And vacant courts dull the suspended soul,
> Till expectation wears the cast of fear;
> And fear, half-ready to become devotion,
> Mumbles a kind of mental orison,
> It knows not wherefore —

show how far this style is from any originality or novelty of effect.   The only other product of the movement which we need examine is Lewis' *Castle Spectre* (1797), which attained immense popularity by its ingenious accumulation of all the stock devices for arousing terror.   There is of course no real thrill in them, and the appearance of the spectre at the end of act iv is almost wholly a matter of stage management, with its music and lights.   When at the end the spectre once more appears, to intervene in the combat between the villain and the long-lost victim, it is in absolutely futile fashion, neither prepared for nor necessitated by the action. The *Castle Spectre* represents the lowest conceivable point in the degradation of the supernatural, and has not the remotest affiliation to genuine tragedy.   With it the English tradition reaches its lowest ebb and requires a complete change of direction if anything vital is again to be achieved.

We have thus traced a steady decline in the handling of the supernatural from the time of the Restoration down, and seen the absolute futility in which it ended.   It should, however, not be forgotten that serious drama is the form in which this period expressed itself to the least advantage. We perceive here the beginning of a movement of great significance for our own day — the creation of new avenues for the expression of the interest in the supernatural.   The eighteenth century marks the beginning of prose fiction as a recognized literary form; and we have seen that the romantic impulse which produced the school of Mrs. Radcliffe and her fellows is most active in the sphere of the novel.   Lyric poetry, too, claims a share in the tendency, from the time of Collins and Gray on.   This gradual expansion of the field, which leads beyond the scope of our present study, can be followed in Thürnau's excellent monograph, *Die Geister in der eng. Literatur des 18. Jahrhunderts.*   We must, therefore, realize that by confining our attention to the drama, and to serious drama, we are approaching the period just discussed precisely where it is weakest, and so need not wonder at the poor quality of the plays we have been considering.   What they show is essentially the decay of the strong Elizabethan tradition amid a long series of adverse conditions; and with the close of the century we come definitely to the end of an era.

CHAPTER VII

THE MODERN REVIVAL

THE task which confronts us in this final chapter is by no means a simple one. We have to consider a literary movement which is still in process, with no certainty of being able to reach final conclusions as to the materials at hand. Moreover, the scattered character of modern publishing makes the various plays more difficult to collect as one comes nearer the present day. Finally, the drama is but one channel for the expression of the modern interest in the supernatural, and by no means the most important one; so that our survey can be in any case but partial. Yet on the other hand we do perceive in the past century unmistakable signs of a revival of interest in the tragic supernatural in many quarters; and our study would be manifestly incomplete if we left such indications out of account. Bearing in mind, then, the double limitation under which we labor — the wide scattering of the dramatic field, and its incomplete expression of its age — let us see what can be derived for our purpose from an inspection of certain selected but typical modern aspects.

SECTION I. — THE REVIVAL IN ENGLAND

The new movement in English literature which had its official beginning with the publication of the *Lyrical Ballads* in 1798, and which so speedily changed the whole aspect of English poetry, could not succeed in raising the drama from its rut of mediocrity. Despite the fact that an important contribution of this movement was a renewed interest in the supernatural, the drama remained impervious to its influence. I can detect no sign of a really novel treatment of such a theme in drama before that singular production, *Death's Jest-Book*, by Thomas Lovell Beddoes. It was practically finished by 1826, though Beddoes continued to revise it almost till the end of his life, and it was not published till 1850, after his death. It could thus exercise practically no direct influence; but from a purely literary standpoint it is highly significant. It represents a genuine return to the Elizabethans, of whom Beddoes was a close and sympathetic student; but it infuses into the adopted motives a novelty of feeling which we must recognize as modern.

At the bottom of the play lies the old theme of revenge. Duke Melveric has in the past slain the father of two brothers, Wolfram and Isbrand. Wolfram has forgotten the crime, and becomes the brother in arms of Melveric; but Isbrand broods on revenge, and assumes the disguise of court fool as an aid to his designs. Word is brought that Melveric, who is absent on a crusade, has been captured by the Saracens, and Wolfram sets forth to rescue him. He succeeds in his mission, but the two quarrel over the maiden Sibylla, whom they both love; she loves Wolfram, and Melveric treacherously kills him. It is of course given out that he was killed in battle; his body is brought home, and given honorable burial, but Isbrand suspects the truth, and is whetted in his desire for vengeance. Melveric returns to his realm in disguise, to find that his two sons, secretly incited by Isbrand, are trying to usurp the rule. At this point the supernatural motive begins to make its appearance. In a scene between Isbrand and his friend Siegfried (ii. 3) we learn from the latter that Melveric and Wolfram once made a death-compact, by the terms of which

> Who died first
> Should, on death's holidays, revisit him
> Who still dwelt in the flesh.

This at once rouses Isbrand to the following extraordinary rhapsody, which serves as a good specimen of Beddoes' peculiar power of imaginative expression:

> O that such bond
> Would move the jailor of the grave to open
> Life's gate again unto my buried brother
> But half an hour! Were I buried, like him,
> There in the very garrets of death's town,
> But six feet under earth, (that's the grave's sky),
> I'd jump up into life. But he's a quiet ghost;
> He walks not in the churchyard after dew,
> But gets to his grave betimes, burning no glow-worms,
> Sees that his bones are right, and stints his worms
> Most miserly.

He further says that he has put Wolfram's body into the grave of Melveric's wife, that the murderer may one day be buried beside his victim. This uncanny act becomes the means by which a subtler vengeance than Isbrand designed is brought about. The disguised Duke joins a band of conspirators gathered by Isbrand, who meet in a churchyard (iii. 3). The episode may have been partly suggested by Tourneur, but the result is different enough. After the departure of most of the conspirators Melveric remains in talk with Isbrand and Siegfried, and they come to discourse of the raising of the dead, a theme naturally suggested by their surroundings. Ziba, the Duke's Arab slave, declares it possible, and says that he himself has the power to accomplish it. He explains his method, on the analogy of the raising of a plant, in this weirdly imaginative passage:

> *Duke.* This was a cheat;
> The herb was born anew out of a seed,
> Not raised out of a bony skeleton.
> What tree is man the seed of?

Ziba. Of a ghost;
Of his night-coming, tempest-wavéd phantom;
And even as there is a round dry grain
In a plant's skeleton, which being buried
Can raise the herb's green body up again;
So is there such in man, a seed-shaped bone,
Aldabaron, called by the Hebrews Luz,
Which, being laid into the ground, will bear,
After three thousand years, the grass of flesh,
The bloody, soul-possesséd weed called man.

After the others have gone the Duke puts him to the test,
bidding him raise his beloved wife, whose tomb is near by.
The evocation succeeds, but it brings back to the light the
new inmate of the grave, Wolfram — not a mere phantom,
but in his old body. The Duke tries to convince himself
that he is deluded; but Wolfram parries his sword-thrusts,
and tells him that when he returns to the grave it will be
with Melveric as companion.

The singular novelty of this conception of the ghost is
obvious at a glance. We can see the Elizabethan elements
which helped to form it — Tourneur, as already mentioned,
the *Second Maiden's Tragedy*, which Beddoes greatly
admired, and perhaps the ghost of Jack in *The Old Wives
Tale* — but the result is something essentially new. Beddoes succeeds in combining the eeriness of a departed spirit
with the grosser horror of a resuscitated corpse, and yet in
making the composite phantom awesome without repul-
siveness. The revived Wolfram goes through the rest of
the play, revealing his identity to Sibylla, who dies shortly
thereafter, and watching the fatal quarrels of the Duke's
two sons, one of whom kills the other and afterwards com-
mits suicide when taxed with the deed. Isbrand, who has
usurped the dukedom, is rather casually slain by one of his
adherents, but the Duke's hopes are crushed by the deaths
of Sibylla and his sons, and at the close he follows Wolfram

into the sepulchre. It must be admitted that the plot is rather arbitrarily brought to an end in these latter acts; but Beddoes' imagination succeeds in maintaining the peculiar quality of the play throughout. The final scene is a good instance of this. It is laid in the churchyard, and begins with a dance of Deaths, who descend from the wall, and sport to grotesque song and music. At the end of the banquet which is held by Isbrand, Wolfram bids them return, and dance to cheer the company. In the midst of their dance the body of Adalmar, the murdered son, is brought in. " What's this, another mummery ? " asks the Duke; and Wolfram, with atrocious irony, replies, " The antimasque, I think they call it; 'tis satirical." So Wolfram's vengeance is attained, as he proclaims in the closing lines of the play:

> Melveric, all is finished, which to witness
> The spirit of retribution called me hither.
> Thy sons have perished for like cause, as that
> For which thou didst assassinate thy friend.
> Sibylla is before us gone to rest.
> Blessing and Peace to all who are departed!
> But thee, who daredst to call up into life,
> And the unholy world's forbidden sunlight,
> Out of his grave him who reposed softly,
> One of the ghosts doth summon, in like manner,
> Thee, still alive, into the world o' the dead.

One cannot assert that this singular play is a masterpiece of dramatic construction; but its remarkable imaginative quality, its admirable dramatic moments, and its utter novelty of conception, give it a place apart. Beddoes himself, it should be noted, judged his own work with ruthless and excessive severity, and applied to *Death's Jest-Book* phrases which could not fairly be used by the least sympathetic critic.[1] It was his misfortune to have to work in a

[1] See his *Letters*, published by Edmund Gosse, London, 1894, *passim*.

singularly sterile period, and to be largely deprived, by his peculiar temperament, of stimulating intellectual companionship.   What he accomplished, however, in spite of all obstacles, entitles him to a place for which he has no rivals; and *Death's Jest-Book*, isolated though it is, is for us a highly significant document.

It is undeniable that Beddoes' return to the Elizabethans is an isolated phenomenon, prefiguring no general revival of such themes in English drama.   The most characteristic treatment of them has been in lyric poetry, beginning with the incomparable *Ancient Mariner*, and passing into a variety of shapes—some of Beddoes' own lyrics, for instance, and later the more emotional presentation in Christina Rossetti, who conveys with singular skill the pathos of the ghosts' unheeded return to the scenes of their mortal life. This change in choice of form is also to be traced in French poetry, from Gerard de Nerval's *Vers Dorés* to that haunting line of Mallarmé which sees in all us mortals only *la triste opacité de nos spectres futurs*, and to still more recent productions.   A study of such lyrics, including revivals of the ballad method, would be a fascinating task.   For us, however, in search of evidence of a new use of such motives in the drama, they must be left out of account.   Signs of a real awakening in that field are hardly to be discerned before our own day, when an unmistakably new spirit meets us in certain plays of the Celtic Revival.   Whatever the ultimate success of this movement, it has undeniably restored to the stage a converse with the deeper realities in which the spirit of tragedy resides, and we encounter a new sort of tragic supernatural, of which strangeness rather than sheer terror is the dominant trait.   We turn first naturally to the work of Mr. Yeats, coryphaeus of the school, and find in his *Land of Heart's Desire* an epitome of its peculiar quality.

The theme of the little play is familiar. The scene is a peasants' cottage, and the time May Eve. Maire Bruin, young and newly married, is reading a legend in an old book, despite the scornful words of Bridget, her mother-in-law. Even the priest, Father Hart, remonstrates with her in kindly fashion; but when she strews primroses before the door he commends her,

> Because God permits
> Great power to the good people on May Eve.

In response to mysterious knocks Maire offers milk and fire to unseen visitants, thus giving the house into the power of the fairies. Bridget reproaches her, but she declares that she is glad of what she has done, and wishes the fairies might take her away. The loving words of her husband Shawn bring her back to herself, and when a voice is heard singing in the distance she is afraid. A strange Child enters, and subdues them all to her charm, even inducing Father Hart to take down the crucifix which frightens her. At length she draws Maire to her, and strews primroses between them and the others, bidding Maire come with her

> Where nobody gets old and crafty and wise,
> Where nobody gets old and godly and grave,
> Where nobody gets old and bitter of tongue,
> And where kind tongues bring no captivity,
> For we are only true to the far lights
> We follow singing, over valley and hill.

Shawn calls her back in the name of their love, but the Child pleads against him, and in the struggle Maire dies, while the fairies take up their song in triumph around the house.

The Land of Heart's Desire shows in brief compass the new quality which the Celtic movement contributes to contemporary literature — the " strangeness in beauty " which brings us a sense of secret and incalculable powers, less personified than the familiar figures of classical mythology, and less subjected to the yoke of convention. The Celtic spirit can thus contribute more profitably to us than it could to the Elizabethans, with whom we last noted its possible influence. Then it was still a process of forgetting the ancient Gods; now the downward course is ended, and we can begin to remember. It supplies us with an impulse to the purely imaginative which is sorely needed under present conditions, and for which no other source is so immediately available. In the field of drama it has produced the only movement in the direction of essential tragedy at present discernible in English; and a survey of some of the works produced under its influence is very important for our estimate of tragedy to-day.

Mr. Yeats has made a more ambitious essay in the tragic supernatural in *The Countess Cathleen*, which tells how the Countess sold her soul to save her people, who had themselves been driven by famine to make such bargains with the demons. Her sacrifice enlists the favor of Heaven, and the demons are baffled. It might be objected that the theme is somewhat too theological for the present day, and that it has not the immediate appeal of *The Land of Heart's Desire*; but on any showing it deserves praise for its grappling with a more extended plot, and for its numerous felicities of detail.

With William Sharp, whose work, produced both under his own name and under a pseudonym, presents such a fascinating problem in double personality, we touch another phase of the movement. In 1894 he published under his own name a group of short plays, entitled *Vistas*,[1] suggesting the method of Maeterlinck, but largely written before their author had become acquainted with the Belgian's

---

[1] Chicago, Stone and Kimball (The Green Tree Library).

work.   The piece most relevant to our subject is *A Northern Night*, which may be summarized as a specimen.   Two lovers, Malcolm and Helda, have fled from a merrymaking to a deserted castle.   Helda is to be married to a rich old man, Archibald Graeme; but Malcolm wins her away with him, and they spend their night of love together.   All through the night some strange presence seems to be about them, in a puff of cold air, a sifting of snow against the window, a sound in the corridor, perceptible only to Helda. As they return in the morning they meet a servant, who tells them that Graeme has just been found dead in his bed, and must have died at midnight.   The explanation of the sounds is obvious.   The play is more interesting for its essay toward a new form than for its actual accomplishment, but it does convey its impression of uncanny mystery with considerable skill.

In *The Immortal Hour*, published under the pen-name of Fiona Macleod, we have a poetical treatment of a Celtic theme, the wooing of the fairy Etain by a mortal, and her return to her own world at the call of Midir, her fellow.   The play, by no means metrically impeccable, does produce a very individual impression.   It seems to be enacted on the very verge of mortality, from the gulf beyond which its supernatural visitants emerge, and into which they return. Through it moves the strange figure of Dalua, the Fool of the Gods, a personification of the sinister secret forces of the world, who beguiles the mortal king Eochaidh into his love for Etain, and takes his life at the end, when she has left him, and he cries out despairingly for his lost dreams — " There is none left but this — the dream of death." Quotation can give little idea of the strange charm of the piece, which makes itself felt through a form which is not fully achieved.   It is perhaps the closest approach to an actual embodiment of a Celtic myth in purely mythical terms that the new movement can show.

In J. M. Synge's *Riders to the Sea*, on the other hand, we have a grimly realistic piece.   The scene is an island off the west coast of Ireland, in the hut of Maurya, an old woman whose sons have all save one been lost at sea.   At the opening of the play her two daughters are examining the clothes of a body found in the north, which proves to be that of Michael, the son last drowned.   The sole survivor, Bartley, is about to take ship in order to go and sell a horse; Maurya seeks to dissuade him, but he goes, leaving behind the bread that he is to take with him.   Maurya goes to bring it to him, but soon returns, saying that she saw behind him the wraith of Michael, portending Bartley's death:

Bartley came first on the red mare; and I tried to say ' God speed you,' but something choked the words in my throat.   He went by quickly; and ' the blessing of God on you,' says he, and I could say nothing.   I looked up then, and I crying, at the gray pony, and there was Michael upon it — with fine clothes on him, and new shoes on his feet. . . .   Bartley will be lost now, and let you call in Eamon and make me a good coffin out of the white boards, for I won't live after them.

In a moment a group of old women enter, and Bartley is brought in, drowned as he was crossing a ford.   " They're all gone now," says Maurya, " and there isn't anything more the sea can do to me; " but she is old, and submissive to Fate:

Michael had a clean burial in the far north, by the grace of the Almighty God.   Bartley will have a fine coffin out of the white boards, and a deep grave surely.   What more can we want than that ? No man at all can be living for ever, and we must be satisfied.

The concentrated power of this little play is extraordinary. With absolutely no forcing of the effect we receive a terrifying impression of the might of the sea, a remorseless power which has seized one member of the family after another, and will not be satisfied till it has taken even the last. The sea is magnified by Synge into an elemental force which takes on the attributes of the supernatural.

Finally, we have in the work of a very recent writer, Gordon Bottomley, a noteworthy attempt at the combination of Celtic and Northern feeling in a curious piece, *The Crier by Night*, issued in 1902.[1] A reviewer in the *Academy* declared it to be modelled on *The Land of Heart's Desire* — presumably because that was the only Celtic play he knew. As a matter of fact, it owes something to "Fiona Macleod's" metrical technique, and a good deal to Mr. Bottomley's own imaginative power. The story is very simple. A Norseman, Hialti, and his wife Thorgerd have an Irish bondmaid, Blanid. Thorgerd hates her thrall with ingeniously fiendish jealousy, while Blanid loves her master for the mere human kindness which he bestows upon her. Near their cottage is a ford, haunted by an evil spirit, the Crier of the title. Blanid, to gain revenge on Thorgerd, uses her Celtic knowledge of spells to call the Crier to her, that she may secure her vengeance at the price of her own life. The lines in which she reaches her decision are a good specimen of Mr. Bottomley's style:

> O, I would sleep in that old Crier's arms,
> Enduring silence harder than all else,
> A mote shut into one cold, kneaded eyelid
> Of the dead mere, and dream into the wind,
> And cling to stars lest I should slip thro' space,
> And dream I was the body of him I love
> Who yields me only kindness, never love —
> O me, that misery of hopeless kindness;
> But I'll not die and leave him to her lips;

---

[1] Reprinted by Mr. Mosher in his *Bibelot*, xv. 299 (September, 1909).

Tho' I can never have him she shall not,
For I can use this body worn to a soul
To barter with that Crier of hidden things
That if he tangles him in his chill hair
Then I will follow and follow and follow and follow
Past where the imaged stars ebb past their light
And turn to water under the dark world.

The Crier answers her summons, " a stooping figure swathed in a rain-colored, rain-soaked cloak," and the bargain is made.   The Crier imitates the voices of a party of travellers lost at the ford; Hialti rushes out to their rescue, and is drowned.   The Crier then enters and claims Blanid, who rushes out into the night, after having vainly implored Thorgerd to hate her as she did before, and thus save her from the Crier's power.   The emotions of the play lie far from any ordinary circle of experience, and the characterization is of course very broad; but the piece does convey its sense of a sinister power that preys on human lives, and is clothed in a style of grim but compelling beauty.   Perhaps no more than an experiment, it is none the less individual and significant.

In a later and more achieved play, *The Riding to Lithend*, (1909),[1] we find Mr. Bottomley turning definitely to the North for his inspiration, and choosing from the Njal-Saga the thrilling theme of the death of Gunnar the Outlaw. The scene is in his great hall, where three serving-women talk of the doom that hangs over their master.   His wife Hallgerd, who has been the wife of two men, and the cause of their deaths, before Gunnar wedded her, stirs him to strife, since she knows that his foes are gathering.   The hound who is set to watch suddenly bays, and three hideous old women enter, Biartey, Jofrid and Gudfinn, craving

---

[1] Also reprinted in the *Bibelot*, xvi. 1 (January and February, 1910), and issued by Mr. Mosher as a separate volume, Portland, 1910.

shelter for the night, which Gunnar grants. It is soon evident that they are something unhuman: " Have ye birds'
feet to match such bat-webbed fingers ? " asks Steinvor,
one of the servants. One of the uncanny visitants takes a
distaff and spins; Hallgerd enters, and they converse with
her. A quarrel springs up, and Jofrid reveals a knowledge
of Hallgerd's past shame which makes her drive them forth,
while they chant a prophecy of Gunnar's doom. Gunnar,
entering just after they have vanished, declares that he has
met no one. The foes gather outside; Gunnar shakes his
bill, which sings on the eve of battle. He fights valiantly,
and with success, until one of the assailants cuts his bow-
string, and Hallgerd refuses him her hair to twist another.
At length he is slain, but his slayers will not touch anything
that belonged to him. Rannveig, his mother, tries to kill
Hallgerd, but she escapes. The last picture is that of Rannveig, bending over her son, and lifting up the bill, to find
that it still sings:

> You had a rare toy when you were awake —
> I 'll wipe it with my hair. . . . Nay, keep it so,
> The color on it now has gladdened you.
> It shall lie near you.
>   No, it remembers him,
> And other men shall fall by it thro' Gunnar:
> The bill, the bill is singing. . . . The bill sings!

This brief summary of course gives no idea of the march of
the drama, which is remarkably compact and well-knit; but
it serves to show the skill with which the ominous old
women are introduced to heighten our sense of foreboding.
In this play Mr. Bottomley is well on the road to an individual dramatic accomplishment, and it is a very encouraging
symptom of the possible growth of a new branch of poetic
tragedy.

We have thus briefly considered certain salient manifestations of a new tragic spirit in English drama which are visible in our own day, and which may point to a revival of the tragic supernatural in our own tongue.   The plays here discussed are by no means all that could be adduced, though they are the cases most significant from our particular standpoint.   There are such works as Mr. Hardy's *Dynasts*, with its curious metaphysical machinery of Immanent Will, Spirits Ironic and Sinister, and the rest; or, in our own country, Mr. Moody's noble *Masque of Judgment*.   There are also plays outside the field of tragedy which employ motives bordering on the supernatural, such as *The Witching Hour* of Mr. Thomas — plays which at all events indicate the appeal of such themes to the average playgoer.   Whether these various manifestations really point to an enduring revival of tragedy in our own day is a question which must be reserved for discussion in the light of all our accumulated evidence.

SECTION 2. — HENRIK IBSEN

The Northern element which we have just been discussing in the work of Mr. Bottomley naturally brings us to a consideration of the greatest Scandinavian dramatist of the time, Ibsen.   His plays offer us the interesting phenomenon of a supernatural thread running through a series of pieces, the tone of which is in general realistic.   This state of affairs is not one which is easily covered by the current conception of realism; but it is possible to show why this interest appears in Ibsen's work, and also to appraise its contribution to our discussion.

It must first be remembered that, before Ibsen began the composition of those social dramas by which he is best known, he had produced a number of important works of a

purely imaginative sort.   Always deeply interested in the
annals of his native land, he sets himself, in his first really
individual play, *The Vikings at Helgeland* (1858), to treat a
theme from Norse legend in a manner which combines elements from both mythological and historical sagas.   The
plot is really based on the legend of Sigurd and Brynhild,
but the legendary motive is reduced to the status of one of
the sagas of family history.   This composite method of
treatment naturally involves the sacrifice of the supernatural features of the mythical narrative, except insofar as
they can be retained for decoration, as at the close, when the
child Egil sees in a vision the ride of the dead heroes to
Valhal, with his mother, who has just slain herself because of
her failure to win the love of Sigurd, at their head.   The
supernatural details thus come naturally into the play by
virtue of their existence in its source, whence they could not
fail to be transferred by any observant worker; but they
remain only details, picturesque indeed, but nothing more.

It required some time for Ibsen to work free of the romantic tendencies which he took over from the Danish and
German authors who were in favor when he began to write;
and in his first actual masterpiece, *The Pretenders* (1863), we
find an odd outcropping of this romantic interest.   The
play is a superb treatment of a theme from Norse history,
the struggle of Håkon and Skule for the kingship of Norway,
ending in the triumph of the former.   Into this prevailingly
realistic drama is brought a flagrantly romantic episode —
the apparition of a ghost in the last act.   Bishop Nicholas,
the rascally churchman who has tried to win his own profit
from the struggle, but whose plans are cut short by his
death in act iii, appears to Skule, who is defeated and a
fugitive.   The apparition in itself is not indefensible; the
ghost offers to help Skule to the kingship if he will make

sure that his son, who has committed sacrilege, shall succeed him on the throne.   Skule sees that the offer is designed to deliver Norway into the hands of the powers of darkness, and rejects it.   This certainly is not a faulty basis for the introduction of a ghost: but Ibsen chooses to make the incident essentially satirical, letting the ghost at the end directly address the audience, with an attack on contemporary Norwegian conditions.   This breaking of the illusion is deliberate and inexcusable: and Ibsen's ill-timed satire recoils upon him, to the injury of the artistic value of the incident.   The fault, however, lies in the tone which is given it, not in the introduction of the incident itself, which, as we have seen, has a certain relevancy to the drama as a whole, and certainly testifies to Ibsen's interest in the supernatural.

In *Brand* (1865), which marks the beginning of Ibsen's wider fame, we have some incidental use of the supernatural at the close, when Brand is tempted by a phantom in the shape of his dead wife, while after the avalanche has swept him away a voice is heard proclaiming " He is the God of Love."   There is also a thread of Norwegian folklore in connection with the half-mad gipsy girl Gerd which prefigures the use of such motives in the astounding *Peer Gynt* (1867).   That poem is steeped in the atmosphere of Norwegian popular tradition, now used for purposes of satire, as in Peer's adventures in the Troll-King's palace, now gruesomely mysterious, as in his encounter with the Böjg, the unseen impalpable monster which cannot be successfully attacked.   It is in the last act, when Peer returns to Norway after his life of wandering, that these elements are most prominent.   Peer's encounter on shipboard with the mysterious Stranger, who bargains with him for his corpse after the wreck; the wonderful lyric scene in which he is reproached by voices representing his sins of omission — the thread-balls that are thoughts, the broken straws that are deeds, and finally by his mother's voice — his meeting with the Button-Moulder who intends to melt him in his ladle, and his attempt to get certification from the Troll-King and a parson (who turns out to be the devil) that he has really sinned, and really been himself; and the conclusion, with the Button-Moulder baffled by Solveig's enduring and forgiving love, but still lurking in the background — all this, with its strange mixture of irony and seriousness, makes an employment of the supernatural which it is hard to fit into our definitions, and which is by no means prevailingly tragic, but which demands mention for its imaginative daring and its novel variety.

During the period of purely imaginative composition which produced *Brand* and *Peer Gynt* Ibsen was also preoccupied with the idea of a great historical drama on a Roman theme. This idea came to him as early as 1864, at his first sight of Italy, and after various developments and modifications resulted in *Emperor and Galilean*, not finally completed till 1873. The first of the social dramas, *The Young Men's League*, had been finished in 1869, so that *Emperor and Galilean* has peculiar importance as a transitional work. It has for us an additional interest in that it contains a supernatural element no longer decorative, as in the plays we have previously examined, but vital to the conduct of the plot. We shall therefore discuss this play in some detail, both for its inherent interest and its peculiar value in illustrating Ibsen's treatment of the supernatural.

Emperor and Galilean consists of two five-act plays, which treat the career of Julian from his youth in Constantinople to his death in the luckless expedition against Persia. As a result of the extent of the work, and the time occupied in its composition, Ibsen's ideal and method changed considerably during its course, with a consequent lack of harmony between the two parts.   It was begun as a simple attempt to reproduce antiquity as accurately as possible, the chosen period being that of Julian's vain struggle against the advance of Christianity, a period in which the opposing forces, taking shape in definite personages, made themselves susceptible of dramatic treatment.   During the actual composition of the work, however, Ibsen was in Dresden, and witnessed the stirring scenes which accompanied the founding of the German Empire in 1868 and 1870.   In consequence of this new influence he desired to inform his historical reconstruction with a philosophical concept, the idea of the "third empire" in which paganism and Christianity are ultimately to merge.   This later intrusion of the philosophical idea is responsible for the changes in the character of the work as it progresses, and while it impairs the artistic unity of the whole, it throws a very interesting light on Ibsen's thought in this period of his development.

The first play, *Caesar's Apostasy*, is frankly a reconstruction of antiquity, executed with admirable vividness.   The first act passes in Constantinople, with satire of the warring sects and the imperial court, amid which Julian, scholar and dreamer, is ill at ease.   He is eager to join battle with the forces of paganism, and is urged on by the visit of a friend of his boyhood, Agathon, who has come in consequence of a strange vision.   This vision, it appears, bade Agathon seek out him who should inherit the empire, and urge him to enter the lions' den and do battle with the lions.   Julian is thus confirmed in his resolution; he secures from the emperor permission to withdraw from court, and at length proceeds to Athens, where we find him in act ii.   Satire of the philosophers matches that of the Christian sects in the preceding act; but the plot does not markedly advance until the sophist Libanius, who has returned from a hurried visit to the Piraeus to secure two wealthy youths just landed there, brings news of Maximus the Mystic, and definitely introduces the most fascinating character of the entire drama. The name of Maximus had come out during Julian's colloquy with Agathon in the preceding act, and Julian's reluctance to have him mentioned indicates a secret preoccupation with the man of whom so many marvels are reported. Now Libanius brings explicit tidings: Maximus has averred that he has power over spirits and shades of the dead, and supported his assertion by the working of miracles. Julian is whirled away by a frenzy of eagerness; in spite of sarcasm and entreaty he tears himself away, declaring that he sees a light on his path; he goes " where torches light themselves, and where statues smile."

The third act, which from the standpoint of the mystic element in the plot is the finest in the entire work, passes in Ephesus. Julian has made the acquaintance of Maximus, and has advanced on the road to his hidden wisdom. At the opening of the act, the Christians Basil and Gregory appear, on their way home to Cappadocia. Julian, warned by a vision of their coming, has made preparations to receive them, and is eager to impart to them the new light that he has received. Overwrought with excitement, he tells them of the empire which he thinks himself on the point of attaining. He confirms his expectation by the vision which appeared to one Apollinaris of Sidon, bidding him prepare a purple robe. His wild speeches naturally repel his guests, and after a vain attempt to dissuade him they depart, just before Maximus enters. On this night he is to reveal to Julian the secret which shall make clear his future course. A banquet is prepared, and they seat themselves; Julian hears mysterious rustlings and whisperings beside him, and starts up excitedly, as Maximus proclaims " We are five at table! " A great wind rushes through the house; the table lamps seem on the point of extinction, while over the great bronze lamp which Maximus has kindled rises a bluish circle of light. Julian, gazing into it, sees a strange countenance, which he proceeds to question. He is told that it is his mission to establish the empire, by the way of freedom, which is also the way of necessity. This way is to be found by him who wills. He asks eagerly what he must will, but the voice only wails his name, and the light vanishes. In perplexity he asks Maximus what is meant, and is told that there are three empires: that founded on the tree of knowledge, that founded on the tree of the Cross, and the third which is to come, and which shall unite the other two. Julian hears the whispering again, and demands to be shown his guests. Maximus reluctantly consents. The first of them is Cain, whose voice declares that the fruit of his sin was life, but the ground of life is death; and when Julian asks what is the ground of death, the voice sighs, "Ah, *that* is the riddle! " Julian compels Maximus to summon the second; he proves to be Judas, who was chosen to help in the supreme task. " Did the Master foreknow when he chose thee ? " asks Julian; and the voice again sighs, "Ah, *that* is the riddle! " Julian demands the third; Maximus tries vainly to summon him, and suddenly realizes that his art is powerless, since the third is not yet among the shades. Julian, seizing on a remark that Maximus had let drop, to the effect that the third is with them, seeks to force him to reveal whether he is indeed the chosen one; then, realizing the responsibility he is incurring, he declares that he will not serve necessity in founding the third empire, and that he is free. At this moment a clamor is heard outside; soldiers force their way in, led by the quaestor Leontes, who informs Julian that he has been made Caesar in place of his brother Gallus, murdered for reasons of state. Leontes brings the purple robe, the emblem of sovereignty; and Julian, remembering the vision of the robe in Sidon, accepts it, in spite of Maximus' warning, " Sign against sign! "

Act iv transports us to Gaul, where Julian, as Caesar, has just won a great victory over the Alemanni. His popularity among the soldiers alarms the Emperor, who seeks to overthrow it by demanding that a large part of the Gallic troops be sent to the East, contrary to Julian's solemn promise to them that they should not be called on for foreign service. This naturally causes a revolt, and the situation speedily becomes critical. Julian's wife Helena, who has urged him to seize the opportunity and make himself emperor, is poisoned by fruit sent from Rome, and he learns from her ravings that she has been false to him, with Gallus. This revelation increases his hatred of the Christianity which the dead woman had professed. The soldiers grow more threatening; Julian is summoned to Rome, presumably to meet the same fate as Gallus, but appeals to the army, wins them over by an impassioned speech, and is proclaimed Emperor by them, in a scene of thrilling theatrical effectiveness.

The fifth act, a worthy climax to the whole, shows a return to the mystical aspect of the plot. It passes in the catacombs under the church where Helena's body lies in state. Below in the vaults Maximus is seeking to obtain omens from sacrifice; Julian stands above, anxiously awaiting the issue. His faithful partisan Sallust comes to him, tells him of the growing discontent in the army, and implores him to seize the supreme power ere it is too late. Julian is almost won over; Maximus ascends, declaring that he can gain no knowledge from the omens, and Julian pours out to him all the hatred of Christianity which has been slowly gathering in him, to be brought to a head by Helena's death and its attendant revelations.   Maximus reproaches him with lack of courage to will; and at that precise moment the chamberlain Eutherius descends with the news that Helena's sanctity is working miracles in the church overhead!   Julian's loathing for his former faith breaks into action; snatching the knife and fillet from Maximus he hurries down into the crypt to annul his baptismal covenant by a sacrifice to the old Gods.   The angry soldiers burst in; Julian, stained with blood, comes up from the crypt, wins back their allegiance, and leads them up through the church where the choir is chanting the Lord's Prayer.   So the decision is made, and Julian accepts the burden of empire, free, as he thinks, from all the shackles that have bound him in the past.

This first play is unquestionably an admirable dramatic achievement.   In it Ibsen works with a free hand; and though he rearranges the sequence of events, in certain cases, for the convenience of his plot, and introduces sundry fictitious characters, he presents a faithful picture of this part of Julian's career.   We see him as a studious youth, forced, almost against his will, to plunge into a whirling sea of passions and events, and at length to assume the headship of the empire.   He trusts in his fortune, however, and is determined to reshape the world into conformity with his ideal.   The evolution of his character is evidently dependent on a supernatural element in the plot; such matters have a fascination for him which at length makes them determining factors in his change of attitude.   This mystical element, as we may call it, centres around the person of Maximus, and culminates in the symposium at Ephesus, which has a doctrinal purpose, but also a purely artistic value. Mr. Archer, with that curious aversion to such subjects which is one of the notes of our time, remarks, " There may be some question, indeed, as to the artistic legitimacy of the employment of the supernatural in the third act; but of its imaginative power there can be no doubt." As a matter of fact, it is primarily because of this slighting of this supernatural element in the second of the two plays that it falls into those faults which are so evident in it, and which Mr. Archer so justly deplores.

The main lines of the first play, it must be remembered, had been fixed by 1871; that is, before the change in Ibsen's view of world-history consequent on the foundation of the German Empire. It was undoubtedly as a result of meditation on this new event in European politics that he came to his notion of the " third empire," and to his theory of universal history as governed by the action of a " world-will " which steadily moves toward a far-off goal. He works out this conception by a method which is obviously intended to be more realistic than that of the first play, aiming at a minute reproduction of the period in question; but the result is much less satisfactory. The larger historical truth is mercilessly sacrificed to the petty detail, and the total effect is distorted and inaccurate. Julian, contrary to all the facts of his career, is made a savage persecutor of the Christians; and there is a vast deal of rhetoric in connection with utterly fictitious martyrdoms which is neither true to history nor dramatically sound. The first three acts are almost wholly barren of vital incident. Ibsen seems no longer to trust his own creative power; he paraphrases Julian's speeches and writings, and laboriously accumulates details which fail to give any semblance of actuality. Even the stage effects are inferior to those of the first play. Contrast the finale of act ii, where Julian is cursed for his apostasy by the blind bishop Maris, and the temple of Apollo is destroyed by an earthquake, with any of the climaxes of the first play, and see how much poorer in mere theatrical value the later example is. Some of the episodes in which the martyrs appear would be quite in place in an Elizabethan tragedy of blood.

On the other hand, the scenes in which Maximus figures, with the consequent return of the mystical element, at once rise to a higher level. The most obvious instance is the last scene of act iii. It is night; Julian and Maximus are seen among the ruins of the temple of Apollo. Julian realizes with increasing clearness that he is pitted against a power of incalculable might; that the Galilean lives on potently in the souls of those whom he has brought to his faith. Maximus reminds him of the symposium at Ephesus, and the discourse about the three empires. He declares that Julian has been following the wrong course; he has striven to restore the past, to make the youth a child again. Such an attempt is vain; but in the fullness of time shall come that third empire which shall reconcile Emperor and Redeemer in a higher unity, brought to being in the man who wills himself. Julian, in a sudden burst of resolution, declares that he will reopen the war against Persia, and finish the work of empire which Alexander began; and so he hastens away into the night, while Maximus looks after him thoughtfully. Merely in its ideas the scene is significant; but it contributes directly to the forming of a decision on Julian's part, and so is justified by its relevancy to the progress of the plot.

The last two acts deal with this expedition against Persia, and its end in Julian's defeat and death. For much of their course a medley of details obscures the deeper movement of the drama; but we catch glimpses of the tragic conflict in

Julian's soul. Thus in v. 2 he narrates a vision, in which he thought he had cleansed the earth of Galileans, but at the end Christ passes before him, bearing his cross; and he reflects:

Where is he now ? What if that at Golgotha, near Jerusalem, was but a wayside matter, a thing done, as it were, in passing, in a leisure hour ? What if he goes on and on, and suffers, and dies, and conquers, again and again, from world to world ?

His military position grows constantly more dangerous; at last he joins battle with the Persians, fights desperately in the thickest of the fray, and is borne off mortally wounded. A touch of antique tragic irony appears here; it had been foretold to him that danger threatened him from the Phrygian regions, and now he learns that the battlefield was called Phrygia, from an obscure village in the neighborhood. He realizes that the powers beyond have betrayed him, and that death is sure. It comes indeed almost at once. Word is brought to those around the death-bed that the Galilean Jovian has been proclaimed emperor. Maximus comments bitterly on the news — " Led astray like Cain. Led astray like Judas. — Your God is a spendthrift God, Galileans! He wears out many souls." Yet even if Julian was not the chosen instrument of the new empire, the third empire shall yet come, and offerings of atonement be made to Julian and to his two guests of the symposium.

Two plays more widely different in method and result than the two parts of *Emperor and Galilean* could scarcely be found. In the first of them Ibsen gives his imagination free play, and produces a picture of the time which is accurate in spirit, if not minutely faithful in detail; in the second he subordinates the creative impulse to the imparting of a philosophical concept, and kills the dramatic movement in the process. When we see how much the impressiveness of the first part is enhanced by the presence of the mystical element, and how invariably the second gains in real power when that element recurs, we are justified in feeling that if Ibsen had subordinated to it his accuracy of detail, instead of adopting a contrary course, he would have produced a more satisfactory and unified piece of work.

I have dwelt thus in detail on *Emperor and Galilean* because it is the play of Ibsen's which has the most considerable supernatural element, and because it shows us an important transitional stage in his mental evolution.   With the social dramas we enter that domain of pure realism foreshadowed by the method of the second play, and for a time have no more concern with supernatural themes. Gradually, however, an almost uneasy consciousness of such matters creeps into the social dramas, and results at length in a peculiar and characteristic manner of treating them. Mr. William Archer, whose comments I have already occasionally quoted, and to whose introductions to the several plays [1] I am largely indebted for valuable facts in the foregoing discussion, finds this method perfectly satisfactory, and praises it in several places.   He says, for example,

> He pursues the plan, which was also Hawthorne's, of carefully leaving us in doubt as to whether, and how far, any supernormal influence is at work.   (Introd. to *The Lady from the Sea*, p. xxix).

and again,

> The story he tells is not really, or rather not inevitably, supernatural.   Everything is explicable within the limits of nature; but supernatural agency is also vaguely suggested, and the reader's imagination is stimulated, without any violence to his sense of reality. (Introd. to *Little Eyolf*, pp. xi, xii.)

Now the difficulty, especially in accepting the comparison with Hawthorne, lies precisely in the fact that Ibsen's

---

[1] In *The Collected Works of Henrik Ibsen*, London, 1906–08.

method is to emphasize the ordinary, every-day character of his events to such a degree that the shift to the supernatural implications demands no inconsiderable effort. With Hawthorne the general tone is so subdued and mysterious that we have little difficulty in accepting the writer's invitation to take one step further, and admit that forces not human are at work; with Ibsen the prevailing method is just the opposite, and no natural fusion of the two spheres is effected. We turn abruptly from a sequence of wholly human events to an arbitrary summoning of the supernatural, unprepared for by anything in the plot itself, or, often, in the allusions. Even in *Rosmersholm*, where the idea of the dead as actual haunters finds occasional but striking expression, it is not really woven into the dramatic fabric; and though at the end, when Rebecca and Rosmer have thrown themselves into the mill-race, the housekeeper exclaims, " The dead wife has taken them! " we are scarcely disposed to accept the idea as a positive constituent of the play. It gives a momentary thrill, but demands no real assent. Can we call this a really satisfactory method ? It is purely decorative, and has no real connection with the plot; hence, if our previous criteria are sound, it is not a real solution of the problem, but a begging of the question. If we are not to take the supernatural seriously, why should it be introduced ? and if we do accept it in a narrowly realistic play, shall we feel more interest in Norwegian politics or in the eternal problems of life and death ?

Medieval records inform us that persons who succeeded in calling up the Devil often had trouble in dealing with him when once he had answered their summons. One might say something similar of the appearance of the supernatural in these later plays of Ibsen. In view of his poetical past one cannot call it a concession, nor precisely an intrusion; but it does not seem an absolutely natural consequence of his evolution.   It is apparent enough to cast a strange light on an ordinary train of events, but not sufficiently a part of the dramatic fabric to be really inevitable.   Perhaps it is enough to call it a recognition of something, whether in Ibsen's personality or in the spirit of the time, which is not satisfied with the limitations of the social dramas, but demands a wider vision and a greater range of spiritual interests.   Yet even so, we can scarcely follow Mr. Archer in his approbation of Ibsen's method of conciliating these two tendencies by introducing the supernatural without really making it an indispensable part of his dramas.

Section 3. — Gabriele D'Annunzio

If we now turn abruptly from North to South, from Norway to Italy, we shall discover in Gabriele D'Annunzio a writer who is making a serious attempt to restore to our stage the spirit of Greek tragedy as he conceives it, venturing even to vie with Aischylos on his own ground.   He would show us the ancient fatality still dominating the souls of men, and the ancient curse still at work.   He brings to his task a mind very conscious (perhaps too much so) of the artistic heritage of his race, and a style of striking richness and flexibility; but whether his peculiar gifts are such as to fit him for the solution of the problem he has undertaken is a matter which we may profitably discuss.

The play that is chiefly in question is *La Città Morta*, which may be classified as a modern development of the sepulchral tragedy.   It seems to owe nothing to such a predecessor in its own tongue as Monti's *Aristodemo*, with its sepulchre and unseen spectre.   Here the intention is to subtilize the theme, to play on our souls with a new and atrocious, but spiritual, horror.   The scene is Mycenae, where the archaeologist Leonardo is excavating. With him are his devoted sister, Bianca Maria, and his friend Alessandro with his blind wife Anna. Leonardo's researches at length reveal the resting-place of Agamemnon and the rest, and from the newly-opened tombs exhales the ancient curse of the house of Atreus. Leonardo, with nerves already strained to the breaking-point by the violence of his search, is seized by an incestuous passion for his sister, and can only free himself from it by killing her. Meanwhile Alessandro has also come to love her, and his wife Anna becomes aware of this change in his affections. A singular conflict of desires is thus created, which it is evidently D'Annunzio's aim to intensify, and partly to account for, by the idea of the reawakened curse. Unfortunately his method dilutes and diffuses the power of the conception, so that its impressiveness is largely impaired. He is so anxious to create an atmosphere of foreboding and horror that his means become too obvious — the passage from the *Antigone* which Bianca Maria is reading when the play opens, and in which she seems to discern her own destiny; the incident of the snake-skin which her brother put round her neck on their first visit to Mycenae; paraphrases of the *Agamemnon*; and in general a sacrifice of idea to speeches of admirable literary quality, but with no dramatic movement.

The fact is that the author's method here is that of the novelist rather than the dramatist, as a curious testimony of his own confirms. In that remarkable autobiographical novel *Il Fuoco* occurs (pp. 290 ff.) what is evidently the first idea of *La Città Morta*; and the version in the novel is undeniably the more impressive. It preserves that hallucinated intensity which the play is constantly striving to convey, but attains only in Leonardo's account of his first sight of the bodies of Agamemnon and Kassandra. A comparison of the paragraph of the novel which summarizes the plot with the play itself will show how the unity of the idea suffers in its transfer to the dramatic form. D'Annunzio does not trust the sheer simplicity of his conception; he must enhance, embroider, wax eloquent, until the effort becomes too obvious. The central idea of the curse that hangs about the infected tombs of Mycenae, waiting to be released that it may resume its fatal work, is admirable; but the conception surpasses the workmanship.

The character of the blind Anna is, from our point of view, the most interesting in the play. She is designed to be sensitive to the action of the mysterious forces to which the others are a prey, but of which they are not wholly conscious, and thus to fill the office of the Greek tragic chorus. These sentences from *Il Fuoco* will show how important to the artistic design D'Annunzio intended her to be: " Ella sarà cieca, già trapassata in un altro mondo, già semiviva di là dalla vita. Ella vedrà quel che gli altri non vedranno. . . . Ah, meravigliose parole io vorrò mettere nella sua bocca, e silenzii da cui nasceranno infinite bellezze. La sua potenza sulla scena, quando parla e quando tace, è più che umana. Ella risveglia nei nostri cuori il male più occulto e la speranza la più secreta." Brave words; but promises rather than things accomplished. We have here, in fact, an interesting example of that opening of new avenues for the interest in the supernatural already noted as characteristic of the century. D'Annunzio finds a more natural expression of his art in the novel than in the drama; and the few pages of *Il Fuoco* might be regarded as the program of a drama that has yet to be written, despite the brave attempt to realize it in *La Città Morta*.

The two shorter plays which are all that have yet appeared of the *Sogni delle Stagioni* touch upon supernatural themes, but show a similar suffocation of drama by style. The *Sogno d'un Mattino di Primavera*, which deals with the strange capacities of madness, rather falls outside our limits, though it is the better work of the two. The *Sogno d'un Tramonto d'Autunno* uses the old motive of the melting of a wax image to cause the death of a foe. Here it is the Dogaressa Gradeniga who seeks the life of the courtesan Pantea for having beguiled away her young lover. The plan succeeds; but the dramatic idea is hopelessly smothered under the elaborate decorations and the massive style, against which it has not vitality enough to contend. The play cannot be regarded as a real contribution to the use of the tragic supernatural.

D'Annunzio's failure in the treatment of the supernatural is primarily due to his trust in his style at the expense of his idea. He represents the surrender of inspiration to stagecraft, the reliance on sumptuous scenery rather than on his own imaginative power. He seeks to produce a new tragic substance from the combination of familiar elements in the alembic of his style; but the desired transformation does not take place. He will not let the inherent force of " the stuffs of ecstasy and pain " find its own expression; and his confidence in externalities betrays him. Yet his experiment is an interesting one, and the idea of *La Città Morta* remains impressive, despite all the shortcomings of its treatment.

SECTION 4. — MAURICE MAETERLINCK

Once more we turn to the North, this time to Belgium, and find there, in the person of Maeterlinck, the most significant of all the revivers of tragedy in our time. Appearing quite unheralded in the forefront of the remarkable revival of letters in his country some twenty years ago, he has made himself one of the leading spirits of the epoch.   It is in the drama that his first success was won, beginning with the publication, in 1889, of *La Princesse Maleine.*

Anything less conformed to current dramatic standards it would be hard to find.   In five short acts, each made up of several scenes, written in a prose full of strange repetitions and disconcertingly vivid figures of speech, it could not fail to excite controversy.   Its plot, around which a wealth of curious detail gathers, is relatively simple.   The prince Hjalmar is betrothed to Maleine; but at a feast held in honor of the betrothal their fathers quarrel, and a war breaks out in which the realm of Maleine's father is laid waste, and the royal family slain.   Maleine, however, escapes with a faithful nurse, and after various adventures reaches Hjalmar's court.   The old King, on the verge of senility, has become the victim of a strange queen, Anne, to whose daughter Hjalmar is betrothed.   Maleine's identity is at length discovered, and Hjalmar claims her as his first love.   Anne pretends to acquiesce, but secretly plots Maleine's death, which, with the help of the King, she brings about.   But the King is too weak to keep so terrible a secret: the crime is discovered, Hjalmar kills Anne and himself, and the King wholly loses his mind.

This portion of the plot, the most important, unrolls itself in the precincts of a cavernous palace, amid an amazing series of portents, some impressive, some rather trivial. Maeterlinck has not yet acquired the virtue of selection, and he impairs the effect of his piece by the accumulation of details.   With all its faults, however, the play is curiously enthralling, and the scene of Maleine's murder is exceedingly striking.   The King is so terrified as to be of no assistance, and Anne herself strangles Maleine, despite her struggles.   Hail beats against the window, which blows open and throws to the ground a vase containing a lily, and Maleine's dog scratches and whines without. Maeterlinck's peculiar method of revealing the sinister implications of the most trivial events in a given situation is clearly marked, and comes out again in the scene where the King betrays his crime. He thinks that everyone is staring at him; he sees hanging on the wall a tapestry of the *Massacre of the Innocents*, which has always hung there, but which he thinks has been placed there on purpose; he orders it removed, and there appears beneath a tapestry of the *Last Judgment*. He goes toward the chapel, and the opened door throws a flood of red light across him and Anne. In his final words he reveals the utter collapse of his mind with wonderful simplicity: " Je ne sais pas pourquoi, je suis un peu triste aujourd'hui. — Mon Dieu, mon Dieu, que les morts ont donc l'air malheureux! "

The general Elizabethan character of the piece is obvious. Mr. Archer, in a discussion of it, called its author " a Webster who had read Alfred de Musset," and it does bear an odd resemblance to *The Duchess of Malfi* seen through the wrong end of an opera-glass. There is the same patient accumulation of details, suddenly illuminated by a revealing phrase; and though the new achievement is not of the same calibre as the earlier, it shows the presence of an imagination of no common sort, working according to a novel method. We do not find in the play a definite supernatural element, but are on the verge of such a feature, and are witnessing the development of a method peculiarly suited to its treatment. The emotions which *Maleine* arouses are those most surely called into play by that use of the supernatural to which Maeterlinck is at once to advance.

In the absence of chronological data, one would be justified in assuming that the piece in which he takes the step was the result of a considerable interval of reflection, in which its author's method gradually attained greater clearness and simplicity. As a matter of fact, the piece in question, *L'Intruse*, followed in the next year, 1890. Here the Elizabethan complexity of *Maleine* is replaced by a severity that can only be called classic. The scene is no longer a fabulous castle, but a Flemish house of our own time. A family is gathered about a lamp — a father and his three daughters, their uncle, and their grandfather, who is almost blind. His daughter, the father's wife, has recently borne a child, and been in peril of her life; but they are now assured that all danger is past, and sit waiting for the father's sister, who has promised to visit them. The grandfather, however, is uneasy. The nightingales outside suddenly cease singing, and they think the sister is coming; but no one can be seen on the road. The sound of a scythe being sharpened is heard; it is the gardener, who is finishing his grass-cutting, since the morrow is Sunday. Some one is heard entering the house, but no one ascends the stairs. The servant is summoned, and declares that no one has come in, but that she found the outer door open, and shut it. The door at which she stands is pushed farther open, and it seems as if someone had entered the room; but nothing is visible. The grandfather's uneasiness grows, and gradually infects the others; the lamp goes out, the uncle walks about restlessly and sits down again. They remain in increasing fear until midnight strikes; a noise as of someone rising in haste is heard, and suddenly the baby, who is in another room, begins to cry. As they are about to go to him, steps are heard in the mother's chamber, and the Sister of Charity appears on the threshold, making the sign of the cross to announce that her charge is dead.

The absolute simplicity of the action, and its unwavering march, to which every detail contributes, are unsurpassed. There is nothing superfluous, nothing that diverts the attention from the issue; and the play must be read in its entirety to be really appreciated. Nothing out of the ordinary happens; the characters are rather commonplace persons, whose speech has no strangeness in it; and yet the sense of the approach and entrance of an undefinable hostile power is appallingly conveyed. Out of absolutely simple elements Maeterlinck has called up the very spirit of Greek tragedy; and *L'Intruse* may be taken as a model for the use of the supernatural in drama, displaying, in small compass, an absolutely adequate method.

It is a very interesting fact that Maeterlinck was anticipated in his treatment of this theme by his fellow-student Charles Van Lerberghe, to whose *Flaireurs*, published a year before *L'Intruse*, he gave full credit as a source of inspiration. He expressed himself publicly to this effect in the program for the first performance of *Les Flaireurs* at the Théâtre d'Art in 1892.[1] The play, first printed in 1889, treats, in three brief acts, the theme of death's coming, with a special interest in its macabre aspects. In a poor farmhouse a girl is watching her dying mother, and to the door come mysterious visitants, speaking a coarse and distorted language. One is " the man with the water," and at his departure the clock strikes ten; the next is " the man with the linen," and as he departs the clock strikes eleven. The daughter will not open, despite their repeated knocks, and the mother, in her delirium, thinks that the lord and lady of the château have come to visit her. The identity of the unseen visitants is sufficiently clear; but in act iii no doubt is left. A third creature joins the other two, declaring himself to be " the

[1] This program is reprinted in *Vers et Prose*, xii. 60 (Dec., 1907).

man with the thing," and, when pressed, "the man with the coffin." " Perhaps you weren't expecting me ? " he adds ironically.   The daughter still refuses to admit them, and amid renewed knockings they decide to break down the door. The mother, dimly realizing what is at hand, begins to sob desperately.   The noise of wheels is heard outside, and the dispute is renewed.   The door begins to yield to the assault, and the daughter thrusts vainly against it; midnight strikes, and the door collapses, letting in a blast of cold wind which quenches the lights.

In swiftness, and in power of evocation, *Les Flaireurs* certainly surpasses *L'Intruse*, developing all the sinister implications of its untranslatable title.   Van Lerberghe emphasizes the horror, the grotesque suddenness of death, while Maeterlinck converts its implacable approach into a thing of pure beauty.   By so much he surpasses his forerunner, as well as in the extent of his work; and we cannot feel that the praise which he so generously bestows on his friend at the expense of himself is wholly deserved.   Yet *Les Flaireurs* remains a strikingly vivid piece, and even apart from its own merits its service in pointing out his way to Maeterlinck would make it noteworthy.

In Maeterlinck's next play, *Pelléas et Mélisande* (1892), we find the supernatural withdrawn from the foreground, and used rather sparingly, as an aid to the creation of atmosphere — chiefly in the form of premonition, as when the servants of the castle enter Melisande's deathchamber unsummoned, and kneel at the moment that she dies.   In two of the " three little plays for marionettes," however, issued in 1894, we have a return to the supernatural, though after a somewhat different method.   In *Intérieur* we look across an old garden, at dusk, into a house where a family sits around a lamp.   An old man and a stranger enter the garden, and we learn that a young girl, one of the family, has drowned herself, and is now being brought home. The problem is how best to break the news to those within. The longer the old man waits, the harder does the task grow; and it seems that his deliberations with the stranger in some way disturb the unconscious members of the household. "Take care," he says at one point; "one cannot tell how far the soul extends around men." A group of peasants enters with the body; the old man goes into the house, and we see him at length disclose his news. The interest of the piece lies in the transfiguring effect which our knowledge of the impending disclosure produces on our view of the family. "They think themselves sheltered; they have foreseen all that can be foreseen," and yet this thing has occurred which will perhaps utterly change the current of their lives. In a certain sense it is the reverse of *L'Intruse*. There we are within, and perceive the gradual entrance of the terror into our midst; here we watch the impending calamity as it gathers itself outside.

In *La Mort de Tintagiles* we have the most perfect result of what we have defined as Maeterlinck's peculiar method — the charging of perfectly simple events with a surpassing terror. The little prince Tintagiles is guarded in an old castle by his two sisters and a faithful old teacher, Aglovale. He has been brought thither by order of the Queen his grandmother, who wishes to reign alone. She dwells in a tower of the castle, and no one ever sees her except her servants — but men say that she is ugly, and is growing huge. Ygraine, one of the sisters, tells Tintagiles of her life there, and how she has been under secret watch: "No one seemed to have suspicions . . . but one night I learned that there must be something else . . . I tried to escape, and I could not . . . Do you understand?" The Queen cannot have summoned Tintagiles for any good purpose; but they will do all they can to save him.   In act ii Bellangère, the other sister, learns that Tintagiles' life is indeed in danger, and warns the others; Aglovale says that all have tried to resist the Queen and failed, yet he will do his best to help them.   In act iii Tintagiles is unaccountably afraid, and cannot be comforted.   Steps are heard outside, and the door is slowly opened, despite their desperate resistance; but nothing is seen or heard of those without.   Suddenly Tintagiles utters a cry of joy; the door abruptly closes, and it seems that they are safe.   But the Queen's servants carry off Tintagiles, and in the last act we see Ygraine in front of an iron door, behind which is Tintagiles.   He has escaped from the Queen, but she follows him, and despite Ygraine's frantic efforts and entreaties she strangles him behind the door while Ygraine is left utterly helpless.   The agonizing scene is executed with absolute simplicity.

There is in *Tintagiles* no parade of the supernatural; but the effect of terror produced is that which only the supernatural can inspire.   The malign Queen corresponds perfectly to our definition of a supernatural power: she is a hostile force, with an incalculable capacity to work evil.   All the other characters are subdued to her will, and know that their struggle against her must be vain.   When the door is relentlessly pushed open by her unseen servants we feel exactly the same thrill as when Death the Intruder enters the Flemish household.   Out of a simple incident, the strangling of a child by his jealous kinswoman, Maeterlinck has evoked a terror identical with that which we have defined as the tragic terror of the supernatural.   Is the Queen a symbol ? It does not matter.   Maeterlinck has transmuted his personages into the very essence of tragedy, and yet left them wholly human; the transformation is by some miracle arrested in the very act, and the same event is at once utterly human and charged with all the weight of supernatural dignity.

With *Tintagiles* this phase of Maeterlinck's dramatic development closes, and his further progress does not here concern us, for its course, whatever its success, takes us into another sphere.   But the group of plays which we have just been discussing forms a coherent series, and constitutes the most important contribution to a real renewal of tragedy that our time has known.   We may say that just as the scholars of the Renaissance rediscovered the material form of Senecan tragedy, so Maeterlinck has rediscovered for us the spiritual form of Greek tragedy.   Whether he is fully aware of the significance of that rediscovery is not wholly clear.   His later works, beginning with *Aglavaine and Selysette*, and his later theoretical writings on the drama, seem to show a certain change of front, which we are not here concerned to trace.   At all events, in the preface to the collected plays (Brussels, 1903), he has defined his aim and accomplishment in these early plays with absolute accuracy: " On y a foi à d'énormes puissances, invisibles et fatales, dont nul ne sait les intentions, mais que l'esprit du drame suppose malveillantes, attentives à toutes nos actions, hostiles au sourire, à la vie, à la paix, au bonheur." The correspondance of this with our own preliminary definition is exact.

To compare Maeterlinck with Greek tragedy may seem to some an unjustifiable proceeding; but it is simply the statement of fact.   The form is of course wholly different; but the spiritual kinship between Aischylos and Maeterlinck is unmistakable, despite the difference in scale, while in *Pélleas et Mélisande* we have a subordination of the supernatural which is quite in the manner of Sophokles.   Once more we see how the supernatural must co-exist with adequate emphasis on the human element, if the result is to be artistically satisfying.   Maeterlinck's method contrasts with Ibsen's by its quiet acceptance of the supernatural, and with D'Annunzio's by its simplicity of expression.   Maeterlinck trusts his conceptions, and lets them develop as they will, unconfined by conformity to an uneasy rationalism or a mistaken desire for eloquence; and in this unquestioning acceptance lies his strength.   He is not afraid to return to the primal sources of tragic inspiration, and not afraid to report simply what he has learned.   In his plays lies what is most significantly tragic in the drama of our time, as well as the hope of future achievement for him who can extend his methods to larger fields.   The prospects for the fulfilment of that expectation may better be discussed when we have retraced in its entirety the historical course of the tragic supernatural, which is the task of our conclusion.

CONCLUSION

FUNCTION OF THE SUPERNATURAL IN TRAGEDY

We have now completed our survey of the supernatural in tragedy from the earliest Greek drama down to our own time, and are in possession of at least the most important documents, with enough auxiliary material to fill out the historical development. As we examine this material in its totality we perceive in it two tendencies in the treatment of the supernatural, which we may call the spiritual and the mechanical. The first of these is not an unbroken current, but it appears at different epochs, under the inspiration of similar conditions. We see it first in Aischylos, as the religious element inherent in Greek tragedy by virtue of its origin is revivified by the creative imagination of a supreme tragic poet. Some reflex of this is discernible in Sophokles, and in the *Bacchai* of Euripides; but there the expression of it in Greek, and indeed in antiquity, ceases. In the Middle Ages a parallel movement begins in the miracle-plays, which have a religious origin analogous to that of Greek tragedy. The resultant interest in the supernatural perpetuates itself in England as a distinct method, which in time combines with a purely native tradition to create Elizabethan tragedy. This movement, too, gradually dies out; but in our own day appear tokens, not wholly independent of older influences, of a revival of a really vital interest in the tragic supernatural.

The mechanical treatment, on the contrary, has a perfectly traceable and continuous ancestry. It begins with Euripides and passes from him to Seneca. The Renaissance, especially in Italy and France, accepts Seneca as the great tragic master, and models its supernatural, so far as it takes it over, on his practice.   Hence the lifeless Senecan ghosts which appear in the learned tragedies of Italy, whence they pass to France, so far as that country cared to copy them.   England shows little interest in them during the great dramatic period; but when the Elizabethan impulse has spent its force they reappear in Restoration tragedy, and there practically come to an end.

It is obvious that the first of these tendencies is as productive of excellent work as the second is sterile; and the coincidence of the first with the great periods of tragic achievement is a striking fact.   No praiseworthy introduction of the supernatural into tragedy has been effected in a period which did not carry the drama to a high pitch of excellence; and no such period of dramatic culmination has been without its tragic supernatural, in one shape or another. This intimate association suggests that a real causal connection underlies the simultaneous appearance of the two elements; a view strengthened by the closely parallel results of the independent Greek and Elizabethan evolutions.

We saw that Greek tragedy was forced by the circumstances of its origin to enstage the action of supernatural forces, and that it possessed in the chorus, its constituent principle, an unsurpassed aid to the accomplishment of this end.   The tragic chorus maintained the standard of excellence established by the preceding independent lyric poetry, and was thus enabled to perpetuate itself as an indispensable part of the tragic form.   The Middle Ages witnessed a similar development of the choral aspect, as a result of the liturgical origin of the sacred drama, of which antiphonal singing was a natural feature.   In this case, however, there was no literary tradition which could support the chorus as a necessary element of drama.   As a result of the altered conditions of production attendant on the secularization of the plays this choral aspect was not preserved as a constant feature; but such pieces as the *Sponsus* and the York *Creation* testify to its existence, and, in the latter case, the admirable result to which it might lead.   But apart from this specific point of resemblance to the Greek, the English miracle-plays possessed a similar general interest in the supernatural, which led to the unconscious formulation of a definite method of dealing with it, and left that method as a legacy to the purely secular playwrights who followed.

I said at the outset of my remarks on the medieval drama that the chief service of the return to antiquity was the recovery of a formative influence, which should supply a standard not to be found in the fluctuating conditions of the Middle Ages.   This service was, however, chiefly valuable for the structure of drama, not for its content, and certainly has no direct bearing on the revival of the supernatural. The admiration of scholars was lavished on Seneca; and we have seen how little vitality his use of the supernatural could boast.   The Senecan ghost may, however, be called a formative influence, in that he furnished a centre about which indigenous interest in the supernatural could gather, claiming a classical sanction for its entrance into the dramatic field.   This is precisely what happened in England; but in Italy and France the divorce of tragedy from the life of the time made such a result impossible.   The learned playwrights of those countries merely reproduced the Senecan formula, without seeking to give it any new content; those of England availed themselves of it only for the sake of propriety, and abandoned it as soon as the native tradition had won a firm foothold.   As a result, England produced an intensely original drama, while France, having broken with her own medieval past, adhered to classical models, and

Italy produced no serious drama of importance whatever. Not until the Elizabethan tradition begins to break down under the new conditions of the Restoration does England reach a stage of definite decline in the drama; and even then the persistence of an interest in the supernatural in the face of the hostile French influence is a notable tribute to the strength of the native dramatic impulse.

When we turn to our own epoch, we do not find a wholly independent resumption of the spiritual tradition, as at the beginning of the Middle Ages.   There is a conscious reversion to Greek and Elizabethan models; but after all the difference in time is so great that a minute imitation is no longer possible.   We must, I think, admit that Beddoes' return to the Elizabethans is an isolated *tour de force*, which produces a singularly interesting play, but does not point out the road to a generally serviceable method. Maeterlinck, on the contrary, looks back to Greek tragedy for spiritual inspiration, not for a copiable form.   He aims to devise a new form, which shall convey impressions similar to those of Greek tragedy, but in a fashion suited to our own tastes and habits of mind.   Consequently he is not fettered by a minute adherence to externalities, and comes closer to the essential spirit of tragedy by the very simplicity of his means.   As we phrased it, he has rediscovered for us the spiritual form of Greek tragedy.

The question whether such indications as these really prefigure a significant revival of the tragic supernatural in contemporary drama is not easy to answer.   On the one hand, the variety of the indications is a hopeful sign; it would seem to imply a rather widely diffused movement, and a genuine interest.   The fact that others beside Maeterlinck, such as Van Lerberghe and Sharp, were seeking, independently of his influence, a new dramatic form which

approximates that which he devised, seems to show that
such a form is demanded by something in the spirit of the
time.   The almost reluctant tribute of Ibsen in his later
plays to the interest in the supernatural seems an analogous
phenomenon.   On the other hand, the drama seems to lack
a vital connection with the life of our age, to be a consciously
supported survival rather than a spontaneous outgrowth of
present conditions.   Especially is this true of serious
drama, of anything which can fairly be called tragedy.   Our
age seems not to desire that intense scrutiny of all phases of
humanity from which tragedy springs.   We prefer the sur-
faces of things to their depths.   In the particular matter of
the supernatural, our imaginations have been largely
atrophied by the modern tendency to sumptuous scenery;
we look to the externals of drama, not to its soul.   D'Annunzio is in this regard a typical modern playwright.   In
view of this disinclination to penetrate beneath the surface
of things, and this inability to respond to imaginative suggestion, the prospect of a genuine revival of tragedy is perhaps not very bright.   Mallarmé has summed up this modern
attitude toward the theatre in a trenchant paragraph:
" Notre seule magnificence, la scène, à qui le concours
d'arts divers scellés par la poésie attribue selon moi quelque
caractère religieux ou officiel, si l'un de ces mots a un sens,
je constate que le siècle finissant n'en a cure, ainsi comprise; et que cet assemblage miraculeux de tout ce qu'il
faut pour façonner de la divinité, sauf la clairvoyance de
l'homme, sera pour rien." [1]   Yet after all a certain diffused
interest in the supernatural does seem to characterize the
drama of the present day; and we have seen that the supernatural, if properly handled, implies a strong possibility of
tragedy.   Hence we may go so far in the way of prediction

---

[1] See *Divagations* (Fasquelle, 1897), p. 191.

as to say that if a revival of tragedy is feasible at the present day this interest in the supernatural is an encouraging factor in its promotion.

Thus much for historical recapitulation, and a slight essay at prophecy; let us now see whether our concrete instances confirm the theoretical principles on which we have conducted our investigation. We declared at the outset that our subject possessed a fundamental unity, by virtue of its origin in a universal instinct. This is confirmed by an inspection of what we have distinguished as the vital tradition, historically discontinuous, but spiritually unified, with manifestations akin to one another through their common source. Whereas direct imitation leads only to lifeless conformity, the independent following of the primitive impulse creates works singularly alike in essence, however different in aspect. In the case of Greek and Elizabethan tragedy the similarity of the conditions of origin is a favoring factor. The medieval English tradition passes over intact into the chronicle-play, and the chronicle-play in turn produces Elizabethan tragedy as an independent form; so that the spiritual kinship of Aischylos and the Elizabethans is partly the result of a real likeness in the forms which they employed, as well as of similarity of native genius.

Our next principle was that the supernatural, when given shape in a concrete figure, must preserve that element of incalculable power which is the essential cause of the supernatural terror. This condition is certainly fulfilled by all the good supernatural figures which we have inspected. Take the ghost of Banquo as a convenient example. Macbeth's words as he confronts him:

> What man dare, I dare:
> Approach thou like the rugged Russian bear,
> The arm'd rhinoceros, or the Hyrcan tiger,
> Take any shape but that, and my firm nerves

> Shall never tremble. Or, be alive again,
> And dare me to the desert with thy sword;
> If trembling I inhabit then, protest me
> The baby of a girl —

are really a statement of doctrine. Before a wild beast, however formidable, or before a mortal foe, his physical courage knows what course to take; but against a ghost such means of defense are of no avail. Yet the ghost, as he stands there with gory locks, and twenty mortal murders on his crown, is a perfectly definite figure; it is no vagueness in his aspect, but the incalculable power which he is felt to be capable of exercising, which makes him specifically supernatural. In the same way, the Furies and the Weird Sisters are perfectly definite beings, made indeed as concrete as possible by their authors; but the power which they exercise is wholly distinct from any human power. This truth has been sufficiently elucidated in the analyses of the plays in question, and needs only to be recalled to our attention at this point.

In considering the specific use of the supernatural in drama, we declared that it must manifest its power in action, and that the criterion of its dramatic necessity is its effect on the mortal characters. Illustrations of this principle have been abundant, and have enabled us to formulate a further principle — namely, that the proper presentation of the mortals is necessary to the artistic use of the supernatural. The more definitely we conceive the individual mortals as creatures like ourselves, the more readily shall we share the emotions which they feel in the presence of the supernatural. Hence a realistic setting — realistic in the broad sense of true to human life — is demanded, if the treatment of the supernatural is to be really artistic. Brutus in his quiet tent at Sardis is the more effectively confronted by the phantom because of the possibility of fitting contrast; and Maeterlinck's peaceful homes in *L'Intruse* and *Intérieur* are all the more suitable settings for the intrusion of the supernatural because of their sheer humanity. Conversely, unsatisfactory instances of the employment of the supernatural almost always occur in dramas which are feeble as dramas, apart from their use of this particular element.

One ready means of effecting contrast through the mortal characters is by the introduction of skeptics, who are confuted by the course of events, and compelled to change their opinions. This means is so closely related to our subject, and so interesting in itself, that it is worth while to inspect a few examples. In Greek tragedy we have Klytaimestra, indomitably resolute at the time of her deed, but later stirred to a frenzy of fear and feigned repentance by the boding dream which reveals the unsleeping wrath of the slain; we have Kreon, outwardly contemptuous of any higher power, but eager to attempt reparation when it is too late. In Elizabethan tragedy we have on the one hand rather crude examples, such as Tourneur's Charlemont, convinced of the ghost's reality by the material evidence of the gun-shot; while the same author's D'Amville, whose atheistic pose is shattered at the sight of what only seems his victim's ghost, and gives place to a momentary but absolute collapse of reason and will, shows the psychological method. On the other hand, we have such a subtly-drawn figure as Horatio, whose skepticism is based on reason, and requires reasonable proofs for its confutation. The course of the play furnishes him such proofs; and his conviction that the ghost is real is a very powerful agent in producing a similar conviction in us. We see that his attitude is absolutely unprejudiced, and hence his testimony has all the weight that intellectual integrity can give it. He is as far above the skeptics of other Elizabethan plays as the ghost is above his fellow-phantoms.   There is an inherent irony in this conversion of skeptics which becomes explicit in such characters as Pentheus and Macbeth.   Pentheus thinks Dionysos is in his power when the situation is absolutely the reverse; Macbeth thinks he can force the Weird Sisters to do his will when he is really their helpless victim.   Macbeth is of course no skeptic; but the irony which is so conspicuous in his fate forms a certain bond of union with the skeptics pure and simple, through such an intermediate type as Pentheus, who is in some degree skeptical.

We thus see that the introduction of the supernatural into a drama does not open the way for mere disordered fancy, but demands for its successful treatment peculiar care in the drawing of the mortal characters.   This is true even of a purely decorative apparition, that of a ghost, for instance. We noted that the isolated prologue-ghost can secure the needed contrast only by expository speeches which diminish his supernatural character; on the other hand, so noble an example as the ghost in *Hamlet* derives no little of his impressiveness from the skill with which Horatio and the rest are drawn.   There is, I think, no instance of a satisfactory use of the supernatural in a play in which the mortal characters are feeble or incredible as mortals.

The sharp opposition of mortal and supernatural is of course only possible where the two factors are set in close relationship, as in the apparition of a ghost.   This will not always be the case with the intrinsic supernatural, which, as we saw, requires powers who are supernatural in essence, and not in virtue of anything they have passed through. Hence the problem of securing proper contrast is not one of mere juxtaposition; nor is every type of supernatural being equally suited to dramatic treatment.   The situation in

Hamlet would be after all conceivable if the information which the ghost imparts were in the possession of some mortal, and revealed by him. In the actual circumstances of *Hamlet*, only the ghost has this information, and hence his apparition is strictly necessary for the individual play, as Shakespeare conceives it; but we have here only a single instance, not a dramatic type. When, however, as in the *Oresteia* or *Macbeth*, we have a sequence of events stated in mortal terms but dependent on something beyond mortality, we have a form of tragedy in which the supernatural is essential, not adventitious. It is interesting to note that in both the cases named the ghost is introduced as a decorative figure, but in a way that gives him a peculiar value. The ghost of Klytaimestra personifies that sleepless wrath of the dead which brought about her own undoing in requital for her deed, and from which Orestes must be delivered if he is to find safety. It is in consequence of his deeds of blood that Macbeth is doomed to fall; and the apparition of the ghost of one of his victims, Banquo, impresses on us the horror of the crime, and the unfailing retribution that must follow, in a degree that no other means could compass. The ghost thus derives from association with the higher supernatural powers an impressiveness which he does not possess in himself; at the same time he retains his connection with his peculiar function of securing revenge, and so preserves his individuality as a ghost. In virtue of this combining of diverse supernatural elements into a coherent whole without incurring any loss of the individuality of each, the *Oresteia* and *Macbeth* are from our present point of view the greatest tragedies that have ever been written — a judgment which might also be sustained on other grounds.

On the basis of the facts which our investigation has revealed we may venture to set forth, in very broad terms, a method for the successful use of the supernatural in tragedy. The supernatural forces must clearly influence the characters, in a manner evidently unlike that of any mortal compulsion. Fitting allusion and description must give us a due sense of the reality of these powers, and of their dominance of the action; and actual exhibition, whether of the forces personified or of their visible effect on one or more of the characters, must at some point be introduced. Such actual exhibition should preferably be brief; the audacious complexity of *Hamlet* is not a model for the average playwright. The attendant allusion must be genuinely imaginative, and evocative of atmosphere; and though it need not employ supernatural themes, it must be consonant with them. The phenomena of death are convenient sources for such allusion, especially where ghosts are in question; but the most widely available method is the use of mysterious sound, as we have so often had occasion to remark. These elements are susceptible of indefinite elaboration, and the ends at which they aim are attainable in various ways under different conditions; but they must appear in every tragedy which achieves a satisfactory treatment of the supernatural.

We have thus completed our chief task — the inspection and classification of our dramatic material, and the deduction of certain principles which confirm and develop the propositions according to which we conducted our study, and which seemed properly resultant from the mere inspection of the problems in question. At the outset we stated the obvious fact that the supernatural seems to have a natural affinity for tragedy, though the resultant manifestations may vary much in merit; we further indicated a possible reason for this, in the essence of the supernatural as we defined it. Can we, however, give a more detailed explanation of this connection on the basis of our accumulated material ? · It is clear that the two epochs at which tragedy has chiefly flourished — the Attic and the Elizabethan — are those in which the supernatural is most diffused in tragedy, and also attains its highest development and expression; and that the tendency toward a revival of tragedy in our own day is attended by a parallel revival of interest in the supernatural.   Here are undoubted facts, for which we ought at least to attempt to account.

The explanation lies, it seems to me, in the very nature of tragedy.   We must agree that tragedy is that form of drama which seeks to penetrate as far as possible into the mystery of existence, and to reveal the secret sources of human action.   It is inevitable that this should involve some opinion of those forces beyond man of whose existence, however to be conceived, we must be conscious.   But such forces are precisely what we understand by the supernatural, taken in its widest and also its deepest sense.   When a writer has penetrated to the very verge of human existence, he must confront the question, What lies beyond ? and it is in some aspect of the supernatural that he will find whatever answer he chooses to give.

This is but a brief mention of one of the implications of our study, which might, if developed, lead to a new theory of tragedy.   I cannot here do more than point it out; the limitations of our present study require us to be satisfied if we have sufficiently revealed the historical continuity of our subject, and thus furnished a basis for further investigation. This continuity has, I think, really been demonstrated by our discussion of the plays we have examined; but we shall be more interested in the task if we can grant that the study of the supernatural in tragedy is not that of an arbitrarily limited field, but the tracing of a necessary connection between the two terms.   If we feel, at this stage, that the supernatural really contributes to the most perfect expression of the tragic spirit in drama — if indeed it be not essential to such expression — we must also feel that our investigation has really contributed to our appreciation of the true significance of tragedy as well as of the importance to it of the supernatural.

BIBLIOGRAPHY

BIBLIOGRAPHY

This bibliography is designed to consist only of books or articles which deal specifically with some aspect of the supernatural in tragedy. Partial discussions of the subject in individual periods, such as are easily accessible in works of reference, are accordingly not included. It is hoped that the list here given is reasonably complete; but some of the items I have not been able to examine myself. Such cases are indicated by an asterisk prefixed to the name of the author. In view of the relatively small number of titles, I have decided to adopt a chronological order under the several headings, which correspond to the divisions of the text.

PART I — ANTIQUITY

GREEK TRAGEDY

GENERAL.

E. Roux, *Du Marveilleux dans la Tragédie Grecque*, Paris, 1846.

*E. Thomas, *De vaticinatione vaticinantibusque personis in Graecorum tragedia*, Paris, 1879.

E. Mueller, *De Graecorum deorum partibus tragicis*, Giessen, 1910.

SECTION 1. — AISCHYLOS.

I have found no special consideration of the supernatural in Aischylos.

SECTION 2. — SOPHOKLES.

A. Geffers, *De deo ex machina in Philocteta Sophoklis interveniente commentatio*, Göttingen, 1854. (Program.)

SECTION 3. — EURIPIDES.

F. V. Fritsch, *De deo ex machina*, 1843. (This item is listed by Mr. Norwood in the bibliography of his *Riddle of the Bacchae*. It is certainly in some way erroneous. The author's name would seem to be a misspelling for Fritzsche, whose initials are the same, but I can find no such title among his publications.)

H. Schrader, "Zur Wurdigung des deus ex machina," *Rheinisches Museum* xxii. (1867) 544, and xxiii. (1868) 103.

A. Duhr, *De deo ex machina Euripideo*, Rostock, 1873.

*Kuhlenbeck, *Der deus ex machina in der griechischen Tragödie*, Osnabrück, 1874. (Program.)

PART II — THE MIDDLE AGES AND THE RENAISSANCE

THE MEDIEVAL SACRED DRAMA

H. Wieck, *Die Teufel auf die mittelalterlichen Mysterien-Bühne*, Leipzig, 1887.

P. Heinze, *Die Engel auf die mittelalt. Mysterienbuhne Frankreichs*, Greifswald, 1905.

I find no specific references for the miracle-plays in England, nor for The Renaissance in Italy.

THE ELIZABETHAN AGE IN ENGLAND

SEPARATE VOLUMES.

*Albert Roffe, *The Ghost Belief of Shakespeare*, London, 1851.

T. A. Spalding, *Elizabethan Demonology*, London, 1880.

T. F. T. Dyer, *The Folklore of Shakespeare*, London, 1884.

*E. Heuse, *Ueber die Erscheinung des Geistes im Hamlet*, Elberfeld, 1890. There is a review in *Englische Studien*, xvi. 290.

H. Ankenbrand, *Die Figur des Geistes im Drama der englischen Renaissance*, Leipzig, 1906. (Münchener Beiträge, xxxv.)

Margaret Lucy, *Shakespeare and the Supernatural*, Liverpool, 1906. With a bibliography of the subject by William Jaggard.

J. P. S. R. Gibson, *Shakespeare's Use of the Supernatural*, Cambridge (Eng.), 1908.

Helen H. Stewart, *The Supernatural in Shakespeare*, London, 1908.

J. E. Poritsky, *Shakespeares Hexen*, Berlin, 1909.

ARTICLES.

C. Dedrickson, " Shakespeare's Spirits," *Shakespeariana*, ii. 534. (1885.)

A. Doak, " The Supernatural in Macbeth," *Ibid.*, v. 341. (1888.) " The Ghost in Hamlet," *Ibid.*, v. 389.

C. Stopes, " The Weird Sisters in Macbeth," *Ibid.*, vii. 251. (1890.)

A. Doak, " The Supernatural in Shakespeare," *Ibid.*, ix. 213. (1892.)

A. H. Tolman, Notes on Macbeth: 1. — " The Weird Sisters," *Publ. Mod. Lang. Ass.*, xi. 200. (1896.)

J. H. Hudson, " Shakespeare's Ghosts," *Westminster Review*, cliii. 447. (1900.)

M. F. Egan, " The Ghost in Hamlet," *Catholic University Bulletin*, 1901, 393. Reprinted in *The Ghost in Hamlet and other Essays*, (1906.)

F. E. Schelling, " Some Features of the Supernatural as represented in Plays of the Reigns of Elizabeth and James," *Modern Philology*, i. 316. (1903.)

L. Wurth, " Geisterscenen in Shakespeares Tragödien," in *Beiträge zur neueren Philologie*, J. Schipper dargebracht, 1903.

F. W. Moorman, " The Pre-Shakespearean Ghost, *Mod. Lang. Review*, i. 85. (1906.) " Shakespeare's Ghosts," *Ibid.*, i. 192.

E. E. Stoll, " The Objectivity of the Ghosts in Shakespeare," *Publ. Mod. Lang. Ass.*, xxii. 201. (1907.)

A. de Berzeviczy, "Le Surnaturel dans le Theatre de Shakespeare," Paris, 1913. (Previously in *Revue de Hongrie*, from January, 1911.)

W. Strunck, Jr., " The Importance of the Ghost in Hamlet," in *Studies in honor of J. M. Hart*, New York, 1911.

PART III — SOME MODERN ASPECTS

For Part III the only reference that I find is

C. Thurnau, *Die Geister in der eng. Literatur des 18. Jahrhunderts*, Berlin, 1906 (Palaestra, lv.).

There are doubtless others concerning the modern section, but I have not been able to secure any.

INDEX

INDEX

Achilles (Loschi), 187.
Acripanda, 198.
Adam, 123 ff.
Agamemnon (Aischylos), 29 ff., 48.
Agamemnon (Seneca), 101.
Aias, 60.
Aischylos, 19 ff., 62, 89, 90, 93, 94, 229, 343.
Alaham, 219.
Alexandraean Tragedy, 219.
Alkestis, 65.
Alphonsus, 222.
Altile, 196.
Andromache, 69.
Antigone, 53 ff., 58, 105.
Antonio's Revenge, 236 ff.
Archer, William, 327, 330, 337.
Arcinda, 199.
Aristophanes, 92, 99.
Aristotle, 9, 66, 100.
Atheist's Tragedy, 244 ff., 267.
Awntyrs of Arthur, 205 ff.

Bacchai, 82 ff.
Balder's Dreams, 6.
Barnes, 264 ff.
Battle of Alcazar, 224.
Beddoes, 306 ff.
Birth of Merlin, 263.
Bodel, 128.
Bottomley, 315 ff.
Brand, 320.
Brome *Isaac*, 157.
Bussy d'Ambois, 240 ff.

Caesar and Pompey, 248 f.
Caesar Borgia, 296.

Cammelli, 189.
Canace, 197.
Cappello, 199.
Castle Spectre, 303.
Catiline, 220, 295.
Cecchi, 185 f.
Changeling, 278.
Chapman, 240 ff., 286.
Chester Plays, 153, 156, 164.
Choephoroi, 35 ff., 49, 51, 104.
Cibber, 300.
Cicero, 100.
Città Morta, 322 f.
Cléopatre (Jodelle), 146, 291.
Constantine the Great, 296.
Corraro, 188.
Countess Cathleen, 312.
Coventry Plays, 153, 164, 168, 173.
Cresci, 199.
Crier by Night, 315 f.
Crowne, 296.

D'Annunzio, 332 ff., 344.
Death's Jest-Book, 306 ff.
Decio da Orte, 198.
Dekker, 266, 270.
Devil is an Ass, 266 f.
Devil is in It, 266.
Devil's Charter, 264 f., 272.
Devozioni, 177 f.
Dido (Gager), 210.
Didone (Pazzi), 191 ff.
Digby Plays, 149.
Dryden, 294.
Du Bellay, 146.
Dublin *Isaac*, 157.
Duchess of Malfi, 260 f.

Ecerinis, 187.
Edward I, 223.
Edward IV, 235.
Elektra (Euripides), 67.
Elektra (Sophokles), 52 f., 58.
Elfrid, 299.
Emperor and Galilean, 321 ff.
Ennius, 100.
Eriphyle, 301.
Eufimia, 196.
Eumenides, 40 ff., 49, 61, 255.
Euripides, 63 ff., 91, 95, 97.
Eusebius, 116.

Fair Penitent, 299.
Faustus, 231, 263, 272.
Filostrato e Panfila, 189.
Fischer, 234.
Fisher, 275.
Flaireurs, 339 f.
Fleury Plays, 120 f.
Ford, 270.
Friar Bacon, 222, 241.

Garnier, 292.
Giraldi, 194 ff.
Gorboduc, 210 f.
Greban, 137 ff., 145, 170, 174.
Greene, 222 f.

Hamlet, 243, 249 ff., 283, 354.
Hardy, 292.
Hardy, Thomas, 318.
Hearn, L., 4.
Hekabe, 89, 101.
Helen, 70.
Henry V, 93, 225.
Henry VI, 225, 263.
Herakles, 78 ff., 102.
Hercules, 98.
Herodes (Goldenham), 210.
Herodotos, 5, 19.
Heywood, 235, 269.

Hilarius, 121 f.
Hill, 299.
Hippolyte (Garnier), 292.
Hippolytos, 73 f., 78.
Home, 302.
Homer, 17, 105, 282.

Ibsen, 318 ff., 344.
Immortal Hour, 313.
Intérieur, 340.
Intruse, 338.
Ion, 71.
Iphigeneia in Tauris, 71, 76.
Iron Age, 235.

Jean de la Taille, 292.
Jeu de S. Nicolas, 128 ff.
Jew of Malta, 232.
Jodelle, 146, 291.
Jonson, 220, 266.
Julius Caesar, 246 ff., 280.

King John, 225, 226, 239.
Kyd, 217 ff., 224, 238, 248, 277, 284.

Land of Heart's Desire, 311 f.
Late Lancashire Witches, 269 f.
Laudun, 293.
Lee, 295 f.
Lewis, 303.
Libertine, 297.
Locrine, 214 ff., 280.
Looking Glass for London, 221.
Loschi, 187.
Lucan, 105.

Macbeth, 255 ff., 268, 272, 350, 354.
Maeterlinck, 335 ff.
Mallarmé, 349.
Marcus Brutus, 300.
Marlowe, 229 ff., 285.
Marston, 236 ff., 243, 254, 255, 285.

Martelli, 193.
Massinger, 274 f.
Merry Devil of Edmonton, 263.
Middleton, 268 f., 278.
Miracles of Our Lady, 132, 205.
Misfortunes of Arthur, 212 ff.
Mithridates, 296.
Monti, 332.
Moody, 318.
Mort de Tintagiles, 341 f.
Mussato, 177, 187.
Mysterious Mother, 302.

Nero (Gwynne), 210.
Nero (Lee), 295.
Newcastle *Noah*, 167.
Norwood, G., 86 f.

Octavia, 102.
Oedipus (Dryden and Lee), 295.
Oedipus (Seneca), 103.
Oidipous at Kolonos, 58 ff.
Oidipous Tyrannos, 57 f., 104.
Old Wives Tale, 223, 308.
Orbecche, 194.
Orestes, 68.
Otway, 298.

Passion, 137 ff.
Pazzi, 191 f.
Peele, 223 f.
Peer Gynt, 320.
Persians, 22 ff., 48, 49.
Philoktetes, 61, 78.
Pindar, 17, 99.
Plautus, 97, 101.
Poliziano, 185, 186.
Polyxena, 62.
Porcie, 292.
Pretenders, 319 f.
Princesse Maleine, 336 f.
Progne, 188.
Prometheus, 25 ff., 49, 231.

Propertius, 106.
Revenge of Bussy d'Ambois, 243.
Rhesos, 81 f.
Richard II, 225.
Richard III (Cibber), 300.
Richard III (Shakespeare), 79, 227 ff.
Riders to the Sea, 314 f.
Riding to Lithend, 316 f.
Rival Queens, 295.
Roman Actor, 274.
Roman Revenge, 299.
Rosmersholm, 331.
Rosmunda, 190.
Rowe, 299.
Rowley, 263.
Rucellai, 190.
Rutebeuf, 130.

Sacre Rappresentazioni, 179 ff.
Sampson, 275.
Sappho, 17.
Second Maiden's Tragedy, 273 f., 308.
Semiramis, 301.
Seneca, 97 ff., 186, 207, 233 f., 280;
Italian translations of, 189; English translations of, 208 f.
Settle, 297.
Seven against Thebes, 26 ff., 49, 54.
Shadwell, 297.
Shakespeare, 225, 246 ff., 285.
Sharp, 312 ff.
Sheffield, 300.
Sogno d'un Tramonto d'Autunno, 335.
Sophokles, 50 ff., 91, 93.
Sophonisba (Marston), 239.
Sophonisba (Trissino), 190.
Spanish Tragedy, 217 ff., 235.
Speroni, 197.
Sponsus, 119 f.
Stoll, E. E., 281.
Suppliants (Aischylos), 21, 48.
Suppliants (Euripides), 66.

Synge, 314.
Tamburlaine, 229 f.
Tancred and Gismunda, 211 f.
Teofilo, 183 f.
Tertullian, 116.
Theokritos, 107.
Théophile, 130 f., 184.
Thyestes, 101 f.
Tourneur, 244 ff., 267, 308.
Towneley Plays, 155, 162, 166, 169, 172, 205, 206, 239.
Trissino, 190, 200, 292.
Troades (Euripides), 64, 76, 92.
Troades (Seneca), 103, 104.
True Tragedy of Richard III, 228.
True Trojans, 275.
Tullia, 193.
Tullia Feroce, 199.

Ulysses, 299.
Unnatural Combat, 274.

Van Lerberghe, 339 f.
Vergil, 105, 107, 115.
Verrall, A. W., 75 ff.
Viel Testament, Mystère du, 133 ff., 145, 173.
Vikings at Helgeland, 319.
Vistas (Sharp), 312 f.
Voltaire, 301.
Vow Breaker, 275 ff.

Walpole, 302.
Warning to Fair Women, 235.
Webster, 259 ff., 337.
White Devil, 259 f.
Witch, 268 f.
Witch of Edmonton, 270 ff.
Woodstock, 226 f.

Yeats, 310 ff.
York Plays, 151, 154, 158 ff., 166, 172, 174.